# NEVER GIVE UP

## MYRA JONES

*As told by Drolan Chandler To Myra McDonald Goode Jones*

SUMMARY: This is Drolan Chandler's personal story of his front-line jungle combat and harrowing prisoner of war experiences during World War II, in the Philippines—including the Death March, Bilibid Prison, Camp O'Donnell, Camp Cabanatuan, transfer by hell ship, Clyde Maru, to Japanese Camp 17, and slave labor in unsafe coal mines. His humor and bulldog determination to survive is inspirational and entertaining.

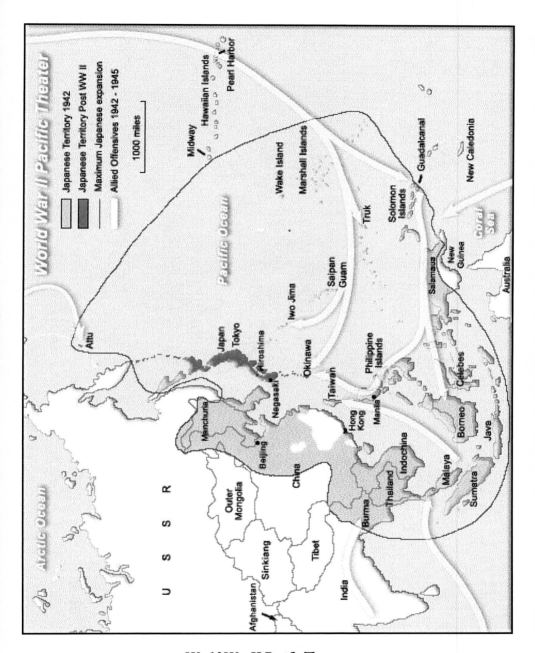

**World War II Pacific Theater,**

*Map courtesy of U–S–History.com https://u–s–history.com/pages/h1693.html*

**The Philippine Islands.** *Public Domain. Courtesy of University of Alabama, Geography and Map Division, Library of Congress.*

**Map – WWII - Island of Luzon in the Philippine Sea,**
*getdrawings_com/drawing_tag/Luzon. Free Downloads*

# PROLOGUE

THE defense lines had crumbled. Starving, disease-ridden Filipino-American troops fled in panic. We met people out from Mariveles who were traveling toward Bagac. They told us troops were to meet at designated places—Infantry in one, Marines in another, and Navy and Air Force at other locations—and they told us how to get to the checkpoint for our units.

**April 9, 1942:** We got word that Major General Edward King, who was in command of Luzon, and Lieutenant General Jonathan Wainwright had gone to Corregidor and surrendered our forces on Bataan to Lieutenant General Masaharu Homma. The Japanese had not yet appeared to take prisoners.

Arriving at the appointed place for the Air Corps, our officers informed us, "This is it. We don't know what's going to happen: your guess is as good as ours. Every man is on his own."

Jim Dyer and I, along with four other guys, talked it over and decided to head for the mountains on foot, armed with guns and ammunition.

Before long, we ran out of water from the long hike. We were hot and dry from the heat wave that permeated the area.

"Cover for me, and I'll get us some water," I told the rest of them and set out for the creek we could hear nearby, which ran down the side of the mountain. I looked in all directions, but didn't see anyone. Keeping an eye out for the enemy, I laid my gun on the bank, slid down to the water, and dipped the canteen in the stream.

"Don't get that water. It's contaminated." I whirled around, startled, and came face to face with a Japanese officer. I hadn't seen him standing nearby underneath a washed-out ledge. I was astounded that he spoke English better than I did!

"Get some out of this barrel," he instructed. "It has been boiled."

I sloshed over to the barrel, filling the canteens, and as nonchalantly as possible, started up the bank, hoping to ease over to my gun. He wasn't interested in playing my game.

"Come here," he ordered, as two other officers joined him. I decided the odds were against me and obeyed. He reached out, grasped my dog tags, and read them aloud.

"Drolan Chandler, Detroit, Alabama. Is that close to Sulligent?" he asked.

"Yes, sir, it is." I spoke from my shocked state.

I was so stunned you could have knocked me over with a feather! Most Americans have never heard of Detroit, located in the northwest corner of Alabama. I'm not even sure it was on the map at that time. And if Sulligent was on the map, it was only a minute dot, ten miles southwest of Detroit, near the Alabama and Mississippi state line.

"Have you eaten?" he inquired.

I told him I hadn't, so he ordered me to eat since they had already finished. My knees were weak while I puzzled over the strange encounter and the gravity of the moment.

I was captured!

# CONTENTS

# CHAPTER 1

## Growing Up Is Hard to Do!

I guess you could say I'm just a good old country boy at heart. Always have and always will be.

Born Drolan Chandler, on June 15, 1919, in Detroit, Lamar County, Alabama, to Juler Elizabeth Real Chandler and Minos Nelson Chandler. I was the eldest of five children: Roberta—we called Birdie, Rayburn—nicknamed Yank, Doyle, and Diane—pronounced Deon.

Through the years, our family moved around following Dad's quest for jobs, although we basically stayed in the same area of the country, in Mississippi and Alabama. He always had a garage business on the side, whether he was farming, hauling lumber, or whatever else he could find. After the war, he established his own garage business to feed all those hungry mouths. He was a humdinger of a mechanic, and I picked up a lot of know-how from helping out.

Acquainted with farm work from an early age, chopping wood, slaughtering hogs, and so on, I started working in the fields at ten, plowing and planting cotton, vegetables, or whatever else would put clothes on our backs or food on the table.

Back then, we used two mules and a middle buster plow to go down a row of cotton and bust up the middle ground. Later, we'd go back with one mule and a turning plow to make a mounded bed to plant the seed in. Dad did the middle busting with that pair of mules. Next, he singled them out and took one while I took the other to go back over the ground and plant cotton.

I plowed with the mule named Bill. He had a fairly mellow disposition and was amiable about whatever you wanted him to do or wherever you pointed him.

Dad took Frank, who was a good deal ornerier to deal with. After resting on Sunday, he felt pretty good on Monday and always had a mind to explore the thickets at the edge of the field more than staying on the row. It didn't take much to scare him or tick him off, so he'd take off at a fast trot, carrying Dad across the field. When Dad finally got him stopped, he'd take him loose and give him a strapping, then hitch him back up. It always took a heavy hand to get him in the right frame of mind. He had to be retrained every Monday. If you didn't whup him on Monday, he got it by Tuesday to conquer him and get his mind right.

I got my share of whuppings, too, when I got a mindset like Frank, contrary to Dad's intentions or instructions. Mother could swing a hickory switch pretty good as well, when one of us five kids got out of line. She was a big-boned, strong woman who liked working in the field or garden better than in the house. Dad was a small-framed man but maintained a firm hold on us kids.

I remember Dad's whuppings good because they tended to be pretty rough ones when they happened. Guess that's why I could take the hard treatment I went through later on. I figured, if I had lived through tough stuff growing up, I could make it through anything anyone else could shovel out.

I got into the usual mischief kids do. When I was fourteen, I got strapped for something I'm sure I must have been guilty of, but before Dad laid the first whelp, I told him, "You'd better get all you want, because this is the last time you're gonna' whup me." I was bigger than him by then and it was pretty big talking, but I pretty big meant it.

When he let up, I said, "Just remember, this is the last time." It set him off again and he made it a good one, nearly beating the devil out of me, more for my impudence than the crime. But he never tried to take me on again after that one.

My mouth got me in trouble more than one time—at home, in school, in the army, and later in the war.

\* \* \* \* \* \* \*

I attended ninth grade at the high school in Sulligent, Alabama. Unfortunately, I came down with double pneumonia and nearly died. I took sick in November and didn't get out of the house until March.

The next year I stayed with Grandma and Grandpa in Hamilton, Alabama, about fourteen miles northeast from Detroit, and made up ninth grade classes while attending the tenth grade at Hamilton High.

Miss Rhodes was my ninth-grade English teacher and hailed from Kentucky. One day she asked the question, "What's Kentucky noted for?" Some smart buck said, and memory fails me as to who might have had the sass to answer such, "Fast women and pretty horses!" It triggered a tirade, so we pulled that stunt every chance we got.

The next year I went back to Sulligent, where I played football with the second team when we practiced against the first team.

Back home where I grew up, when a boy started to a new school, the others felt it necessary to test his mettle. Every time I changed schools, I had to stand my ground or get run over.

I was always big for my age, and with the work I had done, helping Dad farm or in his mechanic shop or lumber jobs, I was a hefty youth who could lift my weight again. More than the brawn, I had enough Joe-Daddler-Chandler in me until I didn't believe in being pushed around. I never started fights except one, and it was the only real whuppin' I ever got! The boy was considered to be a coward, but when I cornered him, I learned he wasn't as yeller as I thought. I caught hold of him, and then I couldn't turn loose.

I usually whipped the biggest bully first whenever I changed schools, which was often, because Daddy Mike was hauling lumber and moved wherever work could be found. That usually saved a lot of other fights while working your way to the top.

To my way of thinking, you don't call it getting whupped until you give up. That mental attitude became so ingrained through my growing-up years that, without realizing it or putting my philosophy into verbal credence, my personal motto throughout the years to come, and especially during my tour of duty, could be summed up in three words that a great man, named Winston Churchill, made famous in a speech: *"Never give up!"*

**Map of the State of Alabama, 1943** - *see Hamilton, near northeastern/ upper left corner of the state. Old historical city, county and state maps of Alabama from University of Alabama Library, Geography and Map Division, Library of Congress.*

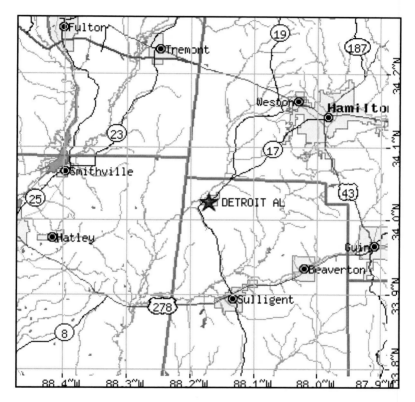

**Map close-up of NW corner of Alabama –**
*See distances for Hamilton, Detroit, Guin, Beaverton, Sulligent.*

# CHAPTER 2

## I'm in the Army Now

I managed to stay in school and graduate. My senior year at Sulligent, 1938, was a good year. Weighing in around 185 to 190, height of 5'8", I played fullback on our football team, which went undefeated.

After graduating in 1939, I drove the school bus in the mornings, worked at Hall's Chevrolet as a mechanic during the day, and then drove the bus home in the evening. When Dad quit, I picked up his old bus route, which he had driven for twelve years for extra income. Later, in my spare time, I worked alongside him as a mechanic in his garage where he set up shop in the one-horse town of Detroit, Alabama.

One Wednesday, Mother's brother, Uncle Carly Real,[1] came by to visit on the way to Barksdale AFB, Bossier City/Shreveport, Louisiana. He had been in the army for nearly twenty-five years. A bunch of us boys, at Detroit, had already planned to enlist in the army the following Saturday.

"Why don't you go to Birmingham with me? I'll get you signed up where I'm going to be stationed in Shreveport for a while," he suggested.

"I've already promised my friends I'd enlist with them," I said.

He said he was going to spend the night and give me time to think about it. I got out that evening, since there were no phones, and hunted up the other fellows. They decided they would wait to be drafted, which we figured would start soon enough, foreseeing the United States' involvement in the war in Europe was inevitable.

The next morning, I asked Dad to drive the school bus until I got back. I loaded up with Uncle Carly and went to the Birmingham Post Office, Court House and Federal Building, at 1800 Fifth Avenue North, which was where everyone signed up back then.

---

1 See Uncle Carly's photograph in Chapter 42 - Honoring Our Family Members.

Carly informed the recruiting sergeant, "This is my nephew and he's going to Shreveport with me." He outranked the Buck Sergeant, so the man obliged and granted his request.

While I was getting my examination, I looked down the line and saw Jim Dyer.[2] We had gone to school together and been best friends since we were kids. I thought Jim would be in Corpus Christi, Texas, by then, because Dad and I had worked on his car getting him ready to go.

"Where are you going?" Jim asked.

"Shreveport, Louisiana," I replied.

"I'm going to Jefferson Barracks, in St. Louis, Missouri. Come on and go with me," he coaxed.

"No, I'm going to Shreveport. My uncle is out yonder in the café eating lunch and he's already got it arranged."

Jim decided he wanted to go to Louisiana with me, so we went to the recruiting sergeant to request the assignment.

"No, I've got a quota I've got to fill for Jefferson Barracks, St. Louis, Missouri," he barked.

I left the Post Office and crossed the street to the café. After I told Uncle Carly that Jim wanted to go with me and what the sergeant had told me, he slapped the table and stood up.

"Well, we ought to be able to fix that!" he stated with finality.

He strode over to the recruiting sergeant. "These boys grew up together and they're going to camp together."

About the time the sergeant finished taking care of Jim, another guy, Grady Palmatier, came in the office. He had been in the Infantry and lived in Birmingham, and he told the recruiting sergeant, "I've decided I'm going to join up again. I aim to join the Air Force in Savannah."

"No, you're going to Jefferson Barracks," the recruiting sergeant snapped, his patience beginning to thin.

Fur flew, but the recruiting sergeant relented and then sent the three of us packing to the hotel to stay, just to keep us away from other recruits. I guess he was tired of messing with Uncle Carly.

---

2  See Jim Dyer's post-war photograph: Chapter 39 – James Fred Dyer.

\* \* \* \* \* \* \*

**October 11, 1940:** I was sworn in and joined the U.S. Army Air Corps at age twenty-one. I weighed in at 165 pounds.

Uncle Carly took us to the Savannah Air Base in Georgia. However, the base was not yet set up for recruit training.

While the Air Force was putting up tents and gearing up for the recruits, I went over to Fort Screven, Tybee Island, a coast artillery eighteen miles out of Savannah on the peninsula, and trained with the National Guard who had been called in.

After that training, I went back to Savannah Air Force Base to finish basic recruit training.[3] I was officially assigned to duty in the U.S. Air Force Headquarters Squadron 27th Bomb Group, Transportation Group, which furnished trucks for the 27th Bomb Group.

I wore a civilian dress suit when I joined up and drilled in it throughout most of basic. The United States was gearing up for war, and it took time to get enough uniforms for everyone to wear. Later, I got a pair of dungarees and drilled in them until they sent me to duty.

Captain William Hipps graduated from West Point, U.S. Military Academy (USMA), made pilot and joined the Air Force, but was assigned to the recruits because he had Infantry training. He was a tough old geezer and later accompanied us overseas.[4]

I finished basic in December of 1940.

\* \* \* \* \* \* \*

We were told there wasn't any need to put in for a furlough for Christmas because all the leave time had been granted.

Five of us slept to a tent. One of the guys in my tent worked as an administration clerk in the orderly room. Being a friend, he applied for

---

3 November 1940—Savannah Air Base became a Recruit Training Center. Lt. Hipps was promoted to Captain." Info from the "27th Bombardment Group, 39th Anniversary Program & Memorial Service," November 2–4, 1979, Shreveport-Barksdale, La., *Chronological Events of the 27th Bomb Group (L)*.

4 Promoted during the war, Brigadier General William G. Hipps, 16th Bombardment Squadron, financed the first of the annual 27th Bomb Reunions, which was held twenty-nine years later in April, 1975.

leave on my behalf, starting January 3, but didn't bother mentioning it to me.

My first day of duty, I was issued my dress uniform, and I sent my other clothes to the laundry.

General Lewis H. Brereton[5] arrived by plane; his driver didn't know he was due back that day and was nowhere to be found. They frantically hunted a man in uniform to go to the airport to drive the General's car and serve as his escort. I was the only one they could find on short notice.

They handed me a trip ticket, stuck a star in the window, and sent me after him. A vehicle is not allowed within a certain distance from the airplane, but being a greenhorn, I didn't know the rules. I drove under the wing and circled out the other side.

I slid to a halt and saw that the General was talking to someone. I parked the car with the right-hand side toward him and sat there waiting for him to get in. Unaware of military protocol, I didn't realize I was supposed to go around and open the door for him.

When he finished talking, he opened the car door for himself and got in.

"Where to?" I asked.

"To the new barracks," he stated. The barracks were being constructed at the other end of the runway.

I drove out from under the plane wing and headed down the middle of the taxiway, also against regulations, straight to the barracks. It seemed to be the logical thing to do since it was the shortest distance from point A to point B. The airport guard thought otherwise and came running out in a panic, then, confused when he saw the star on the jeep, threw up his hand to salute. We bounced off the end of the airstrip onto the street, and I screeched to a stop at his command.

---

5 From July 1939 to October 1940, General Lewis H. Brereton was on duty at Barksdale Field, La., as base commander and then was assigned to command the 17th Bombardment Wing, General Headquarters Air Force, with station at Savannah, Ga. In July 1941, he was assigned to command the Third Air Force at Tampa, Fla. Upon the outbreak of World War II, he commanded the Far East Air Force in the Philippines Islands. U.S. AIR FORCE – BIOGRAPHIES, https://www.af.mil/About-Us/Biographies/Display/Article/107651/lieutenant-general-lewis-hyde-brereton/

"Let's get out and inspect these barracks," General Brereton said. So, he got out on his side and I got out on mine. We walked through inspecting the barracks, with me putting in my two cents worth, and then returned to the jeep.

"Let's go," he said, opening the door on his side and sitting, while I sauntered around to mine.

"Let's go to Camp City," he ordered.

Dutifully, I wheeled around and drove back down the flight strip, taking the shortest route to reach our tents on the other side. Again, guards ran out attempting to wave us down, but threw up a hand to salute when they saw the General.

At the PX on the other end of the landing strip, the General motioned for me to pull over and said, "Stop there." I bounded off the landing field and bolted up to the PX.

In the meantime, the regular driver appeared on the scene. Nervous because he had missed his call to duty, he jumped into action when the General came out of the PX. The guy ran up to him, opened the door, and helped him carry his purchases to the vehicle.

"Sir, do you want me to drive for you?" he asked in a sweat.

"No, I've got a driver," General Brereton replied. Then he turned to me and asked, "How long have you been in, soldier?"

"Today is my first day on duty," I proudly announced. I believe he had figured that one out for himself.

"How long are you going to stay in?"

"Twenty years, I guess." (Later, after my tour of Japan, needless to say, I changed my career plans.)

I delivered him to his appointed address, where he exited, unassisted, and wished me good luck. I suppose he knew I needed it.

How embarrassing it was to recall the episode when it dawned on me later, after obtaining more training and better sense, how many blunders I had committed during my initiation duty day.

\* \* \* \* \* \* \*

**January 3, 1941:** Saturday morning, I started to the mess hall to eat breakfast. As I passed the orderly room, Capt. Hipps stepped out. I snapped to attention and saluted him.

"Chandler!" he said.

I froze on the spot, not knowing what to expect.

The first day we were assigned to duty, Capt. Hipps said, "Alright, men, there's two ways I'm going to know you're in my outfit—if you mess up, or if you are outstanding—otherwise, I won't even know you're here."

"There's a furlough for you on my desk that starts Monday morning at 6:00 a.m. I can't give it to you until Monday morning."

I was dumbfounded!

"Look on the duty roster and see if you're listed for duties," he said. I checked, but there wasn't anything posted. "I'm going to breakfast," he added and left the building.

I went straight into the orderly room and found the furlough. Passing up the mess hall, I ran back to the tent. Two guys from Louisiana, who had a car, were packing to leave.

"Are ya'll crowded?" I asked.

"Nope," he replied.

"Which way are you going?"

"Through Montgomery, Alabama," he said.

"You've got another passenger," I informed them, tossing my bags in with theirs.

When 6:00 a.m. on Monday morning rolled around, I was turning in at the forks of the road at home with a ten-day furlough.

* * * * * * *

Upon my return, I discovered that the tents were deserted. Everyone from my group had left on maneuvers. Also, the construction of the new barracks for our transportation group was finally completed.

Robert (Bob) Harp[6] and I struck up a friendship in basic that would last a lifetime. As a carpenter, he had been left on base to build packing crates. A guy by the name of Baskin, from Arkansas, was helping him. Not yet having an assigned job, I pitched in with them.

During that time, I qualified with the machine gun on the range and then was assigned as bomber gunner and started getting flight pay.[7]

I remained assigned to Transportation, Motor Pool, until March 13, when I boarded a train to Chanute Field, Rantoul, Illinois, where I was being sent to airplane mechanic school. That was right up my alley because I grew up tinkering with motors around Dad's garage.

I graduated the Air Mechanic school in September and got another ten-day leave, hitchhiking from Illinois to Jackson, Mississippi, where Uncle Ace Real lived, and then from there to Detroit, Alabama. When I got ready to leave home and head back, Dad said, "I'll run you south to Birmingham, Son."

"No, Dad, just drop me out at the highway at Beaverton." Beaverton was a little town seventeen miles from home. That was the last time I saw him until 1945, after the war.

When I got back to base, my outfit was away again on maneuvers at Fort Charles, Louisiana.

I was supposed to be assigned to the maintenance crew on an airplane. However, I stayed with the 16th Bomb Group until my group came back into camp, exuberant from winning on maneuvers.[8]

\* \* \* \* \* \* \*

In the interim, I was assigned to motor pool duty to drive for officers, including a Jewish doctor with a captain rating. He and I didn't see eye to

---

6 See post-war photograph of Bob in Chapter 38 - Robert R. Harp.

7 "March 1941, Savannah Air Base received A-20 (Havoc-American medium bomber, attack aircraft, night fighter) and A24 (Dauntless-Banshee) airplanes. April 1941. The recruits completed their training and joined the 3rd and 27th, then off to school for advanced training." Ibid, *Chronological Events of the 27th Bomb Group (L)*.

8 "September 1941—The squadrons returned from maneuvers in Louisiana, the recruits returned from training schools, and the 27th was chosen for "Operation Plum," which meant we were going overseas. Ibid, *Chronological Events–27th Bomb Group*.

eye and, invariably, got into heated arguments while I was driving for him (more about him later in the war).

I'd take the officers to the airfield, then go to the armament to clean guns and do assorted armament work. Later, I'd go back to the airfield to pick them up, or any other officers who came in.

After I arrived, General Brereton, commander of the post at Shreveport and who had participated in the 1940 maneuvers, had been sent to the Philippines, where he had previously been stationed during 1916-1917. After the 27th won the maneuvers, he requested them to be sent to join him. We started packing; our luggage tags read "Operation: PLUM."

And that's how I got to make the wonderful trip of a lifetime!

\* \* \* \* \* \* \*

***Additional Information:*** General George C. Marshall planned mock battles with 350,000 U.S. soldiers, 50,000 U.S. Army vehicles, pursuit planes for dogfights, A-20A attack and Navy dive bombers, tanks and trucks, and newly formed paratroops, as well. Medical units and rear-area combat hospitals' preparedness was tested. Exercises were enacted on 3,400 square miles of marshy mud roads, pine forests, and deep swamps full of quicksand, in Louisiana and East Texas. Loudspeakers blared recorded sounds of battle, canister smoke shrouded the battlefield, and bags of sand were dropped from aircraft to simulate impact of artillery shells.

Training consisted of two events in Spring and Autumn 1940 and two more in 1941, the most important held September 1941. Marshall crafted a thirteen-week basic training regimen, challenging and instructive, which revealed weakness in plans and leaders. The events honed combat leadership skills of future generals, including Bradley, Clark, Eisenhower, Krueger, McNair, and Patton. Eisenhower won the first set; Patton, won the second. Three months later, the forces were sent to the battlefields of Europe and the Pacific. It became known as "combat college for troop leading."[9]

---

9 For more info on these interesting training battles, see: "*Louisiana Maneuvers (1940–1941),*" HistoryNet.com. Also: Oct. 6, 1941, issue of *Life* magazine. (For actual video – see YouTube: "Your Army in the Making – 1942 – Carolina Maneuvers" by WWII Public Domain, 08/11/13)

**Drolan in uniform.**

**Drolan at home on leave. Front Row *(L-R)* Diane Chandler, Doyle Chandler; Back Row: Minos "Mike" (Dad) Chandler, Juler (Mother) Chandler, Drolan, Yank, Roberta Chandler Rye and Ordle Rye**

# CHAPTER 3

## Operation: PLUM

THE train ride across the states to the West Coast was a new experience and a real eye-opener in more ways than one. I had never strayed far from the backside of my woods, and chugging across the country on the steam train allowed me to see this beautiful "sweet land of liberty." However, young soldiers can find more ways to entertain themselves than gawking at scenery.[10]

We passed time on the trip, and later on the ship, by gambling whenever we got a chance. I had never gambled, didn't even know how, until I went into the service. After I learned to roll the dice, I'd break up a game when I joined it because I had a good case of beginner's luck!

The first sergeant of the 16th, a big-time gambler, got the dice and jumped on me. About the third or fourth pass I made, he said, "Somebody else get him." So, the next guy moved in on me. The first sergeant put his money down with mine and pulled the money while I rolled the dice. Every time I went to the table, he'd do that. He wouldn't fade me.

(At the first POW—Prisoner of War—reunion I attended after the war, a fellow named Finch, out of the 17th, strolled up to me and said, "How are you, Drolan Chandler?"

I looked puzzled. "I don't think I know who you are, but you seem to know me."

"Yeah, I know you. When a man makes thirty-two straight passes on me, I remember him," Finch exclaimed.)

---

10      "October 1941—Everyone was issued winter clothes. Three troop trains, traveling separate routes, took us to San Francisco. Capt. Eubanks lost his golf clubs, and our luggage went into the Bay. NO SHORE LEAVE. Angel Island was our Port of Embarkation." Ibid, *Chronological Events–27th Bomb Group*.

\* \* \* \* \* \* \*

**The luxury liner, USS President Coolidge.**
*Photo courtesy South Pacific WWII Museum and Coral Quays Resort.*

**November 1, 1941:** We sailed out of San Francisco, aboard the *USS President Coolidge*, a former luxury ocean liner, which had been commandeered as a troop/freight ship. It had two swimming pools on it. We left the United States, destination: PLUM, which was kept secret from us until we docked at Manila in the Philippines. PLUM, we found out, was the code name for U.S. Army in Philippines.

(It's sad to say, but that grand liner, later in the war, hit a mine in the ocean before docking and sank.)

**November 6, 1941:** "The ship docked in Honolulu and we had shore leave from 0800 until 1400 hrs. It was a good time for all. We sailed the remainder of the way under blackout condition, with only one stop at Guam."[11]

Bob Harp spent the day with his brother, Woodrow, who was in the army. (Woodrow Harp came through the Pearl Harbor bombing without getting injured. He was sent to New Guinea to fight, and came home to the States after his big brother, Bob Harp.)

---

11      Ibid, *Chronological Events of the 27th Bomb Group (L)*.

**November 25, 1941:** "We arrived at Manila Pier 7 on Thanksgiving Day and were transported by truck to Ft. McKinley. No planes had arrived yet. We drilled in the a.m., played softball in the afternoon, and went into Manila in the evening. Ray Holland bought a monkey and a rooster. Harrison from the 17th bought a rooster also."[12]

Results were cock fights, something new to the majority of our guys. Cock fighting was a big sport in the Philippines.

A few days later, unknown to us, the war would start, on December 11, but my buddy and I almost started our own war with the civilians that first night in the Philippines.

\* \* \* \* \* \*

I had a big roll of money burning my pockets from gambling aboard ship. Although we weren't supposed to be off base that night, Bob Harp and I slipped out of camp and hired a taxi driver to show us around town.

Filipinos took advantage of the new guys, and instead of the usual six pesos (3 dollars) fare, he charged us tenderfoots 6 dollars. None the wiser, we shelled it out. It proved to be a bargain, considering he accompanied us all night and saved our necks a time or two.

When most of the better places closed at midnight, we were still in a partying mood and ended up on the seedy side of town. We ventured into one Filipino dive, which had to be entered through a maze of chicken coops and across a hog pen.

We ordered a couple of drinks, and I handed the bartender a hundred-dollar bill.

"I don't got change for that. Got to go get it. Wait here," he said and left the bar. When he returned, he didn't have it all in American money; some of it was in peso notes, some in dollars. He proceeded to count alternately in pesos and dollars, and I suspected he was trying to swindle me. Being pretty well tanked up by that time, and lacking better sense, I threatened to take the place apart.

---

12      Ibid, *Chronological Events of the 27th Bomb Group (L)*

Our cab driver, sober and aware of the potential danger, grabbed me by the elbow and shoved us outside, trying to quiet me down before I lost more than my change. We staggered back through the web of animal pens.

"We're still thirsty," we grumbled to the cabby as he mopped his brow and sped away from the scene.

"There's nothing open. Nowhere else to go," he responded.

We badgered him until he relented. "Well, there's a place out in the country I know of."

We bounced over rutted roads so far out in the boonies we could never have found our way back to base had he decided to ditch us.

He pulled to a halt outside a native hut. "Drop your money in that trough," he instructed. We deposited the required amount into a slot and heard it slide down inside. Shortly, a bottle of booze rolled out a second trough, which slanted back toward us. Satisfied and soused, we headed back toward Fort William McKinley.[13]

He dropped us off at daylight as roll call commenced. The first sergeant shouted, "Drolan Chandler," just as I staggered out of the cab. I yelled "Here," and he looked ominously in my direction. By the time he bellowed, "Bob Harp," Bob was still crawling out of the taxi.

Needless to say, that was the last of our celebrating for a while to come.

* * * * * * *

The U.S. Air Force Headquarters Squadron 27th Bombardment Group was composed of Headquarters & HQ Squadron, 16th, 17th, 91st, and 48th Material Squadron, and 454th Ordinance Squadron, including Radiomen and Communications, although I never had contact with them until we were crossing the ocean on the liner.

---

13      After Philippine independence on July 4, 1946, the U.S. surrendered to the Republic of the Philippines all rights of possession, jurisdiction, supervision, and control over the Philippine territory except for the use of their military bases. On May 14, 1949, Fort William McKinley was turned over to the Philippine government. The facility became the home of the Philippine Army and, later, the Philippine Navy, and was renamed Fort Bonifacio. Wikipedia: Fort Bonifacio.

Our new quarters in the Philippines consisted of tents lining the golf course at Fort McKinley, an infantry base, even though we were Air Force. Bob Harp was assigned to a different area of tents than Jim Dyer and me.

Our Radio and Communications men were assigned on location at the airports to set up operations and were there when the war started. Filipino Scouts were housed in the barracks until they went to the front.

The fort was approximately five miles from downtown Manila, but was considered part of the city.[14] We had permanent passes and went to town any time we weren't on duty.

Upon arrival in the Philippines, the 27th Bomb Group, which was to have worked on aircraft at Nichols[15] and Eber Air Field, was assigned to a motor pool because our airplanes hadn't arrived, so I flew low in jeeps and trucks instead. We were kept busy moving the trucks and equipment off the ship. Driving in Manila was confusing because they drove on the left instead of the right like we did back home.

We were trained mechanics for a heavy bomber group. I also qualified as crew member aerial machine gunner, and heavy bomber, and I was supposed to be on flight pay.

\* \* \* \* \* \* \*

Before the war started, I received a few pieces of mail while in Manila.

At that time, land was selling for a dollar per acre around our homestead, and I had instructed Dad to invest the money I was sending home in as much land as he could acquire.

My problem was that the military had a purchase limit of one fifty-dollar money order per day. I had a wad of money from my gambling

14      Manila, pre-war, was considered to be the Pearl of the Orient and the most beautiful city in the Far East. Hotels, theaters, department stores lined the street. "Victims of Circumstance" and "Manila Nostalgia" by Lou Gopal, Feb 29, 2016.

15      Nichols Field later became the headquarters of the Philippine Air Force. First named Nichols Air Base, it is now named Villamor Air Base. Wikipedia: Nichols Field. "Eber Air Field was on the hill as you went to Nichols, so they were right there close together," Drolan Chandler.

aboard ship and was buying a money order daily to send home airmail on the next flight of the China Clipper.[16]

As my luck would have it, the China Clipper got shot down, and the money never made it to the states. Later, I was unable to reclaim any of it because all my receipts were lost while I was a POW.

Had it made its destination and Dad had bought a bunch of that land, I'd be sitting easy now, because not only has the value of the land soared, but oil was discovered in the area and a number of folks hit pay dirt, literally.

**PanAm's China Clipper.**
*Photograph from picryl.com, GetArchive.net – Public Domain*

---

16      Collectively known as the China Clipper (each clipper was given individual names), the flying boats built for Pan American Airways, inaugurated the first commercial transpacific airmail service from San Francisco to Manila, beginning in November 1935. The clippers were "luxury flying hotels", with sleeping accommodation, dining rooms and leisure facilities ... the price of a return air ticket, say San Francisco to Honolulu, was 1,700 dollars (equivalent to 29,000 dollars in 2018—by comparison, a brand-new Plymouth automobile cost about 600 dollars in the late 1930s.) "Pan American Airways wins Collier Trophy for Pacific Plan Service," *Life* magazine, Aug. 23, 1937, pp. 35–41. The entire PanAM Clipper fleet was pressed into military service during WWII.

*USS President Coolidge was converted to a troop ship in 1941, and painted grey. Photo courtesy of South Pacific WWII Museum. National Archives photo no. 36983.* [17]

---

17  Pre-war, *President Coolidge* ran voyages for sun seekers in the Pacific and Far East. June, 1941, it became a troopship; 1942 properly converted, painted gray, with guns mounted. Oct. 26, 1942, as the ship entered the harbor of Espiritu Santo, the ship struck one of our own mines and sank. Capt. Nelson ran her aground and ordered troops to abandon the ship. Over the next ninety minutes, 5,240 men got safely ashore, with only two casualties. The ship is now a protected wreck and dive site. Divers see guns, cannons, Jeeps, helmets, trucks, chandeliers, mosaic file fountain, etc. Wikipedia. Also, see: Hello-Kiwi Tagebuch – Vanuatu3 (USS Colidge) for dive info. *Note:* In 2013, after 73 years, the remains of Capt. E.J. Euart were found by his dog tags. He had repeatedly rescued men who could not get out, but then was unable to escape himself. Per DPAA.mil News Release 16–65, 08/24/16.

**Manila, downtown pre-war.**
*Photo Courtesy of Lou Goupal, author, www.Manilanostalgia.com*

**Manila tranvia (trolley) car on rails drawn by horses.**
*Photograph courtesy of Lou Goupal, author, Manila Nostalgia.com*

**Philippines, Manila – Pier 7.** *Photograph courtesy of Mansell.com/ lindavdahl/omuta17/photo_gallery/photo_gallery.html*

**Fort William McKinley, entrance.**
*Source unknown. Image may be subject to copyrighted.*

**YMCA***

**Infantry Barracks**
*(occupied by Filipino soldiers; we had tents on the golf course)**

**Officers' Quarters***

**Cavalry Barracks***

**Drill at the Fort.** *Training - firing 37mm anti-tank gun.**

**Fort McKinley - tanks lined up in background** *The above photos are courtesy of Pinoy Kollektor: Collection-copyright B McIntosh 2011 (permission granted)*

# CHAPTER 4

## ATTACKED!

**DECEMBER 7, 1941:** The Japanese came like a thief in the night. The U.S. Pacific fleet at Pearl Harbor on the island of Oahu, Hawaii, was devastated (Luzon and Hawaii are on opposite sides of the International Date Line).

We were eating dinner when the shocking and sad news was broadcast that Japanese planes had hit Pearl Harbor. Apprehension filled the air, and everyone was eager for retaliation.

"Don't get out there and get excited and start shooting," the officer cautioned me when he put me on guard duty around 9:00 p.m. that night. "You'll scare everybody to death. Be sure it is enemy planes before you start firing."

Ten hours after the attack on Pearl Harbor, the Japanese turned their attention to the Philippines and attacked our U.S. Air Force bases, including Clark Field, 60 miles northwest of Manila. I heard the planes and knew they weren't ours by the sound. I waited like a sitting duck for a warning signal.

My first sergeant started blowing his whistle, so I commenced to firing into the air to signal the men. Soldiers poured from their tents.

In the event of attack, we had planned to use a gully-like embankment for trenches. The women's barracks lined its banks. Our tents were pitched on the parade ground with a golf course situated between the banks and us.

With enemy aircraft strafing us left and right, the men ran across the open golf course, making a beeline for the banks. The ladies scattered and dove under their barracks.

When the commotion started, the first sergeant, a small man, blew his whistle and dashed toward the ravine, pumping for everything he was worth. The rest of the guys followed on his heels.

"Big Stoop," a tall, slender fellow who wore a size fifteen shoe and was too uncoordinated to master the art of marching because he stumbled over his own feet, came out of the tent on his hands and knees. He never made it to his feet, but passed everything in sight yelling, "Don't leave me boys, don't leave me boys!" As he sped past the first sergeant, he shouted over his shoulder, "Stand there and get killed if you want to! I'm outta here!"

I was out in the field beyond the tents, on duty, and was one of the last ones coming in. With tracers zipping all around, my feet nearly ran out from under me. By the time I reached the bank, I was practically airborne and would have sailed completely over, except for an abrupt slap in the face by a banana stalk growing out of the bottom of the ravine. Grabbing hold of the stalk for dear life, I tumbled down the fifteen-foot ditch like Jack sliding down the beanstalk with a giant in hot pursuit.

After the assault was over, we counted off and found we were one man short. Nobody could remember seeing the guy. When we got back to the tent, we found him sleeping like a baby. Enemy aircraft had crisscrossed his tent, strafing both ways, up the side of his body through the cot and all the way out the tent with a .50 caliber machine gun. He had not moved a muscle and didn't have a scratch on him. Had he awakened and jumped up to run, it's highly probable he'd have gotten killed because the Japs had riddled the tent from both directions.

There are just some things you can't explain, and my life for the next four years was full of mysterious incidents and close calls. Someone back home must have been getting hold of Someone upstairs!

* * * * * * *

The Japanese attack crippled our defenses. We still had no planes, and after the first raid, our pilots were flown out of the Philippines to another location. Ground crews with very little combat training were left to take up arms. Capt. Mark Wohlfeld obtained some First World War Springfields and Enfields, and we all learned to shoot the rifles. I already had plenty of experience with hunting for game back home.

**December 18, 1941:** "A group of our pilots flew out with Capt. Fred Hoffman. They headed south to get our planes and return. Little did we know it would be years until we met again. Neilson Field had an air raid; the hangers were burning when Sam Moody jumped into a ditch. He felt someone grab his legs every time a Jap strafed the field. When he could turn around, he saw it was Gen. Brereton."[18]

After the war started, only twenty-eight survivors stationed at Eber Air Field escaped and joined us. The rest of the radiomen and communications were slaughtered. The Japs had already parachuted in and were setting up post at the airfield, although they had not completely secured the area.

A large supply of oil, .50 caliber machine guns, and ammunition had been deserted at Eber Air Field; also, the chemical masks and chemicals (solution used for neutralization) to be used for counteracting mustard gas had been left there. Mustard gas had been used in the First World War, and we couldn't predict whether the Japs planned to use it on us. Unsure of Japanese intentions, it was essential that we rescue that supply located at the airport as a precaution, considering it was the only stash of it on the island.

Our officer called us together and said, "We want fourteen volunteers to go to Eber Air Field and bring out the oil, ammunition, supply of chemical masks, whatever else we can salvage."

No response. We stood silently, waiting for the other guy to step up.

"We want fourteen volunteers *NOW*," his voice boomed again.

I had been in the service long enough to know they were going to get fourteen men one way or another. To avoid wasting more time, I reluctantly stepped out and said, "I'll go."

Raymond Demers, a draftee from Tacoma, Washington, stepped out and said, "I'll go, too." We didn't have many draftees, but he was sent to fill our quota of men before we left boot camp.

After we broke the ice, other guys began stepping out. Seven trucks, seven machine guns, and two supply officers were assigned for our task.

---

18    Ibid, *Chronological Events–27th Bomb Group.*

"You are to go to Eber Air Field and load these trucks with everything you can confiscate. Bring it out as quickly and quietly as you can manage. Don't stop or report to anyone, Filipino, Americans, or anyone else. That's your mission."

# CHAPTER 5

## Mission Impossible!

### *Reconnaissance Missions*

**Bataan Truck Convoy.** *Battlingbastardbataan.com*

NIGHT caught us at a small *barrio* (village) named Del Monte, after the Del Monte Company that canned pineapples and other fruits and vegetables. We pulled our trucks into the large Del Monte warehouse, out of sight from enemy aircraft.

By daylight we headed out again and encountered Filipinos who attempted to stop us, but we didn't slow up, according to orders. It wasn't necessary to use the machine guns, which were loaded and braced for action.

We reached Eber Field about dusk and hid the trucks in a building close to the airstrip. One man was left to guard the trucks while the two officers and remaining thirteen men climbed on one truck and nervously pulled out.

Under the cover of darkness, without lights, we patrolled around the field for whatever we could find. We knew Japs were in the area, so we weren't taking much time for sightseeing. From what little we could make out, since we were running "blackout" without lights, it wasn't a pretty sight anyway. Craters gutting the runway had to be dodged, as well as the dead bodies littered here and there. Only twenty-three men had survived and come to us from that field.

When one of us lucked up on oil or ammunition, we signaled for the truck, scrambling to load it as quickly as possible. Ordinarily, two men would have difficulty picking up a drum of oil and loading it on the truck—twenty-, thirty-, fifty-five-gallon drums at 8 pounds liquid per gallon—you get the idea! But, with our adrenaline pumping full speed, it wasn't a strain. Two of us would pick up a full drum of oil or a case of ammunition and toss it onto the truck like a bag of beans. When the truck was loaded to the hilt, the driver raced to the warehouse and exchanged it for an empty vehicle while we continued our scavenger hunt around the field and base.

When all seven trucks were loaded, we breathed easier, relieved to have the worst of the mission behind us. Within hours, we were on the road rolling and spent the night at the Del Monte warehouse again.

On the return trip to Manila the next day, Demers got behind the wheel. I rode in the back, manning the machine gun, agreeing to pound on the top of the cab if we needed to stop.

We came to a long stretch of open highway with no trees in sight, only a straight blacktop road as far as the eye could see. Hearing a roar overhead, I looked up in time to count seventy four-engine bombers in formation. To me, it felt as if a bull's eye target was painted on top of the cab because of the ammunition we were hauling. I cringed and held my breath, thinking that we were the prey.

I performed a Watusi drum rap on the back of the cab to get Demers attention before clearing out. The whole convoy, traveling 60 mph, came to an abrupt halt simultaneously. Demers shoved the gear in low, cut off the switch, and jumped out, all in one instant, at the same time as the guys in the other trucks. I bailed out the back, landing spread eagle on the ground, tensed for the first wave of explosions.[19]

Amazed when they didn't dump their lethal cargo on us, we listened as a small town within close proximity caught the brunt of their attack and was demolished in one fell swoop. Evidently, the planes were designated to bomb certain towns and took turns dropping their loads. From there to Manila, every town we came across was ablaze.

Fortunately for us, the Japs missed a splendid opportunity to see a magnificent fireworks display!

**WWII Imperial Kawanishi H8K "Emily"** *flying boat, high performance, four-engine bomber, reconnaissance and transport aircraft, long-range and good defensive armament. Photo from Seaplane International, www. seaplaneinternational.com/2015/05/14/ some-interesting-pictures-of-ww2-seaplanes/*

---

19       Demers and I got separated sometime during the war and didn't see each other again until 1966 at a POW reunion in Shreveport, Louisiana. I was surprised to see him. After the war, he had married a woman from Shreveport and moved there.

\* \* \* \* \* \* \*

As the Japanese landed, the Filipino scouts who were living in the barracks were moved to the frontlines, which were beginning to form. We stayed at Ft. McKinley until Christmas Day.

The tempting aroma of turkey and dressing wafted through the air as we marched into the mess hall for a welcome holiday meal. Before being served, however, orders came over the loudspeaker: "Everybody outside!"

Mouths watering for the neglected festive Christmas dinner, we shuffled outside, grumbling, and loaded into the line of waiting trucks. We were taken down to the dock where we stayed until nightfall. They didn't bother to give us food or water.

A bunch of our troops were ordered to burn Neilson field and evacuate to Port Area. By evening, Ft. McKinley was evacuated. It was like a ghost town. Manila was the same. At midnight, they boarded a freighter, thinking they were headed south to join our planes.

Instead, they were transported across Manila Bay to Mariveles, where they unloaded and marched to the Bataan Picnic area. They learned the road to Manila was open, so they loaded the trucks with food, whiskey, candy, champagne, beer, parts for aircraft, clothing, shoes, and as much medicine as they could carry.[20]

I was held over, along with others, to drive a truck in the motor pool to help move cargo out of Manila around the coast to a warehouse in Bataan.

Before pulling out that night, a buddy from Montgomery, Alabama, and I were told by the Commanding Officer, "You boys protect this load. There's 50,000 dollars' worth of equipment in this van."

We joined the procession and got as far as a small *barrio* outside of Manila before we pulled over to the shoulder of the road during the wee hours of the morning to sack out. More tired than hungry, we lumbered wearily out of the vehicles, slid down a bank to a soft, grassy area, and were all snoring within minutes.

Filipinos didn't confine their animals in pens. The next morning, hogs rooting around rudely awakened several of us.

---

20    Ibid, *Chronological Events—27th Bomb Group.*

We scouted up a bite of breakfast, a tasty morning-after Christmas treat of sardines, but we ate like pigs. Maybe it was the company we kept.

After unloading at the designated warehouses in Bataan, we made several trips back to Manila on reconnaissance missions to transport our equipment to safety.

\* \* \* \* \* \*

A night or two later, I drove a gas truck filled with twelve hundred gallons of airplane fuel, in a convoy, back around the coast to Bataan. We were running blackout so that enemy planes couldn't sight us. Army trucks had blackout lights on the rear, about the size of a silver dollar, which emitted a sliver of light for the following vehicle.

As the head vehicle led the way for the convoy, I was cautiously tailing the blackout lights of the truck in front of me. Suddenly, they mysteriously disappeared. I braked slightly and squinted into the pitch dark. Sitting high in the cab, I peered through the large windshield, which was almost tall enough for a man to walk through, and over the hood, straining to see the road ahead.

Suddenly, like a spotlight beaming from the portals of heaven, a full moon popped out from behind the cloud screen and shone brightly down on a river in front of me. In a split second, I caught sight of the ledge of the bank, only a few feet directly in front of my truck, which dropped approximately fifty feet to the river.

By instinct, I jerked to the right, miraculously swerving onto a plank runway, which our engineers had hastily erected after the attack. It was slightly offset from the damaged end of the bridge and veered around the rubble to join the remainder of the bridge further out in the river. God only knows—and probably had something to do with it—how my wheels found that narrow ramp by mere inches, just in the nick of time.

As soon as I swung onto the new bridge, I was able to detect the blackout lights of the truck ahead. He had anticipated the detour somehow, but when he had zigged, I had zagged.

I don't know what might have happened to the aviation fuel had I plunged fifty feet down, whether it would have exploded or whether we would have just sunk to the bottom. Either way, it could not have been a gracious exit. When that moon popped out, that's all that saved me.

* * * * * * *

It took several days' travel to reach a former recreation area on Bataan, called the Salian Camp, somewhere between Orion and Mariveles.

While at the Salian Camp, I remember hearing an occasional Tokyo Rose broadcast out of Manila before we went to the frontlines. The program was difficult to pick up most of the time. She played just enough music to make you homesick, then slipped in messages about where the 31st Infantry, or other groups, were located. She had all kinds of information on the units.

One evening she said, "27th Bomb Group at Salian Camp, you've got a good place to rest." She told who and where we were, supplying information to the Japs!

We didn't want to listen for long because it was too depressing and infuriating, a real morale killer, when we did intercept it. We knew Jap reconnaissance planes had been reporting our positions for her to broadcast the word to their troops.

**Iva Toguri, dubbed "Tokyo Rose",** *By David Shapinsky from Washington, D.C., United States – Public Domain: WWII.*[21]

\* \* \* \* \* \* \*

**January 1, 1942:** "Some men of the 27th were returning in one truck when a Jap Betty tried to strafe them. They hid in the fields and under buildings. When he came in real low, they all jumped out, shooting up into

---

21      *Tokyo Rose* is the name coined by South Pacific Allied troops for English-speaking female broadcasters spreading Japanese propaganda in the Second World War. Read the unfortunate story of Iva Toguri D'Aquino (07/04/16–09/26/06) in biograph. com/military-figure toyko-rose. Falsely convicted of treason, this American citizen served six of the ten-year-sentence, before being pardoned by President Gerald Ford in 1977.

the plane. He didn't have a chance. The plane burst into flames and crashed. Our first downed plane for the 27th had been shot down from the ground."[22]

\* \* \* \* \* \* \*

The secondary line ran from Orion, across and below Bagac, where the majority of our outfit had settled in. The Army learned there were about eight thousand airmen on Bataan. They divided us into two groups; 1st and 2nd Provisional Infantry. The 1st was assigned the left flank, while the 2nd took up their place on the right.[23]

Clyde Hillhouse drove the chow truck awhile, carrying food to the frontlines. When Clyde got hit with a piece of shrapnel, Bob Harp replaced him.

I continued with the motor pool. A few of the roads were paved, but most were so bomb-pitted that travel was torturously slow and dusty, with hairpin curves. As quickly as the engineers made repairs, the Nips struck again.[24]

One night, after setting up a temporary location for the motor pool near the Salian Camp, another buddy and I rode to Mariveles to get parts for repairs. On the way back to our camp, a van passed us at breakneck speed. Dust boiled up from his wheels as he whipped by, nearly choking us to death. Through the whirling clouds, we watched as the back door of the van banged open and shut, three or four times.

"Something fell out of that truck," buddy exclaimed.

We slid to a stop, jumped out, and fumbled around in the dark. A huge loaf of field bread had toppled out of the delivery truck, which was headed for the kitchen at the frontlines. Field bread will keep well because it has a half-inch thick crust to preserve it for five or six days without refrigeration, up to eight days in the winter. It can hold up to rough handling in

---

22      Ibid, *Chronological Event–27th Bomb.*

23      The Army tried to focus the majority of its forces in the northern part of the peninsula to defend the front, "Abucay Line" in early January 1942.

24      'Nip' was slang for *Nippon*, the word for Japan or *Nihon*. Nippon means "the origin of the sun". Since the sun rises in the East, Japan's flag had a crimson-red disc at the center representing Hinomaru, the "circle of the sun" or "Land of the Rising Sun".

transport, too. The idea is to break open the hard crust and, inside, you've got good, tender eating.

"We've got bread now and nothing to go with it," my buddy said.

"There's food hidden out at the Salian Camp we had taken off the trucks," I recalled, since we were in the vicinity. "If we go scratch around, we might find something to go with this bread."

We detoured off route toward the deserted camp. Not a soul was in sight, so we went in and foraged blindly, not daring to show a light, and getting that creepy "eyes watching in the dark" feeling, we didn't let moss grow under our feet.

One of us stumbled across an unlabeled gallon can and dug it out. Unsure of the contents, but concerned about attracting the attention of unwanted Japanese dinner guests, we hightailed it out.

Back at the motor pool campsite, we eagerly opened the can. Ugh! Boiled beets. We cracked open the loaf and filled up on bread and beets. I hate beets, but it was a feast that night.

FIELD BREAD JUST OUT OF OVEN.

**Field Bread with thick crust for better preservation.**
*joyoffieldrations.blogspot.com. Image may be subject to copyright.[25]*

---

25        See YouTube US Army Field Bread R1916 by Atomic Viking 06/29/15; See YouTube WWII Field Kitchen Overview-2/15/18

\* \* \* \* \* \*

Our motor pool progressed as swiftly as possible around the peninsula, considering the poor excuses the Filipinos called "roads," with hairpin curves and roller-coaster dips and hills, almost impassable at places. About the time we got our gear unloaded and set up camp at a place we thought was safe, we'd have to load it all again and move out because the Japs kept encroaching on our lines, inching our men further back. The motor pool trailed behind with equipment and trucks.

**January 9–23, 1942:** The Abucay line held for a while but was slowly pushed back to a road that ran from Pilar across to Bagac.

At the beginning of the attacks, our officers told us that because we were Air Force and not trained infantrymen, we wouldn't be sent to the frontlines. Our outfit set up machine guns on a secondary line at Orion.

But we didn't have to go to the front. It came to us when they pulled out all the infantry at Pilar/Bagac. We were left wide open!

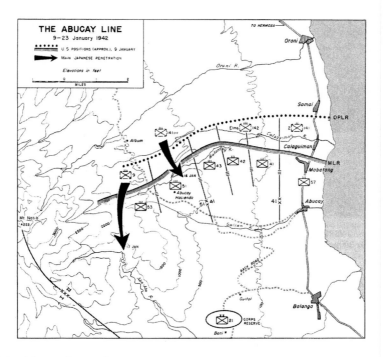

**The Abucay Line – Jan 9-23, 1942.** *U.S. Army Center of Military History, Mansell.com/lindavdahl/Omuta17/maps_charts_lists*

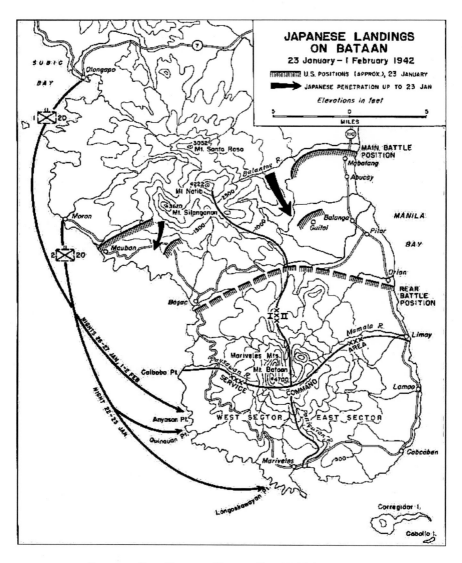

**Japanese Landings on Bataan-Jan 23-Feb 21, 1942.**
*The US Army Campaign of WWII, Public Domain*

VFW Post 7591

**Map of Bataan Mountainous area,** *VFW Post 7591, Photograph courtesy of Mansell.com/lindavdah/omuta17/maps_charts_lists/*

# CHAPTER 6

## Motor Pool

WHEN the line was first established, Vernon Richards and I were placed in charge of the motor pool. I had drawn corporal's pay, but I had a specialist rating and was only a private. He was a corporal and had the stripes, so he was the ranking man.

While the line was being dug in at Orion, we were hidden out in the mountain area near Limay with the trucks. The two of us had the demanding task of keeping a hundred and ten trucks ready to go at a moment's notice.

Our trucks were concealed under the natural camouflage of bamboo thickets and trees. We knew better than to cut the bamboo for cover. When it died and turned brown, the Japs would suspect something was amiss.

The Filipinos had a battery of artillery near us. Although we couldn't see them, we could definitely (and *deafeningly*) hear them. One night a Filipino came running into our camp in a frenzy, shouting, "The Japs have shelled our guns and we've got wounded men. We need an ambulance to take them down to the hospital at Mariveles. Pronto!"

I didn't think it was a good idea to leave the trucks, but Vernon decided to go, and I couldn't stop him since he outranked me. He raced out of camp in the ambulance.

After he left, I got busy gassing up trucks with one of the tankers. When it ran out of gas, I stashed the empty truck back in the brush, broke out another tanker that was full, and brought it around to fill up the remaining vehicles. There may have been two or three gas trucks in the whole fleet. A number of the trucks were ten-wheelers.

On edge, I thought I heard noise overhead and slammed on the brakes. Japanese artillery was trying to take out the Filipino artillery below us. A shell whizzed over the tanker, then exploded by my left front wheel. Shrapnel usually blows forward, so luckily, it didn't even puncture my tire.

The windshields had been removed to prevent sun glare, which acted as a reflector and would inadvertently signal the Japs as to our whereabouts. In the space of a heartbeat, I jumped up in the seat and dove through the empty windshield, across the hood, tumbling to the ground.

After we had sailed from San Francisco, we discovered some bozo had left all our truck keys back in the states; thus, all the vehicles had to be straight-wired in order to crank them. When I came to my senses, I realized I had ripped all those wires out the window in my clenched fists.

I remembered pulling the truck up beside a trench, and scooting on my elbows around to it, I hunkered down in the hole. Shells were singing everywhere. The Japanese artillery was hurling them in rapid fire.

Finally, it dawned on me: *What kind of fool am I? Lying under this gas tanker with them throwing shells left and right!*

Then I thought of a hole out yonder a little way and skittered toward it like a sand crab. I heard a shell coming, *woof-woof-woof!* When you've been under enough of them, you know just about where its target is, and I knew I was it!

My brain was clicking like a slot machine and I recalled another hole over to the right. I felt like the last turkey at a turkey shoot, dodging harum-scarum. I practically sprouted wings and sailed through the air into it. By the time I kissed the bottom of it, I was suffocating to death. I had to come up to catch my breath before the shelling stopped.

Surfacing for air, I saw the reason. A truck, parked next to the hole, had been hit by a piece of shrapnel, blowing off the rim of the tire; all its air burst out and shot dust down on me.

I ducked again just as shells hit several of the ten-wheeler trucks that I had been about to gas up. Fortunately for me, being empty, they didn't explode.

After the attack subsided, much to my amazement and relief, all of the vehicles could still move. I had to put a new tire on the one that blew out by my refuge trench and reinstall the wires in the first truck, which I had jerked out during my quick ejection escape. I figured I got off lightly!

* * * * * * *

From the time Vernon and I could barely see daylight until we couldn't see our hands in front of us at night, we worked full tilt to keep all the trucks in top condition. Each one had to be ready to move out posthaste, either to the front or to another location. That meant keeping them gassed and revving each one up daily to keep the battery charged. We were driving ourselves pretty hard since there were only two of us.

We were already asleep one night, tired to the bone, when the Japs started their infernal shelling again. The place was worse than trying to snatch a few minutes of sleep in a hospital!

Our living quarters consisted of a scaffold with a blanket thrown across it under the bamboo trees. Approximately thirty feet away, we had constructed an improvised air raid shelter, which amounted to a little trench with poles covering it—scant protection, but we felt safer burrowed down in it than staying topside.

*Boom-boom-boom!* The night lit up in a brilliant display of fireworks from the bomb explosions. Vernon sprang from his cot to rush to the air raid shelter. He made it, but I didn't make it out of the tent.

When the shelling stopped, he was convinced I had been hit. Apprehensive that he'd find me blown limb from limb somewhere outside, he eased back to the tent and anxiously looked around. His jaw dropped open when he discovered me sitting on my bed sound asleep, snoring, one shoe on and holding the other as if about to put it on. Being physically bushed and wrestling with bouts of malaria was beginning to take its toll.

A truck, parked no more than twelve feet from our makeshift bed, had been hit while I was sitting there dead to the world, so to speak. It hadn't hit me, so it didn't bother me or disturb my catnap.

That's what war will do to you!

* * * * * * *

After two weeks or so, our outfit returned in order to move the trucks out at three o'clock in the morning. The shelling had increased and we had been hit a number of times. The sergeant decided the Japs knew our hideout, and we had better move on to another location.

Only two of the hundred and ten trucks stalled and refused to crank. The old sergeant got mad and cussed a blue streak. I got mad, too, listening to him rant and rave after all we'd been through, but I held my temper for the moment.

He ordered me to drive a truck that was hitching a trailer. We moved to another remote site lower in the mountains. It was dark by the time we halted to set up camp.

The sergeant stood adjacent to the truck as I was backing it under the brush. I could feel the trailer buck, so I pulled up to straighten out and reversed.

The sergeant was still fuming because of the vehicles that wouldn't crank and commenced to cursing and snorting, using me for his whipping post. He let out a big ugly word and roared, "Back it!" And I did. I stomped down in reverse, the trailer buckled, and I rammed the truck back over it.

He flew into a rage. He had a bad habit of grabbing his gun and would stand there waving it around in a guy's face while cussing him out. As soon as I backed over the trailer, I reached for my Colt .45, shoved the door open and jumped out.[26]

"Sergeant, you reach for your gun and I'm going to kill you. Just like that. You ain't going to stand and hold a gun on me or cuss me." I threw a shell in the chamber and repeated, "You ain't going to cuss me without holding a gun on me and you damn sure ain't going to put a gun on me," I repeated. He believed me and backed off.

When the other drivers started loading up to go back to the frontline, I clambered onto the truck with the rest of them.

"You can't go," the sergeant yelled.

"You watch me," I said. "I can go to the front and you can't stop me. At the front, I might not be allowed to come back here so easy, but I can leave here and go to the front any time."

I figured it was safer to take my chances with the enemy than back there with that blockhead after our gun-pointing episode.

---

26    During World War II about 1.9 million M1911A1 (aka the Colt .45) .45 caliber pistols were procured by the U.S. Government for all the armed forces. "Ready for Battle: The Personal Equipment of a World War II Soldier," www.armyheritage.org.

**WWII Colt .45** – *Armslist.com.*
*Image may be subject to copyright.*

# CHAPTER 7

## ON THE FRONTLINE

**Browning M2 air-cooled .50 caliber machine gun.**
*US Army WWII Archives*[27]

THE artillery group came to our outfit and asked for volunteers for front-line duty at Pilar-Bagac, to help keep the enemies' planes off our artillery. The biggest artillery we had were 155-mm M1 guns, also known as M1

---

27      Total weight of gun, complete, on M3 mount equals approx. 128 pounds (gun weighed 84 lb/tripod 44 lb); maximum range (M2 ball) equals 7,400 yds; maximum effective range equals 2,000 yds/maximum range 4.22 miles; cyclic rate of fire equals approx. 450–550 rpm. Called "Ma Duce" for short. Tabulated data from FM 23-65, December 1955. Olive-Drab.com.

"Long Tom". Four guns made up a battery, and that was the only battery we had in the Philippines.

They brought us in there at night, and it was so dark that you couldn't see your hand in front of you. The officer was ahead, and every man was fanned out across the line. He got to a place and said, "Everybody dig in right where you are."

I had a little folding shovel we carried in our packs. I poked it down in the dirt a time or two. It just slid and bounced because the dirt was like concrete. I was exhausted and it was the middle of the night, so I just laid down right there and went to sleep.

We didn't realize we were so close to the big artillery. They must have known we were out there not far behind them, but we didn't know exactly where they were until, sometime in the night, that battery of 155mm's began unloading on the enemies' tanks. One of the guns would bust a rotating bearing and make an awful noise; we talked about it and wondered what that sounded like on the other end. When those tanks came in close, we found out when they fired into our area at close range. The 155mm's make a big concussion behind them when they fire.

I was rolling across the ground, trying to get hold of something to stop me, wondering what the thunder was happening. By the time I realized they were within forty feet of us, I had done had my britches scared off of me. I was ready to dig a hole to China with my hands to crawl into to get away from those guns.

One little Filipino sergeant in charge of firing would get his instructions as to where to load out to, and after he set his guns, he'd go back and say, "Count your men, Tojo!"[28]

*Boom, boom, boom.* "Now count 'um!" he'd holler out to them.

They made a counterattack, pushing the line back, and came after us.

Ironically, they pulled the big guns out and moved us up to the new position. When they moved, we were left there, stranded like sitting ducks,

---

28    Nickname for Japanese soldiers after Hideki Tojo, the Japanese premier and chief of the Kwantung Army. Post War: Tojo was executed by hanging with six other top Japanese leaders for war crimes in Tokyo, December 23, 1948. Over time, there were 5,600 Japanese prosecuted in more than 2,200 trials; many were given life sentences. History.com

with our toy machine guns. They had already spotted us and were throwing everything they had at us.

**US 155mm Gun M1 (Long Tom)** *on Rendova Island, Rickard, J. http:// www.historyofwar.org/Pictures/pictures_155mm_gun_rendova.html; historyofwar.org/weaponsframe.html. Known for mighty blast and long-range accuracy. Manned by 8-10 men, it could fire a 45.36 kg (100 lb.-) shell to a maximum range of 22 kilometers (13.7 mi)*

\* \* \* \* \* \* \*

Cullen Barrett—one of two brothers, Cullen and Cecil, in the same outfit—and I wanted a piece of the action! Cullen, an old cavalryman, was supposed to be very rough and tough, but neither of us felt very tough later that night.

We tested out a Browning M2 air-cooled .50 caliber machine gun, which had been removed from a P-40, U.S. fighter. It weighed approximately over a hundred pounds and sat on a tripod. After gathering our duffle bags, we came back to pick up the gun and accompanied the unit to our position.

The Japs kept bombing and strafing without letting up. The lines broke then, and the Japs got between us and our frontlines, but we didn't know it. We hunkered down, close to exhaustion.

The Japs had already found them. The next morning, they started strafing and bombing the place to kingdom come. Cullen and I tried to get a shot at the planes who came in at a low altitude and sprayed our troops, but our machine gun fired one time, then jammed. Every time we tried to use it, it pulled the same stunt, hemming and hawing. We field-stripped it and fired. It balked again. We took it apart and got off another shot, but it hung up again. We did that several times, and it played the same trick each time. We quit firing and took cover in a foxhole. When you're out in the open, standing under a plane that's throwing bombs fast as spitballs, and you can't get but one shot at a time, you don't stay out there for many tries and misses.

We figured out later that someone had hoodwinked us out of the one we had tested; while we went to get our backpacks and other gear, they took off with it, leaving us the lemon.

Weather was sunny and hot, often as much as 110 degrees Fahrenheit. We could hear a creek running nearby. Craving drops of fresh water to wet our whistles, I took a chance and crawled down the hill. I had just gotten my feet wet, with barely enough time to dip my canteen in the cool, clear stream, when those blasted Japs sent me running with dangerously close strafing.

I went back a second time a short while later and they did the same thing. We remembered there was a spigot with artesian water near a schoolhouse up above us. We could see it from where we were crouched down. Cullen had been with the cavalry and was reputed to be a pretty tough guy. He said he was going up there to get water.

"Those slope heads aren't going to keep me from having some of that water. I'm going up yonder, no matter how many Japs there are!" he exclaimed. I handed him my canteen, slapped him on the back, and wished him, "Good Luck!"

He got halfway up the bank, crawling through the thickets that were lined all the way up the hill, using them for cover. The Japs spotted him and began strafing. He came running back and dove into the hole with me.

"Where's the water?" I asked.

"I'm not even thirsty," he replied.

We camped in that hole for forty-eight hours before the colonel who had carried us up there came back around dark. He almost fainted when we stuck our heads out of the hole.

He said he had come after the gun because he didn't expect us to be alive. We informed him the gun was a dud and said that we'd be happy to go back with him. He carried us back to the kitchen and they fed us breakfast.

While we were chowing down, the colonel mentioned they lost two men that night: a staff sergeant and a tech sergeant. "If you guys will stay with this unit, we'll give you those ratings," he graciously offered.

"Is that a request or a command?" I asked, looking him straight in the eyes.

"A request," he stated.

"Well, if you don't have any objections, I want to go back to my outfit. I know those men down there and like their company pretty well," I responded with certainty.

A guy by the name of Osterika volunteered and went back in my place to the post. He never returned.

Osterika had been sitting on the bank of the Pasig River and was dug in to where the Japs couldn't get him from the other side where they were trying to cross the river.

His unit found him, buried to his waist in empty .50 caliber hulls and the Pasig River was running blood. The Japs couldn't put him out of commission from the other side, so they sent a plane to kill him and the other guy, who was feeding the ammunition, by a direct hit.[29]

\* \* \* \* \* \* \*

---

29      I met that same officer on April 7, 1942, after the lines had broken when we were on the road to surrender. He remembered Osterika had taken my place up there. "You know about Osterika?" he asked. "No," I said. He told me the sad story about what had happened to him and his immense bravery.

Shortly after that incident, I was taken in an ambulance to the hospital with malaria, running a 105-degree temperature. A sick man was a liability on the unit's hands when they were desperately trying to plug up a line. No time to tend to him. They wanted a lieutenant and me out of the way, so we caught a truck down the mountain to the hospital, located somewhere between the frontline and Mariveles on the main road.

That's when I found out there were five other Chandlers that had come over to Manila from the states; three of us were put in the same room.

The Japs bombed the town and hospital that night, wiping out a lot of people. It didn't catch fire because they dropped fragment bombs instead of incendiaries, but it was blown to smithereens.

The next morning, I was only in the way because I couldn't help with the injured victims. Medics were scurrying around, trying to bring the chaos under control.

I discharged myself, got out on the road, and thumbed a ride on a truck. They used flatbed trucks like a bus. They'd pick up everybody they came to, and when it got to where not another person could get on, they'd load fifty more on it. They hauled animals, with the humans, and sometimes humans carrying animals.

When they stopped to pick me up, I said, "There's not enough room for me on that thing."

They said, "Nothing else is coming this way."

So, I got on too. Further down the road, I looked over and saw my officer hanging on, too. He saw me about the same time.

"Where have you been?" he asked.

"Hospital. Where've you been?" I replied.

They had brought him in another ambulance. "Were you properly discharged?" he asked.

"Yes, sir, this morning at 5:00 a.m.," I said.

"Me, too," he laughed.

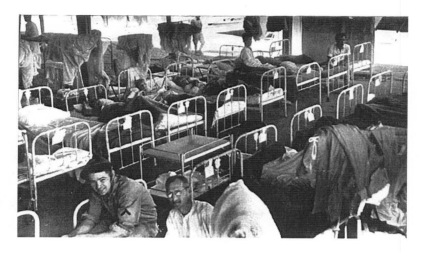

**Hospital in Bataan – WW2 Military Hospitals,** *Courtesy of WW2 US Medical Research Centre – www.med–dept.com*

**Abandoned flatbed trucks were used as buses by Filipinos.**

*Photograph courtesy Lou Goupal, author, Manila Nostalgia.*

# CHAPTER 8

## BACK TO THE FRONT

WHEN we got back to our unit, no one was there except five truck drivers. The line had broken in the mountains, and they had come back from taking a load of men to the front to plug up the hole in the line. We didn't usually fight with the Filipinos, but they were fighting with them, attempting to reestablish the line.

We were all sitting around in a circle talking, when I heard something that sounded like *glug, glug, glug*. I had been under fire when I volunteered to the front. Nobody else in that bunch had been up there. After a while, you get to be a good judge of where it will hit by the sound of the incoming. I said, "Hit the ground boys, that artillery is fixing to hit home plate."

I fell where I was and two of the others fell with me. Two men shot off through the thicket where holes had been dug for trench cover.

Well, that shell hit right between us, blowing up dirt and dust. They lobbed another and it hit over yonder a good way, then another one, way out there. We couldn't figure what was going on, because artillery is usually put in a pattern. We heard tanks roaring, then everything got quiet.

After the shelling stopped, the two fellows that ran for the thicket could be heard cussin' and talking loudly.

"What's the matter, boys?" we asked as they limped back into camp.

"We spent all that time looking for a trench and couldn't find one. Then, on the way back, we fell over in one and nearly broke our necks."

The next morning, we learned what had happened. The Japanese had slipped a 75-mm antitank gun, bound on a barge, past our shore patrol. It cruised along, down the hill below us, and fired the first random shell our direction. Our camp was near the coastline. When the concussion whipped it around, they put another shell in the way it was turned and set that one off. That woke up the tanks and they went into action; they took good care of those slippery pirates.

\* \* \* \* \* \* \*

Three or four days after I got back to the front, my pistol-waving motor pool sergeant strode up, requesting me to return and help with the trucks. He had eighteen guys working on them, but he decided he needed me after all. He was in a better humor by then, and after getting a frontline view, I guess I was, too. The first sergeant told me I could leave, so we did.

The new area seemed fairly safe, so we had it pretty good. When the Japs tried to aim a shell in our direction, it'd hit the top of the mountain and blow up before reaching us. If they raised it up, it'd sail over the other side past us.

You tend to get a little careless when you feel really secure. We had three or four trucks pulled out from under the camouflage to work on.

I was tinkering around underneath one of them with J.P. Lollar, a friend from back home in Vernon, Alabama, about forty miles from my hometown of Detroit. When I slid from underneath the truck and started for the latrine, he said, "Get us a bottle out."

The two of us had been driving the maintenance truck, and on the way out of Manila, we had dumped all the tools into the bed of the truck and filled the toolbox with fifths of vodka and Four Roses whiskey. We were the only ones with a key to it.

I took out a bottle and handed it to him under the truck.

The latrine was a nice little walk up in the woods from the trucks. It was nothing more than a straddle trench, hardly more than a shovel wide.

As soon as I had assumed an awkward pose, I heard a noise overhead. I looked up and saw a squad of four-engine planes. I thought, "If they open those bomb doors right now, I'm really going to be caught with my pants down!"

As if those thoughts were radar signals to the pilots, every plane up there threw his doors open and turned loose their loads. I lost mine, too! I panicked and tried to get in that hole, but I was too big!

Man, those mothers were screaming as they showered down on us, and I think I might have been screaming with them. Our enemy had decided that, since the artillery couldn't paste us, their air power would have to clean house. They meant to wipe out that whole transportation area.

After the shelling simmered to a stop, I got my pants down from around my ears and struggled downhill to see if anyone else was still kicking. Due to an unusually long dry spell, and the ruckus stirred up during the air raid, choking clouds of dust billowed all around. I floundered through it, coughing, and hollering, "Everybody OK?" while working my way past each truck down the line.

"Yeah," someone replied.

I felt my way around to the next vehicle, "You alright?" I asked tentatively.

"Barely," the guy sputtered, and I moved on, checking on each guy in our unit.

Incredibly, the closest bomb to hit anywhere overshot the last truck by approximately fifteen to eighteen feet. The dense jungle thicket bordering below the truck area was so cleared out, you could have planted a crop. J.P. was under the last truck, closest to the bombed area.

I got down on all fours and looked for J.P. under the last truck. "You OK, J.P.?"

He was still underneath, but all I could see was his blinking eyeballs. "I won't know until I feel and see!"

When the dust settled, I spied the empty bottle rolling around.

"That dirty dog poured out our whiskey," I huffed, thinking the sergeant must have found it.

"Naw, he didn't pour it out," J.P. admitted sheepishly.

"You tell me what happened," I asked.

"I had just turned it up to take a sip when those rascals flew over and I never turned it back down." He had inhaled a whole bottle, mind you, but you couldn't tell it on him.

Under the circumstances, he killed that fifth of whiskey before they could kill him!

* * * * * * *

Jim Dyer and I returned from patrol one time, bone tired and hungry. However, we decided to save our bread because we heard we were getting a rare treat of real meat for supper. Real meat!

We stretched out on our makeshift beds, which had been constructed by propping a door across two school desks. Our foxhole was centered between the two of us with our meager gear and food stored neatly in the desks.

About the time we got comfortable, a guy came up and said, "First Sergeant wants you to go down yonder, about a hundred yards away, and dig trenches."

"Tell Fish Face," First Sergeant F. F. Bietler's nickname, "that we just got in from patrol and we need some shut-eye."

Before long, he came back and said, "Bietler don't care where you've been. Get your ass out there and dig the trenches. Now!"

Jim sent him back, repeating that we were too tired to dig.

The third time the guy came back with the same command, we decided we weren't going to get any rest until we followed orders. Cursing Fish Face, we grudgingly headed out.

We had trudged a few yards when a Japanese plane flew over, dropping a shell right into the foxhole between our beds.

We gulped and ran back to look, shaking our heads in disbelief at the close call. Everything in the vicinity was fried to a crisp, including our bread, which was then burnt toast. We decided right then that every meal would take care of itself and not wait for another.

"Fish Face," Jim mused, "I take back everything I've ever said about you."[30]

* * * * * * *

Our main outfit was located down the mountain below the frontline, and we knew if the Japs broke through above, they could come down the blacktop road and be in our outfit before you could whistle "Dixie". Ten

---

[30]      Sgt. Bietler died May 31, 1942.

men stayed at an outpost above the road, rotating guard duty out on the road.

Dusk was settling when I returned from a patrol at the back of our outfit to make sure the Japs didn't surprise us from the rear. Jim Dyer and Grady "Shorty Red" Palmatier, from Deland, Florida, waited for me out on the road.

"You ought to have been here earlier," Jim exclaimed. "Chickens have been crossing over yonder about a hundred yards up the road all day."

We weren't supposed to be shooting anything but Japs, so as not to give away our location.

"Wish you had been here," he repeated.

"What did you want me here for?" I wanted to know.

"You might could have killed one. We ain't been able to kill one," Jim said.

"Why, yeah," I boasted. "I could kill one that far away."

Precisely at that time, a chicken strutted across where they had been pointing.

"Look, there's one now!" Shorty Red whispered. "Shoot 'em."

"No, I left my gun back at the tent on my blanket," I said, trying to make an excuse.

He shoved his gun into my hands anyway, so I swung it around without thinking or aiming and pulled the trigger. The hen flopped over in her tracks.

Shorty Red took off running, picked her up, and then came walking back with the dead fowl hidden behind his back. "Where did you hit her?"

"Shot her through the head, both eyes," I wisecracked.

He came up a little closer and asked again, "Where did you say you shot her?"

"Shot her through the head, both eyes." Sure enough, my bluff was right on target, clean shot through both eyes. Pure stroke of luck! I could barely see the chicken, much less her beady little eyes.

Our mouths watered in anticipation of tasting the tender morsels while we cleaned and dressed her, then dropped her in a bucket of water to stew. Rations were pretty low, having been cut to one-fourth.

We built a fire in the foxhole and, waiting patiently, savored the wonderful aroma. We tried to cover it enough to keep the smoke and flames to a low roar. When it was done, we set it out on the bank to prepare our picnic.

*Boom—boom—boom.* We heard the Japs coming and dove for cover. Whether their shot was pure luck—like mine—or not, they put a shell dead center of the pot and blew our feast to bits.

Don't tell me Japs can't hit. They saw that fire and zeroed in. But that wasn't the only time they dashed our hopes of an entree to complement the C-rations.[31]

---

31        "The first Type C ration consisted of a 16 ounces (450 g) 'meat' unit (M-unit) (reduced to 12 ounces (340 g) after being field-tested during the 1940 Louisiana maneuvers). In the initial Type C ration, there were only three variations of the main course: meat and beans, meat and potato hash, or meat and vegetable stew. Also issued was one bread-and-dessert can, or B-unit. Each daily ration (i.e. enough food for one soldier for one day) consisted of six 12 oz. (340 g) cans (three M-units and three B-units) ..." Field ration, Type C (1938–1945), C-Ration, Wikipedia.

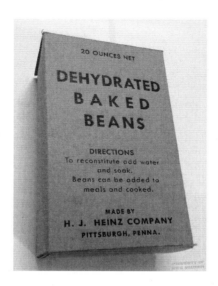

**Dried Baked Beans.** *Photograph courtesy of WWII Soldier.com.*

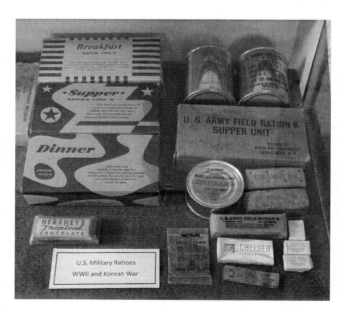

**Typical WWII Military Rations –**
*Photograph courtesy of K. Fossey, Fort Devens Museum, Devens, MA*

After rations became so meager, most of the troops had been living off the fat of the land. Unfortunately, now the land was pretty lean. The Filipinos had already harvested their rice and stacked it in piles around poles like a haystack to be thrashed afterward. When the war came on, the natives were either captured or in hiding; thus, the rice crop was abandoned in the fields. This section of land between the Japs and us became "No Man's Land."

Five men would venture into the danger zone together: four to tromp the rice and one to guard. We figured if the Japs wanted that rice, they better bring more than five men and be hungrier than we were. We'd gather it up and carry it back to the kitchen to boil.

The pineapple fields had been harvested for the farmers—with the help of Uncle Sam's army. Cane fields had been picked clean, too, but you can't live long on cane juice. Doesn't stick to your ribs very well.

Even the monkeys got scarce. Soldiers were so hungry they caught the little clowns and brewed them to eat. Anything that moved was fair game: rats, snakes, cats, dogs, you name it. I had opportunities to sample various delicacies, but never would—didn't get that hungry, I guess, although I did dine on dog over in Japan later on—can't say I've craved it any since then, either.

We had a guy we called Arizona, a real live cowboy, not a drug store cowboy, who occasionally lassoed a wilderness wild carabao (water buffalo) for us. He took a big seagrass rope, tied it to the bumper of a jeep, and climbed on the fender when we saw a carabao out in the field. We would take out after the carabao; Arizona threw the lasso and snagged us real meat to eat. We'd follow up with a maintenance truck that had a hoist on it to tie the animal down. Next, we put belting under him, hoisted him up in the truck, and took him to the catch pen built out back of the kitchen. That was good eating for a day or two.

Back at headquarters, they found out what we were doing and gave us a bad time about it, even though our rations had been cut severely. We were trying to survive, but they didn't want bad will with the citizens. I don't think our enemy was as sensitive to the locals' feelings.

When the war started, the Filipinos moved their civilians up into the mountains and woods, up toward Mariveles, for safety. They couldn't take their animals—the carabao, ponies, and so on—with them; the animals were left to forage for themselves.

They left their ponies, which were a little bigger than a Shetland pony. They worked with them and paired them with a cart or *carretela* (carriage), especially in the cities, where they were used as a kind of taxi.

**Carabao pulled freight carts** *(notice the long horns).*
*Source of photo: www.Manilanostalgia.com Author: Lou Goupal*

When we first came into Manila, the ponies had the right of way on the roads; everybody drove on the left-hand side. But when our eighteen-wheeler trucks came through, it didn't take but a few days after the GIs got there before the pony drivers were running off the road, into a store or whatever they had to scatter, to get out of the way. They learned to move over fast.

We ate horsemeat in soup occasionally on the frontlines. Whenever one got killed, the meat was distributed, if it was still edible.

The 26th Cavalry truly etched itself into history, when on January 16, Lt. Edwin Ramsay made the decision to fight back against the Japanese invasion of Morang, Bataan. With the Japanese infantry reinforced by mortar rounds and automatic weapons, and far outnumbering the troopers, Lt. Ramsay made the decision to charge – with M1 Garands in hand.

The gallant 26th Cavalry Philippine Scouts made a daring charge on Jap tanks, trampling soldiers in the process. After they charged the tanks, we didn't have a 26th any more. But they helped slow the tanks. They'd gallop alongside, jump off the horse onto the tank, jerk open the hatch and toss M1 grenades inside.

With the Japanese infantry reinforced by mortar rounds and automatic weapons, they far outnumbered the 26th Cavalry who lost their magnificent steeds. Afterward, they put them on motorcycles.[32]

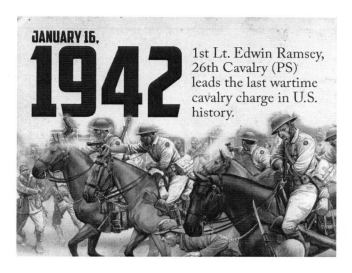

JANUARY 16,

1942

1st Lt. Edwin Ramsey, 26th Cavalry (PS) leads the last wartime cavalry charge in U.S. history.

*Poster inspired by cover of the book, World War II US Cavalry Units, Pacific Theater, by Gordon L. Rottman, illustrated by Peter Dennis. Photo courtesy of the Philippine Scouts Heritage Society.*

---

32        The 26th Cavalry Regiment, consisting mostly of Philippine Scouts, was the last U.S. cavalry regiment to engage in horse-mounted warfare. It would not be until Oct. 22, 2001, when American soldiers would enter combat on horseback again. During the retreat to Bataan, the 26th was heavily outnumbered by an infantry force supported by tanks. They drove off the surprised Japanese. Due to a shortage of food, they found it necessary to butcher their mounts and the regiment was converted to two squadrons, one a motorized rifle squadron, the other a mechanized squadron utilizing the remaining scout cars and Bren carriers. Wikipedia, "26th Cavalry Regiment (Philippine Scouts)." Also, see You Tube: Philippine Scouts Presentation (series) bing.com/videos

Horsemeat has a distinctive flavor, sort of sweet, pretty good meat. I've eaten it here in restaurants when I first came back. Most folks probably didn't suspect what it was, but I recognized the particular taste of it.

Rations got so skimpy; we had a saying that two cans of sardines could feed a hundred and twenty-five men.

For three or four nights straight, an old sow (female hog) came around grunting and trying to poke its head under my skeeter net. I stomped and kicked at her, shooing her out. Then I made the mistake of mentioning my night visitor to my buddies.

"You mean to say a hog has been trying to break into your net and you haven't killed that porker yet?"

"We ain't supposed to be shooting at game," I reminded them.

"It's alright to shoot a hog when you're starving," they argued.

"Alright, if that's what you want," I said. I found a lard (grease) can near a deserted Filipino hut, then a buddy and I risked running back and forth to the well, filling our canteens and pouring it into the bucket.

It isn't wise to go around shooting in the middle of the night when you know everyone sleeps with their gun in their hands. The excitement might cause confusion in the camp, so after my buddies went to sleep, I slipped over and got their rifles and put them in my tent for safekeeping. Shorty Red and Jim, being smaller men, shared the same net nearby.

*Umph, umph, umph.* The hog's grunting woke me. Easing to my hands and knees, I aimed my trusty gun and *bang*! I shot her right between the eyes. Squealing, she ran straight into Red and Jim's net, knocking it down, thrashing about in a blind rage, and trapping them in their own net. They scrambled for their rifles, but couldn't find them. In all the tumult, they tore up their skeeter net and mine. It was heck getting them calmed down.

We skinned and cleaned the hog, then put it in the can and brewed it over the foxhole fire, trying to shield it enough to keep the smoke from giving us away. Toward daylight, the meat was getting tender and juicy.

Near the crack of dawn, "Photo Joe," our favorite Jap reconnaissance plane, flew over and discovered our little barbecue party. He went back and told another old Tojo, who must have gotten a bit miffed that he hadn't been invited and retaliated by putting a shell slap-dab into the middle of the can in our foxhole. Probably went back and had a good laugh about it, too.

But we got the last laugh on him a little while later!

\* \* \* \* \* \* \*

Eighteen men out of my outfit and I went out to establish an outpost line, approximately a mile out in front of the main line. We set our machine gun up on a point. Another man was with me on the gun. An officer was stationed in an old creek bed behind us. The others spread out in a line, hidden by vegetation.

I stayed awake and let the other guy sleep. Around 3:00 a.m., I woke him up and told him to let me have an hour's nap, then I would come back. He agreed and I got up and went around behind our post, leaned back against a tree, and went to sleep.

Suddenly, I woke up to the sound of voices, which I knew weren't American. The sound was coming from across a cane field out in front of our post.

I eased over to the other guy on the gun and found that he was asleep. I shook his shoulder to wake him, whispering what I had just heard. I went back where the officer had set up; he was sound asleep, too. I woke him with quiet urgency. Next, I crawled down to the line, where I found the other men all asleep, waking each one in turn.

We listened intently; the Japs progressed through the cane field, but never came out where we were on standby.

The next morning, I went back to the main line and told the sergeant, "I'm not going out there anymore."

"Why?" he barked.

"I'm not going back!" I stated.

"Yes, you are. I've got to have you because you're the only qualified gunner out there."

"I'm not going back to that bunch." I stood my ground.

"What happened?" he asked.

"They all went to sleep!" I threw up my hands in disgust.

"Is there anybody here you will go out there with?" he said.

"Yes, my friend, Jim Dyer." I explained, "We were childhood buddies, went to school together, and enlisted together. I trust him with my life." I had reasoned, *why not volunteer a friend to share all the fun?*

"Well, tonight Jim Dyer will be up here to go watch your back, and you watch his," he assured me.

At suppertime, Jim came trailing in and we went to the outpost. Jim had been driving for an officer, which was a cushy job.

I stayed on the gun, that time, a total of fifty-two days; Jim stayed out there with me fifty-one days. The fact is, you feel better having someone you trust to cover your backside.[33]

We didn't sit on the gun twenty-four hours a day. Occasionally it happened, but usually one of the guys came to relieve us long enough to eat and rest.

* * * * * * *

**February 14, 1942:** I had just returned from patrol. The Filipinos held the line up above. We were afraid they would let the line break and the Japs would come down the blacktop road that ran down the mountain behind our outfit and be on top of us before we knew; one of the ten of us stayed up there all the time patrolling.

I was standing out on the road, milling around with several buddies, shooting the bull to pass time, when our peaceful interlude was interrupted by two big, four-motor Japanese bombers buzzing over, approximately fifty yards in front of us.

"Head for the foxhole," one guy yelled.

I wasn't very worried, because I figured by the time they made a loop, I could take cover. Distracted, with my eyes and mind on them, I was unaware of a single-engine plane slipping up from behind, skimming the treetops, until I heard him go into a dive. By the way it squealed, I knew he

---

33       Years later, while sitting with Jim, who was sick with cancer, he looked over at me. "I've been wondering all these years how I ended up on the outpost line with you. Did you send for me?" he asked. I grinned. He said, "I think I can guess who volunteered me." "Might be possible," I replied. Sadly, he died a week later. He had never asked or mentioned it before that day.

was loaded for bear; pulling the small plane so hard, it sounded like the engine was going to be torn apart. I heard the bomb whizzing before it exploded. At times like that, you lose track of your movements; it all happens in a flash. I don't know whether I was running, leaping, or flying, but I know enough about explosives that I didn't have either foot on the ground or the concussion would have blown my legs off. The impact blew me off the right shoulder of the road into a ditch, burying me with dirt, rock, asphalt, and debris. The whole road where I had been standing was obliterated.

Before I knew there was a plane back there, the other fellows leaped into a trench. They knew I was out there somewhere because they left me only minutes before to run for the foxhole from the first two planes that I had ignored.

When I came to my senses, the medics—who were within hollering distance downhill from the outpost—were sitting me up and brushing off the dirt.

"That was quick, boys," I said to the medics; I knew all of them.

"What do you mean?" one of them said.

"Well, I no sooner hit the ground than you picked me up," I said. They burst out laughing.

"That happened over an hour ago. We had to find you before we could dig you out. You were knocked out cold all that time."

I was bleeding and bummed up pretty bad. My back wasn't broken, but it felt like it.

The medics tried to persuade me to let them cart me off to the hospital, but I refused, having been there once when it had subsequently gotten bombed. "It's too dangerous in there; it's a bigger target for those Nips to hit," I argued.

"What are you gonna do? You can't stay on that machine gun with your back injury," one of them asked.

"I reckon I can. They said we weren't going anywhere if the line broke anyway. This is the last place we can have a line. Just take me down to my post. I can hold the handles of that machine gun and pull the trigger when

I see the whites of their eyes." So, I stayed on the front with Jim Dyer on the same gun.

The explosion knocked the whole road out. They didn't even try to repair it; they just made another road around it.

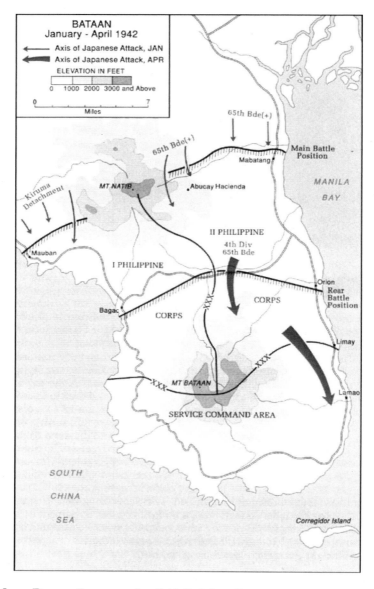

**Map – Bataan, January – April 1942.** *Mansell.com/lindavdahl/Omuta17/ maps_charts_lists. Courtesy of U.S. Army Center of Military History*

# CHAPTER 9

## PHOTO JOE

**Mitsubishi Ki-51 Sonea attack reconnaissance plane.**[34]
*National Archives; WWII Imperial Japanese Navy Air Force aircraft archives.*

WE had orders not to shoot a plane from the ground, so as not to disclose our position; the Japs would see where the gunfire originated and bomb the spot.

However, Photo Joe become a real nuisance, consistently following our outposts, making every curve, and strafing our lines with a machine gun. There was no fear of giving ourselves away; he could practically read our dog tags.

---

34        Mitsubishi Ki-15, nicknamed 'Babs' by WWII Allies & Ki-51 **Sonea** - Japanese reconnaissance aircraft and a light attack bomber. It began as a fast civilian mailplane. Single-engine, crew of two, served Imperial Japanese Army & Navy. Wikipedia (general example of recon planes)

Our officer wouldn't let me shoot or I'd have knocked that sucker out of the sky, but a soldier isn't supposed to disobey orders.

He hung around close to my gun and every time something happened, he'd say, "Chandler, get several men and go check it out."

I received the same pay rate as a corporal, with fourth-class specialist rating. Tech, staff, master sergeants, corporals were out there on that line. Here I was, a lowly private, and he wanted me to order those men to go with me to check out the situation. Of course, those guys weren't rated on their fighting ability any more than I was. They were rated on their ability to operate a radio, mechanical work, etcetera, and were getting on-the-job training, same as me. I guess I got called on more because I had gunner training. None of the guys ever balked or objected when I gave orders.

That officer wouldn't budge from his safe spot to see about anything and didn't want us shooting, either.

Eventually, he blew up and lost his nerve to the point where he couldn't stay out there without endangering his men. He was finally relieved of duty and sent to the hospital.

A new officer named Tucker from another outfit was assigned to our outpost and proved to be a braver soul. The first day he was there, they started throwing knee mortar hard at us. The three of us—Tucker, Jim, and me—dove into a hole dug for one man and still had plenty of room.[35]

---

35    **Japanese knee mortar—a grenade launcher**—was a 10 ¼ lb., 10" barrel/2' long overall, used at a 45-degree elevation. It could lob a 1-lb. 50mm grenade high-explosive shell about 75 yards maximum range, 25 rpm. Effective firing range with Type 89 shell was 131 yd; maximum firing range, 732 yd. Although dubbed "knee mortar," the recoil was known to have broken thigh bones if braced in such a way; typically operated by a crew of three. Optimized short-range combat infantry fighting. Wikipedia. George, John B. (LTC) 1981. *Shots Fired in Anger*, NRA Press, p. 343.

**Knee Mortar.** *U.S. Army Center of Military History*

The Japs were getting so accurate that every second or third shell was showering dirt on us. Unable to stay put, I came out of that hole, scooted over to the big tree where my machine gun roosted for the duration, and shimmied up the backside.

Due to a long dry spell, dust flew up when they fired at us, marking where the bullets were hitting. I came down out of the tree to where the others could hear me.

"One of you, bring me my rifle," I yelled. I had a pair of field glasses and could see the Japanese line. Tucker jumped up with my 1920 model

Springfield rifle, his rifle, and another set of field glasses and climbed up the tree with me.

I watched while he fired; when his bullet scattered dust, I knew whether his aim was true or not. "You're shooting too high," "too low," "too short," I'd say. He got to plunking them right on target. When he gave out, he took a turn coaching me where to place the shots.

We started putting them right at home where they were living. They weren't comfortable with our welcome, so they pulled up and left the neighborhood.

Tucker slid down out of the tree and said, "Chandler, see how many guys want to go with us to see what they left."

I wound up having to stay on the gun because everybody was eager to go with him. They found out the Japs were dug in so good, they even had canned beer and other goodies. The guys brought back whatever they stumbled across. We were near starvation—our rations having been cut to a fourth.

Someone piped up, "Boy, I'd be afraid to eat that candy."

Our officer replied, "They didn't have this up there to feed us with. Won't be any poison in this stuff. They were dug in for duration and planned to wipe us out."

A day or so later, the last day I was on the front, the Japs began strafing our lines again, too close for comfort. Photo Joe came back to pay a visit, following the line, right on course. Wasn't missing a shot. The men burrowed down in their foxholes and he wasn't hitting anybody, but he was shooting right over their positions.

I was under the same tree as always. He came by, flying so low until he had to pull his plane up when he got to my tree. I stayed out that time and didn't jump for cover.

Previously, we had removed all the phosphorous shells, or tracers as they called them, from our belts and weren't using them so they wouldn't ignite to reveal our firing position. With the phosphorous shells, you could see it blazing wherever it struck.

I quickly inserted a phosphorous shell about every tenth one while he was circling back up from the coastline. The officer quietly stood by and watched.

"Lieutenant, you don't want to see none of your men disobey orders, do you sir?" I asked.

"No, I don't," he replied.

"Well, start walking down through that cane field," I suggested.

He turned and started walking down through the cane field.

I had my belt loaded and my mind made up as to what I was going to do when Photo Joe made his rounds again. As soon as he closed in on my tree and turned his belly up like before, I started shooting at one end of his propeller, watching where the tracers were hitting, and froze on the gun. It streaked from his propeller plumb out his tail. He just went off over the side of the hill and down in a flame of glory.

The Japs were heavily concentrated out in the field, so we don't know if any of his troops rescued him or he went with the plane.

When the plane went down, our officer came sailing out of that cane field whooping, "You got him, you got him, you got him!" He hadn't said he wouldn't look back.[36]

From then on, Jim and I shot all the shells we could get our hands on. Can't say how many more planes we took out of action, but we target practiced, every chance we got, orders or not!

---

36      After we were captured, I never saw Tucker again, but I heard reports about him. He wasn't a coward, but he wasn't much of a man either. Rumor said he had no principle and wouldn't help others in the POW camp. A man's character comes out in times like that. You see the sorry or good side of his nature when the chips are down.

**C3n Type 97 Carrier Reconnaissance plane**. *National Archives; WWII Imperial Japanese Navy aircraft archives. www.ijnafphotos.com*

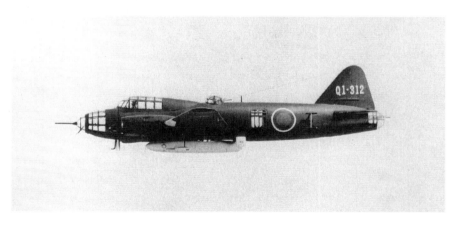

**Jap Betty bomber.** *National Archives – WWII Imperial Japanese Navy Air Force aircraft archives.*

**Zero Reisen Japanese bomber.** *National Archives – www.ijnafphotos.com*

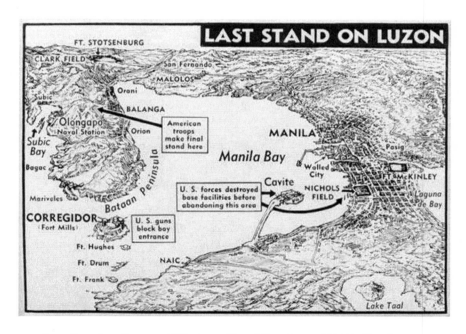

**Last Stand on Luzon.** *U.S. Army Signal Corps' map (1943). Picryl.com, getarchive.net – Public Domain.*

# CHAPTER 10

## CAPTURED!

**APRIL 6, 1942:** Our outfit was a short distance from the Pilar/Bagac line. Just before dark, the first sergeant sent word to the frontlines for Jim Dyer and me to come down to the kitchen to load chow trucks for delivery back up to the front. He sent another guy to take our place because we had been under fire too long.

We worked in the kitchen all day on the 7th preparing food for the men out in the battle zone. Around 10:00 a.m., the Japanese infantry broke through with tanks from the rear. The first knowledge we had that the lines were broken was around 4:00 p.m., when we heard two Jap tanks rolling up the hill to the kitchen.

While the tanks were coming around the bend, Jim and I, along with five others, made a dash across an opening to the creek. They fired a few shots at us, but we escaped by slipping down the steep bank to the road, which looped around and came out directly below the kitchen. We had hidden pickup trucks at the foot of the hill.

We grabbed a truck, but soon learned that traffic had been halted because the roads were bombed out. The highway was jammed so tight with vehicles until you couldn't walk between them. The Japs were flying back and forth over that road, dropping bombs at random, and strafing everything that moved. They were flying so low you could tell whether the pilots were wearing specs or not!

We unloaded off that pickup, crawled over a bunch of vehicles, and struck out on foot through the woodlands toward Mariveles, the same direction everyone else seemed to be headed.

We came across another truck parked along a back road, tried cranking it, put it in gear, and to our surprise, it was able to run, so we loaded up and headed toward Mariveles on a different route.

Before long, however, the backend of the truck hung up. The grease plug had come out and it was leaking like a sieve. We realized then why it had been deserted.

It was getting dark, so we scooted up under the truck and laid down. A truckload of Filipinos came by and saw us under there and stopped.

"What are you doing here?" they asked.

"The truck wouldn't go any further," we explained.

"You've got no business here. The Japs are closing in," they cautioned.

"Well, we can't go anywhere." We shrugged.

Directly, the Filipino's officer came up in a scout car and said, "We need to join up with our other men. You take this scout car and we'll join our men on that truck."

That was fine with us. We all piled in the car and continued to Mariveles. We ran up behind a truck that was hauling food and pulled up close enough for one of our guys to jump from the hood of our car onto the fender of the truck and he precariously passed food back to us.

We arrived at the airport at Mariveles at nightfall. The driver, a guy from Montgomery, Alabama, drove across the airfield and bumped across a crater-like place that had been bombed out. The car turned over, tossing us in every direction. Miraculously, we hung onto the food boxes and none of us got hurt.[37]

**April 9, 1942:** We got word that Major General Edward King, who was in command of Luzon, and Wainwright had gone to Corregidor and surrendered our forces on Bataan to Lieutenant General Masaharu Homma. This ended the Battle of Bataan, which was hard fought, without reinforcements, very little food and medicine, obsolete weapons and lack of artillery or supplies, from January 7th to April 9th—three months and two

---

37        "**April 8, 1942**—We were ordered to evacuate and pull back toward Mariveles Air Field. Capt. Wohlfeld and his merry men to the last position, holding the highway to Mariveles. No one could get by them. Many wanted to take to the hills or go to another island. We were ordered to lay down our arms and were told we would be home by Christmas." Ibid, *Chronological Events—27th Bomb Group.*

days—while fighting a southward retreat down the peninsula.[38] The Japanese had not yet appeared to take prisoners.

By daybreak, we hiked back down to the highway and were surprised to see white flags draped on trees and posts.

The defense lines had crumbled. Starving, disease-ridden Filipino-American troops fled in panic. We met people out from Mariveles who were traveling toward Bagac. They told us troops were to meet at designated places—Infantry in one, Marines in another, and Navy and Air Force at other locations—and they told us how to get to the location for our units.

Arriving at the appointed place for the Air Corps, our officers informed us, "This is it. We don't know what's going to happen; your guess is as good as ours. Every man is on his own."

Jim and I tried to catch a boat over to Corregidor, but they wouldn't let us on board.[39]

We decided it might be safer away from there, so we struck out with four other guys on foot armed with guns and ammunition and extra canteens and traveled up the side of the mountain to find an area to camp for a night.

To further add to our shaken dispositions, unsure of what might happen next, the ground began to tremble. It shook so hard that we tumbled downhill, trying to grab hold of bushes, limbs, or anything else that appeared to be attached to earth and remotely stabilized. Even after the tremors ceased, our knees and nerves kept rattling.

We speculated that our troops were blowing up the TNT storehouses and the big ammunition and artillery shell dumps before the Japs could get to them. We didn't learn, until much later, that part of the rumbling was due to a severe earthquake in our area.

---

38      After the war, April 9th was declared a national holiday in the Philippines. Originally called Bataan Day, the day is now known as Day of Valor, commemorating both the Fall of Bataan (9 April 1942) and the Fall of Corregidor (6 May, 1942). On the peak of Mount Samat, Pilar, Bataan, Shrine of Valor is a memorial cross standing 311 ft high." Wikipedia: Battle of Bataan.

39      Didn't too many men make it off the island, but Cullen Barrett escaped to Corregidor. The Japs attacked Corregidor twenty-eight days after capturing Bataan (May 6, 1942). He got shot during that invasion.

Before long, we ran out of water from the long hike. We were hot and dry from the scorching heat.

"Cover for me, and I'll get us a canteen of water," I told the rest of them and set out for the creek nearby that ran down the side of the mountain. I looked all around, but didn't see a thing. Keeping an eye out for the enemy, the coast appeared to be clear, so I laid my gun on the bank, slid down to the water, and started filling a canteen.

"Don't get that water. It's contaminated!" a voice behind me spoke up.

I whirled around, startled, not only because I hadn't seen the Japanese officer standing nearby underneath a washed-out ledge, but also because he spoke English better than I did!

"Get water out of this barrel," he instructed. "It has been boiled."

I sloshed over to the barrel sitting on a stand, filled the canteens, and as nonchalantly as possible, started back up the bank, hoping to ease over to my gun. He wasn't interested in playing my game.

"Come here," he ordered, as two other officers joined him. I decided the odds were against me and obeyed, walking over to him. Next, he reached out, grasped my dog tags, and read them aloud.

"Drolan Chandler, Detroit, Alabama. How far is that from Sulligent?" he asked.

I was so stunned you could have knocked me over with a feather! Most Americans have never heard of Detroit, Alabama. I'm not even sure it was on the map at that time. And if Sulligent was on the map, it was only a minute dot in the northwest corner of Alabama, thirteen miles from Detroit.

"Have you eaten?" he inquired.

I told him I hadn't, so he ordered me to eat since they had already finished.

My knees were weak while I puzzled over this strange encounter and the gravity of the moment.

I was captured!

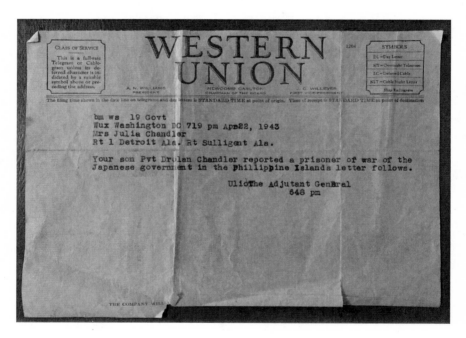

**Telegram sent to my parents, April 22, 1943.**

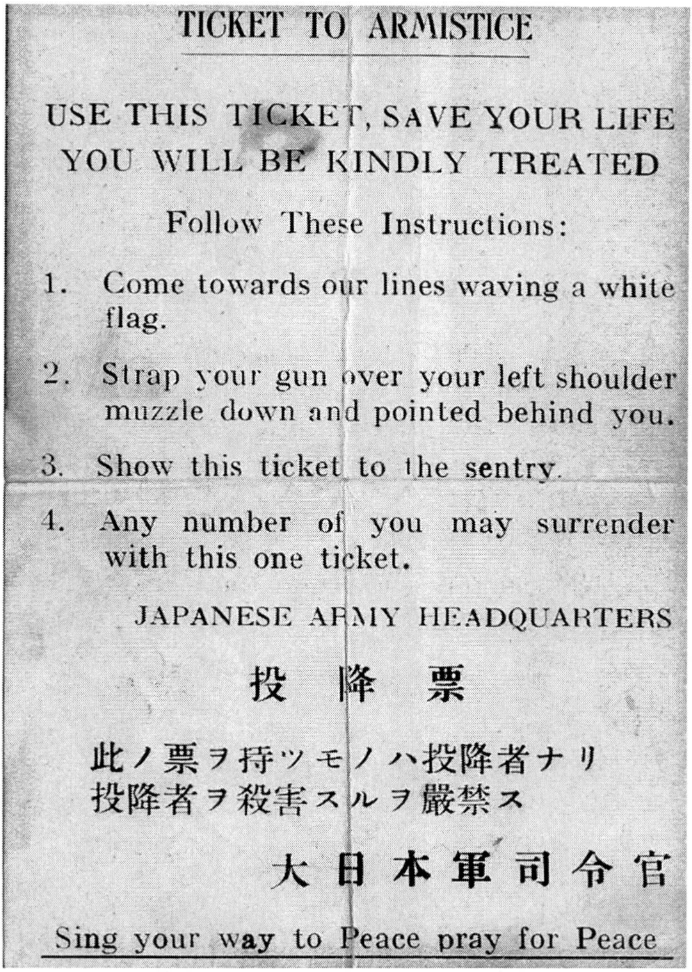

## TICKET TO ARMISTICE

USE THIS TICKET, SAVE YOUR LIFE
YOU WILL BE KINDLY TREATED

Follow These Instructions:

1. Come towards our lines waving a white flag.

2. Strap your gun over your left shoulder muzzle down and pointed behind you.

3. Show this ticket to the sentry.

4. Any number of you may surrender with this one ticket.

JAPANESE ARMY HEADQUARTERS

投　降　票

此ノ票ヲ持ツモノハ投降者ナリ
投降者ヲ殺害スルヲ嚴禁ス

大 日 本 軍 司 令 官

Sing your way to Peace pray for Peace

**Ticket to Armistice.** *Japanese planes dropped propaganda leaflets behind US lines to encourage men to surrender. They often contained sketches or photos of scantily clad or naked pin-up girls to entice them to read the messages. Photo courtesy of Mansell.com/lindadahl/omuta17/photo_gallery*

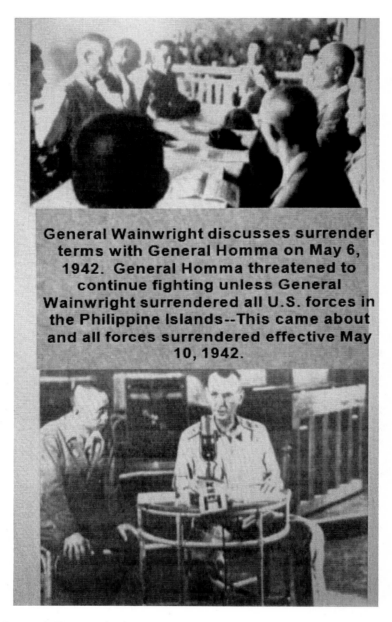

General Wainwright discusses surrender terms with General Homma,
May 6, 1942. *Photo courtesy of Mansell.com*

**Newspaper Headlines.** *National Archives; filipiknow.net.*

**American Officers at surrender to Japanese.**
*Photo courtesy of Mansell.com/lindadahl/*

**Japanese soldiers raise Imperial Japanese Battle flag (red disc with rays).** *From Japanese war film. US National Archives - Awesomestories.com; P.O.W. – www.us-japandialogueonpows.org/slideshow/Slide05.html*

SURRENDER TO THE JAPANESE. *American prisoners sort supplies under the supervision of Japanese soldiers, Bataan, 11 April 1942.*

**Surrender to the Japanese.** *American prisoners sort supplies under the supervision of Japanese soldiers, Bataan April 1942. Courtesy of Mansell.com*

# CHAPTER 11

## Death March

WE camped there for the night.

"Can you drive a car?" the Japanese officer asked me before we went to bed. A captured Filipino civilian had been chauffeuring for him.

"No," I lied.

A short while later he asked again. "Can you drive a car?"

Again, I said no.

But the third time he pulled out a saber and demanded, "Can you drive a car?"

My memory suddenly returned and I answered, "Yes, I can drive a car."

"You are my driver," he informed me and let the Filipino go. He, like many innocent Filipinos, probably wound up on the Death March.

The next morning, the three officers and I hiked down to the highway. We came upon an American-made Ford, which had been "liberated" by the Japs. At the time the car was made, they had sixty-horsepower and eighty-horsepower motors. When I realized this was a sixty-horsepower with little power for climbing mountainous terrain, I got very worried. I didn't have much confidence it would ever get us out of there. The sixty-horsepower cars were fine for driving on level roads, but it would be a challenge in that rugged terrain.

Nevertheless, the old car faithfully struggled up the mountainside, much to my relief. As we neared the crest of the crude, potholed dirt road that had been cut through the mountain pass, the old Ford was in low gear, pulling for all it was worth. Then, it started shimmying and rolling backwards.

One of the Japanese officers, who was the same rank as one of our colonels, knew two words in English: "Go!" and "Stop!" Whenever the car shimmied and rolled backwards, he drew his saber, swung it around slicing air, hollering, "Go, Go, Go!" The car was not a convertible, so the quarters got mighty close and the air pretty thin.

The problem was that there wasn't anywhere to "Go!" but back down the way we came up, and back up the previous mountain, to get another running start. After a few tries, we finally made it over. That happened repeatedly on the journey, often requiring two or three attempts at backtracking and lunging forward before getting a toehold on the next hill.

We had almost conquered another of those mountains, stalling at the top, when the car commenced to jitter and threatened to backpedal again. Before the officer could unholster his saber and start slicing air, and possibly my neck, I desperately motioned for several Filipinos, who had the bad luck of walking down the road beside us at that time, to help push the car. They gave it a shove and we had another hill under our wheels.

The Japs got the idea and began to volunteer pedestrians for the job to the tune of their singing sabers. During the course of the trip, that happened numerous times, and it often took two or three tries to conquer the mountain in the faithful little old car.

We traveled another mile, and then I saw Jim Dyer who had been captured by another group of Japanese soldiers. We waved to one another. He was close enough to the road that we hollered, "See you in a few days." That was April 10, 1942. I didn't see him again until November 9, 1945.[40]

---

40        On April 9, 1942, nearly 75,000 U.S. and Filipino troops at Bataan Peninsula surrendered to the Japanese. Wikipedia.

**Shooting a Straggler (2010.06.53), by Ben Steele.** *Image courtesy Montana Museum of Art and Culture (All sketches are charcoal on paper).*

We rumbled along, zigzagging around hairpin curves and clattering up and down the rutted roads.

As we journeyed, we came across the wreckage of a Japanese airplane. My captor began a heated discourse about how a "murderous damn American" had shot down an innocent observation plane, as if it merely made Sunday afternoon sightseeing excursions.

Of course, the first thing that popped into my mind was that there was no such thing as an innocent observation plane. They reported positions and gave artillery ranges so that the Japs could bomb the heck out of us. Not only that, they strafed our positions. I bit my tongue until it was close to bleeding because I knew if I said a word, it would be my last. Guys who confessed to being in a certain area or boasted of shooting down planes were executed on the spot.

Luckily, the officer didn't ask me if I knew anything about it; he merely made the comment.

I knew, as well as he knew, nothing is "innocent" in war. Everything happens for a purpose; if it doesn't, it's a waste. Some folks might call it bravery; we just called it survival.[41]

My Japanese captors and I traveled to an area where their cavalry had assembled and stayed for several days. I ate with those officers wherever we moved.

A Filipino-American machine gun outfit and a medic outfit had been gathered up and herded there. That was the first large group of Americans I saw. From there, we joined the infamous Bataan Death March.[42]

Being forced to drive a car turned out to be my salvation. It became a chilling close-up view, a horror story, of weary and defeated soldiers. We kept pace with the tattered, hungry, filthy captives along the road, occasionally stopping for a break. I felt helpless to intervene for my fellow soldiers who were being killed, punished, and tortured. I had my own troubles with the car, because not topping the next hill could mean losing my life at the hand of those brutal captors.

As I was driving in the sweltering 100-degree temperature—it rarely got under 90 degrees in the Philippines—I saw a Jap soldier walking behind a fatigued American officer, keeping in step with him. Every time the officer made a step, the Jap maliciously stabbed his prisoner in the hip with his bayonet.

Japanese soldiers stood along the side of the road and beat men with clubs and sticks as they passed by them. Prisoners too weak to continue, many of them sick and delirious, were killed if they fell out of line. Three Filipinos and three Americans were buried alive.[43]

---

41    In total, 10,000 men—1,000 Americans and 9,000 Filipinos—died during the Bataan Death March. Ibid.

42    "The Bataan Death March, a march in the Philippines of 66 miles (or up to 120 miles, depending on where the captured soldiers began their march), 76,000 prisoners of war (64,000 Filipinos, 12,000 U.S.) were forced by the Japanese military to endure in April 1942." *Encyclopedia Britannica*, "Bataan Death March," Elizabeth M. Norman; Michael Norman (March 6, 2017).

43    "Camp O'Donnell" - Provost Marshal Report 19 November 1945

**Jap Soldier with bayonet.** *Photo courtesy of C S Hagen,*
*http://www.weihsien-paintings.org/NormanCliff/Books/Samurai/*[44]

---

44 The Type 30 bayonet was designed for the Imperial Japanese Army to
be used with the Arisaka Type 30 Rifle. Infantrymen were issued bayonets, whether they
were armed with a rifle or pistol, or even if they were unarmed. The single-edged sword
bayonet was 15.75 in. blade and an overall length of 20.24 in. The design was intended to
give the average Japanese infantryman a long enough reach to pierce the abdomen of a
cavalryman. Gordon L. Rottman, *Japanese Army in World War II – Conquest of the Pacific
1941–42* (Oxford, England: Osprey Publishing, 2015; 47).

"Stop the car!" ordered the officer who had first captured me.

Snatching out his pistol, he shot the tormenting Japanese soldier, who died on the side of the road. He never told him to stop or anything.

"Go!" he commanded.

I cranked the car and the other Japanese officers made no comment. I recalled that when I was first captured, the first officer, my captor, had told me I would have it good because his men were not battle-scarred, not as blood-thirsty and vengeful, as those who were bitter, war-hardened veterans. Still, I realized I was in the company of unpredictable people. It registered heavily that they were dangerous enemies.

After journeying further, we paused to cook a meal. I noticed a man straggling alone, straying behind the group ahead and in advance of the following company of men. I don't know how he managed to get separated, because anyone else who had fallen out of ranks had been shot or bayoneted. He trudged in a daze, oblivious to the danger surrounding him. This was the worst type of malaria; those folks were like the walking dead.

"He's a friend of mine. Let me feed him," I begged the Jap officer.

"OK, if you can call him back," he relented.

I yelled at him, pleading for him to come back, but he never looked right or left. It was unbearable to watch him staggering off in the distance, so I started to run after him.

The officer grabbed my arm. "Call him back if you can, but don't get out in the road," he ordered.

My attempts to catch his attention went unheeded as he plodded onward, a zombie on the road to nowhere. I never saw him again.[45]

We followed the Death March northeast until we arrived at San Fernando. From there, men were loaded on trains like cattle and shuttled northwest to Camp O'Donnell, but the officers ordered me to drive to Manila and on to Cabu City,[46] approximately one and a half miles from

---

45     After I got home from the war, I learned that he endured the Death March with the rest of the troops, but died at Camp O'Donnell.

46     There were two cities named Cabu/Cebu. This one was Cabu on the main island of Luzon, not the island of Cebu.

Cabanatuan. It was a sugarcane town, and we stayed in the sugar plantation region near Manila.

Gradually, my Japanese captor and I became better acquainted during the four weeks I was with him, slipping away from the other officers every night to talk. He spoke good English, and I was the only American with them.

He surprised me with the fact he had attended the University of Alabama in Tuscaloosa, where he met a girl from Sulligent. She had mentioned Detroit in their conversations.

"I guess you know Hilma Collier," I said.

His jaw dropped like mine did when he read my dog tag.

"She was a teacher in Detroit and told me about going to school with a Japanese," I explained. And it had turned out to be the same joker who had captured me. I figured that out because he knew so much about the area and had actually been in Sulligent a couple of times.

When the war started, he was forced to cut his studies short and was commissioned to return home to Japan to serve his country.

One afternoon he asked, "Who will win the war?"

"You know who will win," I boasted.

Head down, staring at the ground, he sat quietly for a few moments, then looked up and said, "Yes, you are right. The Americans will win, but it will take five years to do it."

"You must be crazy," I countered. "I'll be home in eighteen months."

"I wish you would be. If you are home in the next eighteen months, perhaps I will be home, too. But it will take five years."

I shook my head, convinced that he didn't know what he was talking about.

During one of our discussions toward the middle of April, he predicted the Japs would capture Corregidor on the sixth day of May.

"You don't know any more than I do when they will capture Corregidor," I retorted.

"I do. The day is already set." It happened exactly as he foretold!

One day he asked how many men I thought we had in service. I admitted that I had no idea.

"America has a wonderful army on paper only," he said with certainty.

I discovered after the war, after all the facts were known, that the truth was really the way he described. Amazingly, he knew the reality of the situation. America did have a fine army on paper, but didn't have many men ready for service. Odd that a foreigner was much better informed than this old Southern plowboy.

* * * * * * *

Upon our arrival at the city of Cabu, my Japanese officer asked if I preferred to become a "trustee," which meant wearing an armband and having the freedom to go anywhere I pleased, or have a guard for my own safety. I elected to wear the armband due to the fact I had only been in the Philippines a brief time before the war began, didn't know any civilians to contact, or anything about the geography of the land. The possibility of escaping appeared hopeless.

The majority of our troops were in bad shape and sick before we were captured. We didn't have much time to think about it before then; we had to do what needed to be done to defend the lines. Our rations had been cut down to one-fourth, but our military still tried to balance what we got and provide protein. That all changed with our captors who weren't really concerned about feeding us, much less protein levels.

I already had malaria, but it hadn't gotten me down. I had managed to stay on the gun on frontlines. Now, after being captured, between malaria and the sorry food, other illnesses began to take a toll.

Being a trustee afforded me the opportunity to mix with the locals. I was permitted to roam about the town, providing I didn't enter their homes or stores. A generous Spanish family gave me money so that I could go to the little market and get food, tobacco, etcetera, although I continued to eat with the Japanese officers.

Actually, I did pretty well while I was with my captor, except for being terribly sick. The Japanese doctor gave me medicine, but it was ineffective. I kept getting weaker. Almost daily I would ask him to allow me to go back to where the other Americans were being held, but he refused to let me leave.[47]

An officer came to me one day and explained that he had a job for me to do that day. I was ordered to drive his car to another *barrio*. He was not supposed to have the car in his possession and I was told to hide out with the car while the high-ranking officer pulled inspection. Later that afternoon, he came for me when the coast was clear.

This same officer ordered me to fix a truck that wasn't running well. "I don't know how to fix a truck," I told him.

"Yes, you can fix a truck. You will fix it," he assured me, using mighty strong language, enforced with a persuasive sharp saber tip nudge.

Left with little choice and great respect for my life, I started tinkering under the hood. Another Jap came by and decided he knew more than I did, but he began tearing up things faster than I could fix them.

I elbowed him back and said, "Get out of the way!" He walloped me with a stinging *binta* (strong slap to the face). Now, he shouldn't have done that! I hit him before he could spit, knocking him to the ground and pouncing on top, trying to pulverize his ugly mug.

Luckily for one or the other of us, an officer overheard the commotion and hurried over to peel me off the sapsucker. He informed me I had no right to fight back because I was a prisoner of war.

"Yes, but I am an American prisoner of war," I declared.

He shook his head and said dourly, "You sure have a lot of learning to do."

It wasn't very long before I got my first lesson.

A fierce case of diarrhea struck me during the night and I trotted to the little outhouse in the field. Guard change took place while I was gone. It so happened that the person they put on guard duty between me and the house was the Jap whose face I had tried to rearrange that afternoon.

---

47      "His Fate Lay Homeward," (article about Drolan's war experience) Tombigbee Electric Cooperative, employee publication, from the "Community Heroes Series," November 2002 issue of *Alabama Living* magazine.01/21/2003. http://www.tombigbee.net/sections/at_home/athome_hero11_2002.html

While realizing my grim predicament and sweating out my options, I began to get the gist of what the officer inferred when he said I had a lot to learn. The guard had the advantage and could get away with murder out in that field, literally. On the other hand, if I tarried too long, they would come after me.

I finally worked up enough nerve to make a move. To my surprise, the guy didn't bother me as I walked past, not looking to the left or the right. It wasn't because he was being merciful either. I found out later he had been ordered to keep his hands off me.

For once in my life, I shrewdly kept my trap shut and let bygones be bygones. I realized that even though I had rights, I also needed to learn the right way to go about things.

* * * * * * *

*Additional Information:* The following Battling Bastards of Bataan logo and verse reflects the strong sense of betrayal felt by MacArthur's troops on Bataan, although he was stuck between a rock and a hard place – abandon his troops or defy President Roosevelt's orders.

On March 11, 1942, MacArthur departed for Australia under the cover of night with his wife, his son, his son's nanny, and a large contingent of his closest and most trusted staff officers. They became known in Australia as the "Bataan Gang." Before leaving them, MacArthur (who promoted self-glorification and was hailed "Hero of the Pacific," who himself had encouraged the myth of his military genius) gave his desperate troops false hope of reinforcements. He knew it was a cruel lie.

Brigadier General William E. Brougher, one of the deserted Americans on Bataan, probably expressed the view of most of the troops when he described the order and lie as: "A foul trick of deception played on a large group of Americans by a commander-in-chief and his small staff who are now eating steak and eggs in Australia." *McArthur Deserts "The Battling Bastards of Bataan" and Escapes to Australia,* pacificwar.org.

## The Battling Bastards of Bataan Poem

*"We're the battling bastards of Bataan;*
*No mama, no papa, no Uncle Sam.*
*No aunts, no uncles, no cousins, no nieces,*
*No pills, no planes, no artillery pieces.*
*And nobody gives a damn.*
*Nobody gives a damn."*

By Frank Hewlett 1942

*(Hewlett was the only US War correspondent left in the islands.)*

### Hear the song, "Hymn of the Battling Bastards" – Now and Then, by Dan Owen, on YouTube

**Battling Bastards of Bataan, 27th Bomb Group insignia**

**Battling Bastards of Bataan Memorial monument.**
*National Archives; Photo by James Litton. May be subject to copyright.*

**Newspaper headlines tell the grim story.**
*National Archives; WWII Headlines.*

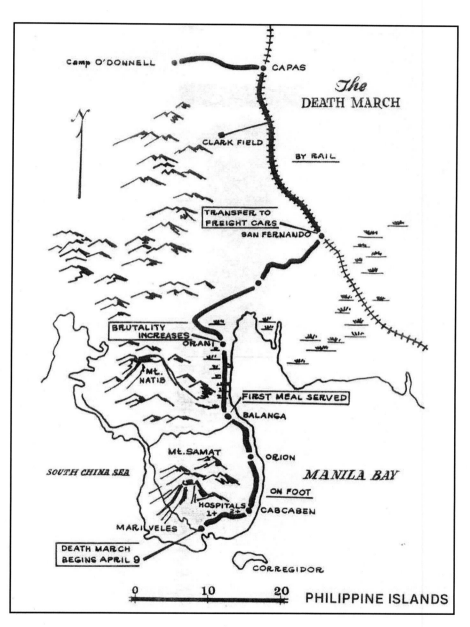

**Death March Route.** *US Army Military History, National Archives*

**The Bataan Death March, (2010.06.01) - Ben Steele, artist.** *The famous WII artist said that, during his imprisonment, art saved his life. He drew images of typical POW life with charcoal or whatever he could find. Image courtesy Montana Museum of Art and Culture (All paintings are oil on panel.)*

**Bataan Death March, long weary journey.**
*Courtesy Bataanproject.com; Public Domain.*

**Jap soldiers examine POW possessions at start of "Death March"**
-*Photographed: Saturday, April 11, 1942, by Alcantara. World War II*
*Multimedia Database, caption by Jason McDonald; Caption ©2007 MFA*
*Productions LLC Image in the Public Domain.*

# CHAPTER 12

## Hotel Bilibid

**Bilibid Prison Gates.** *Photograph courtesy of Mansell.com*

WE stayed at Cabu City through April 28th. The night before departure, my Japanese captor received orders to continue south and offered me a choice: I could go with them and be well cared for, or join my fellow Americans in a prison camp. I refused to go any further and requested to return to my compatriots.

He asked if I felt well enough to drive alone, north to Manila. I was ready, willing, and tolerably able. He strapped an armband on me that would prevent me from being stopped or shot by other Japanese troops. He assigned a truck for my use and handed me the keys, commanding me to return the way we had come. My four weeks' stay with my captors finally ended.

I began the trip, backtracking to the compound holding American prisoners. There was little worry about an escape on my part because the island was infested with Japanese troops, as well as Japanese occupation throughout the Philippine Islands. He also told me a place to stop for gas where fellow Japs would take care of me that night.

I did as he instructed and stayed with the two Japs that night. They issued the promised ration of food and gas to carry me through the remainder of my trip.

The next morning, I drove the truck into Manila and met the Japanese guards at the rendezvous point, the famous Resolute Statue, in the middle of town, where I was to leave the truck. I rolled to a stop at the base of the statue, barely able to drive, because my body was so ravaged with malaria.

Almost immediately, the Japanese soldiers escorted me to the outskirts of Manila to the prison camp at Bilibid Prison.

Bilibid was a large complex already equipped to handle prisoners because it was formerly the main Filipino prison before the war began. (The penal colony at Davao, on the island of Mindanao, was for murderers and rapists and other real hard-core prisoners.) There were no bunks, so everyone had to sleep on the concrete floor. The Japanese army had more sick captives than they anticipated or were prepared to accommodate.

Malaria had almost taken its toll by the time I arrived at Bilibid. I was so exhausted, I almost passed out several times. I vaguely remember going through the gates and being hospitalized.

Hospitals at the prison camp were merely holding tanks for the sick and dying. Very little food or medicine was available. Each person was abandoned to his own care. Few had the strength to help himself, much less his neighbor.

I became so weak I couldn't do anything for myself. I don't know whether they thought I was dead or just wanted me out of the way, but they lugged me over to the old building being used for a morgue and shoved me aside. Fortunately, the camp was so unorganized that no one came to bury me for several days. It's a good thing, because I wouldn't have appreciated being buried alive!

It's doubtful I was conscious much of the time. I was so feeble I couldn't groan or even wiggle a finger, totally incapacitated. Luckily, there weren't any folks in there at the time to keep me company. I reckon they would have let me lie there and rot if I had been dead.

One day a mysterious shadow fell across me late in the evening. For all I knew, it was the Death Angel coming to get me. I lay on my side with my back to the door, staring straight ahead at the wall. I watched the shadow, feeling frustrated that I couldn't grunt or move a muscle to catch its attention. It paused a moment, then moved away.

Next day, the same thing happened. A shadow loomed over against the wall for a minute or two, and then it disappeared. My position never changed.

The third day the apparition appeared, it ventured inside the morgue for a closer inspection. I'd have been decaying by then in the tropical Philippine climate if I'd been dead, although the stench from my diarrhea in which I had lain for days must have been overwhelming in itself.

The shadow took on the form of an American major, who grasped my dog tags. "Chandler, you're the toughest man I've ever seen. You're a fighter. Most people would have given up, but you've hung in there," he remarked as he rubbed water on my parched lips. He told me he had noticed when they brought me down to the morgue, and he had kept an eye to see if my body started to decay.

"I'm going to do all I can to help you pull through. I've got money and access to outside resources. I'll try to get medication for you," he informed me.

He left for a while and returned with water and rice, patiently spoon-feeding me. Afterward, he hauled me outside to a water spigot and bathed my stinking body, then dressed me in the extra set of clean clothes, which I had managed to bring back with me.

The officer continued to dribble food into my mouth. He washed me when I soiled myself until several days later when my strength began to return and I showed encouraging signs of improvement. He moved me out of the morgue, back into the main area, into a three-story block or stucco building, which served as barracks. By a miracle or, more likely by money, he procured a bed on the ground floor, since I was too weak to climb stairs.

One of the prisoners in camp had been a veterinarian in civilian life. The major brought him to examine me. He gave me pills for malaria and fed me a dark liquid medication, which tasted of iron; it's hard to forget the flavor of that stuff. They turned me over on my stomach and gave me a shot in my hip with a horse's syringe and, in spite of my inability to move, I nearly shot through the ceiling!

Malaria chills and fever alternately seized my body, but I gradually improved to where I could sit up and, finally, to shuffle outside to collect my own food a time or two. The Japs didn't bring food around to the sick. They figured if you weren't strong enough to stand through the long lines, you weren't worth bothering with and would be one less mouth to feed. There were few officers there and little authority or discipline. The guards didn't give a hoot if anyone survived. Survival of the fittest was their philosophy. Unless you had a buddy looking out for you, you were out of luck.

At the end of the second week, the major came to me and said, "I have my orders; they're sending me out in the morning. You keep fighting. You're going to make it, Chandler."

Without realizing it, I unconsciously leaned on my "never give up" philosophy. Looking back, I believe it is the gospel truth that "outlook determines outcome." I guess that attitude and determination apply to almost any endeavor, whether it is war, business, daily living, or whatever. But it was undoubtedly the main thing that got me through those purgatory years, assisted by fervent prayers back home.

I'm sure the major told me his name, but my mind wasn't functioning well and I regret that I can't recall it. The malaria fever induced fuzzy memories during that period of time except the fact that his assistance definitely saved my life.

I never saw him again. I don't know where he went or what happened to him. It sure would be nice to know that my Samaritan friend made it home safely after the war.

A few days later, a number of doctors who had been imprisoned during the time we were fighting were moved from Manila to Bilibid, bringing with them desperately needed medicine and equipment. I moved back into the hospital and improved considerably.

\* \* \* \* \* \* \*

Bob Harp and I had been separated after capture. In lucid moments, I wondered about him and Jim Dyer. I sure was glad to see Bob come through the camp one day after one of his details.

He had been in the hospital for nearly six weeks when he first came into Bilibid with malaria and diarrhea. Two one-legged guys, Floyd Lassiter from Bristol, Virginia, and Gene McDonald, had seen him coming and came hopping out to help drag him to the hospital. They brought food and water to him while he slowly regained strength.[48]

There was no activity or work details to speak of, except for burying the dead, and other Americans who could manage to get around were assigned that gory duty. Bob went back out on another such detail and looked pretty ragged, so I gave him my extra clothes. Most of us were at Bilibid for a short period of time before being transferred out to other POW camps in the Philippines.

I didn't see him again until after he came into camp at Cabanatuan, around the time we were going to be sent to Japan. He had been to O'Donnell and worked on the Tayabas Road detail.

---

48      Bob was a real funny character. Floyd and Gene each claimed that he paid them back for their help when he got well by grabbing one of them by his one foot, every chance he got, to tickle them until they cussed and threatened to kill him. He could make them 'hopping mad' (the pun they used), but they really liked him.

**Bilibid Prison Walls, guard tower.**
*Photo courtesy Lou Goupal, Manila Nostalgia.*

**Aerial view of Bilibid compound.**
*Courtesy of Bataanproject.com; Mansell.com*

**Barracks with straw mats.** *armylive.dodlive.mil* www.army.mil; *Public Domain.*

**Bilibid Hospital.** *Mansell.com – Photo in Public Domain.*

**Map: Major POW Internment sites in the Philippines during WWII.** *US National Archives; Bos, Carole "Japanese Internment Camps in the Philippines" AwesomeStories.com. Oct 07, 2013. Sep 23, 2020. Image online, courtesy Wikimedia Commons.* http://www.awesomestories.com/asset/view/Japanese-Internment-Camps-in-the-Philippines.

# CHAPTER 13

## Train Ride to O'Donnell

**Death March Boxcar on display at Capas National Shrine.**
http://www.mansell.com/lindavdahl/omuta17/photo_gallery/Boxcar.jpg

AT 2:00 a.m., the Japanese told us to fall out and herded us to the train depot in San Fernando, where we were loaded into small cattle cars headed for Camp O'Donnell, located at Capas in North Central Luzon. O'Donnell was the first prison camp for the men who had survived the Death March. We were crammed inside the boxcar as tight as we could squeeze together. It reminded me of the way little Vienna sausages are packaged.

The doors slammed shut and bolted, blotting out light and air. We nearly suffocated in the darkened car, gasping to breathe putrid, stale air. Most of us had dysentery, which we were unable to control, and malaria, which caused fever and the sweats. The temperature outside soared to 110 degrees or above that day. I have no idea what it reached inside the car with the body heat pushing up the factor, as well.

At 5:00 p.m. that evening, the train screeched to a halt. As we unloaded, men who had died during the hellish trip collapsed to the bottom of the boxcar as soon as the guy he had been propped against stepped out.

Not a drop of water or bite of food had been issued during the ride, and none was offered before we began the arduous, eight-mile march on foot.

Whooooeee! I was sick. Diarrhea had drained my precarious strength, and malaria fever had my throat parched. It took every ounce of grit left in me to make each step.

Before long, I decided it wasn't worth the effort. I intended to pull out to the side of the road and let them shoot me, which is what happened when anyone fell out of ranks. They were bayoneted and left for buzzard meat.

I staggered over to the side and glanced up the road ahead. My attention was riveted toward the front of the line to an old-timer, about seventy years old, sporting a little goatee, white as snow. As a valiant civilian, he was captured to suffer along with the rest of us.

My guess is that he might have weighed as much as 110 pounds when he was healthy before the war. Now he was a walking skeleton with skin stretched across his frame. He had managed to get hold of or hold onto some tobacco, and his little goatee was jumping up and down as he vigorously chewed.

Watching him, I thought, *If they can't keep that old man from chewing tobacco, or make him want to give up and quit, those slant-eyed Nips can't make me give up either.* With renewed determination, I stepped back in file and started marching again.

Several miles down the choking, dusty road, with pain coursing through my body, I again thought, *I can't make it. A bullet will be a blessed relief to end this misery quickly. I'll just let them shoot me.* I dropped to the shoulder of the road with my feet sore and bleeding.

Again, I spied that little old man, his pointed beard bobbing up and down, still chewing his tobacco as if it was keeping him alive, and plodding along.

*Here I am twenty-three years old and that old man is sticking it out.* I reprimanded myself. *I'm not about to give up,* I thought and set my jaw, determined to hang in there for the duration.

I had never seen him before the march and never saw him afterward, but he was an inspiration. I took courage from his stalwart example and stumbled back in line again.

\* \* \* \* \* \*

**O'Donnell guard shack.** *USMC, US Navy & Army Signal Corp photos.*

I barely survived the trek to Camp O'Donnell. Upon arrival, I became very sick again and was carted off to the hospital, which was in an appalling condition.

There was very little medicine to be found, other than a few aspirin tablets, bandages, and tape. It was rumored that medicine in the form of quinine or sulfathizaole was selling at the rate of five dollars a tablet, but nobody had money to buy.

Patients were sleeping on the floor. Many guys with dysentery were too weak to get up and go to the latrine, so they lay in their own filth---feces, blood, vomit---with flies and mosquitos swarming. The odor was overpowering and could gag a maggot, which were also festering.

For meals, they often served a thin watery soup, the Filipinos called lugao, as the main staple, also, *lugaw* (gruel, rice porridge).[49]

Rice, almost always the main meal, was occasionally "spiced up" with a tablespoon of *camote* (sweet potato), usually rotten, to enhance the flavor. It was known that there were abundant food supplies outside our camp, but the Japs intentionally kept us on a starvation diet.

Nearly everything but our canteens and mess kits were confiscated. The drinking water supply came from three spigots in the center of the camp. For the greater part of the day, prisoners stood in long lines in the scorching heat to fill their canteens and the canteens of their buddies too weak to endure the wait. One doctor said he stood in line six hours and was three men away from getting his water, when the faucets were shut off for the evening by the Nips.

**Typical Vintage WWII U.S. Military issue Mess Kit.** *Lid has folded handle which can be used for pan; bottom portion is divided to hold food or utensils when not in use. US National Archvives; WWII Military Equipment – Mess Kits.*

---

49      The Tagalog word *lugaw* is Chinese in origin. Lugaw is a Filipino dish traditionally thought of a soft food for sick people. But lugaw is enjoyed for breakfast, as a snack, and when you're sick, even as a meal in itself. Some meat is added to the rice for nutritional value. Chicken bones and ginger are favorite ingredients. https://www.tagaloglang.com/lugaw/ "Comment: No meat, chicken bones, spices were added to ours."

**Typical Vintage 1 qt. Canteen and 0.5 qt. cup with folding handle, and carry bag.** *US National Archives; WWII Military Equipment – Canteens.*

\* \* \* \* \* \* \*

Men who were able to walk were assigned to burial details and carried heaps of bodies out to mass graves. These graves averaged fifteen feet long, sixteen feet wide, and only eighteen inches deep in which five bodies were laid crosswise. Sometimes more bodies were piled into the pits, too. It was the practical way to handle the high death rate due to the fact that most of the men on the burial detail did not have the strength to dig deep graves. Several of the men on detail were so weak that they fell into the pits they had helped to dig, and were buried alive.

\* \* \* \* \* \* \*

I was rounded up for transfer and, in the summer heat, we made another arduous nine-mile march to our new home away from home. We stumbled through the ten-foot-high wooden gate to the Camp Cabantuan clinging to life by a thread.

**His Own, by Ben Steele.** *Image courtesy Montana Museum of Art and Culture (All sketches are charcoal on paper).*

**Begging for Rice, Filipino villagers tossing food to prisoners (2010.06.58), by Ben Steele.** *Image courtesy Montana Museum of Art and Culture (All paintings are oil on panel).*[50]

---

50          **Ben Steele's** drawings during captivity were made with charcoal on whatever he could find. When he was to be shipped to Japan, he left them with Father Duffy, a Catholic priest, but Duffy was also destined to be shipped out. The drawings were lost at sea when the hell ship, Oryoku Maru, was bombed and sunk by American Bombers. Father Duffy did survive. Ben later redrew his sketches from memory when he returned home. From War Torn: The Art of Ben Steele, a collection of 68 drawings and paintings gifted MSO from Ben & Shirley Steele. See: https://artmontana.com/article/steele/ for Ben Steele's *Personal Chronicle of from Bataan to Hiroshima.*

**Ben Steele, #359, at Japanese Prison Camp**

\* \* \* \* \* \* \*

***Additional Information:*** "Between the period of April 15, 1942, and July 10, 1942, there were 21,684 Filipino deaths, a mean average of 249+ per day, and 1,488 American deaths, a mean average of 17+ per day." [51] According to Major William E. Dyess, approximately 2,200 Americans and 27,000 Filiinos died at the O'Donnell prison camp from disease, starvation, and brutal treatment.[52]

By July, sanitary methods had been initiated. Old latrines were covered over and new ones dug. Pools of stagnant water were drained. The tall grass was burned to help eradicate mosquitos. Barracks were cleaned out using grass attached to sticks. Water was boiled for drinking. Garbage and refuse

---

51      Camp O'Donnell, Provost Marshal Report, Nov. 19, 1945. "Report on American Prisoners of War Interned by the Japanese in the Philippines."

52      By the end of April 1942, approximately 9,300 Americans and 45,000 Filipinos were interned at this camp. "1931-1945 – Atrocities-Severe Mistreatment-Slave Labor", Edward Jackfert, past National Commander American Defenders of Bataan & Corregidor, Inc.

was burned or buried. A daily cleaning policy in the camp was practiced. Thus, the death rate finally dropped below 100 per day by July 21, 1942.[53]

During June and July 1942, prisoners at O'Donnell were evacuated in small groups to Camp Cabanatuan, approximately one hundred miles north of Manila. Camp O'Donnell, located at Capas, in North Central Luzon, which had originally been a Filipino army camp, was turned into a rehabilitation center for the Filipino prisoners of war.

**Bob Harp in center with pan at O'Donnell POW camp.** *Courtesy of Jim Opolony, BataanProject.com; National Archives.gov-Awesomestories.com; P.O.W. Experience. Bos, Carole "Camp O'Donnell Prisoners of War" AwesomeStories.com. Oct 07, 2013. Sep 23, 2020. <http://www.awesomesto-ries.com/asset/view/Camp-O-Donnell-Prisoners-of-War>.*

---

53       Ibid. Provost Marshal

**American soldiers in front of nipa hut.** *Photo courtesy of Jim Opolony, BataanProject.com; US National Archives; Bos, Carole "Camp O'Donnell" AwesomeStories.com. Oct 07, 2013. Sep 23, 2020. <http://www.awesomestories.com/asset/view/Camp-O-Donnell>.*

Number 6
Picture shows conditions of mass graves at POW
Cemetery, Camp O'Donnell, Capas, Tarlac.

**Mass grave at POW Cemetery at Camp O'Donnell.** *Photo courtesy of Mansell.com/lindavdahl/ODonnell_mass_grave.jpg*

**Burial Detail at O'Donnell** – *carrying bodies in blankets to mass graves.* *National Archives and Records Ad, Identifier 208-AA-288BB-2; ©2011 MFA Productions LLC Image in the Public Domain*

**Burial Detail at Camp O'Donnell (2010.06.04), by Ben Steele.** *Image courtesy Montana Museum of Art and Culture (All paintings are oil on panel).*

**Water Line at Camp O'Donnell, by Ben Steele.** *Image courtesy Montana Museum of Art and Culture (All paintings are oil on panel).*

**Water Brigade at Camp O'Donnell (2010.06.08), by Ben Steele.**
*Image courtesy Montana Museum of Art and Culture
(All sketches are charcoal on paper).*

# CHAPTER 14

## Camp Cabanatuan

**Entrance Gate at Cabanatuan POW Camp.** *i.pinimg.com;*
*http://nadfserver.org/map/cabanatuan-the-great-raid-call-of-duty-5-world-*
*at-war-cod5 - Image may be subject to copyright.*

EVERYTHING went black as soon as I stumbled through the gates at
Camp Cabanatuan. Raindrops splattering in my face nudged me to consciousness sometime the next day. Glancing around, I saw no one else in
sight, except one other man who was sprawled on the ground nearby. I
managed to roust him awake and together we inched along, too weak to
walk, to take cover beneath a bamboo hut built on stilts that served as
barracks.

The Filipinos used coconut palms folded over bamboo poles and nailed to a frame for roofs and sometimes for the sides of huts. It turned the water and allowed airflow; built five to seven feet off the ground, the huts allowed room for animals to live underneath.

We stayed there for three days, during which time a kind soul took pity and brought us a portion of food.

Eventually, we were carried to the hospital across from the Japanese compound and admitted to the terminal ward. I don't remember much from the fourth to the eighth. I had a severe case of malaria, dysentery, and beriberi. You name it, I had it.

The hospital amounted to a place where you didn't have to work. As in O'Donnell, the doctors had no medicine and very little means of treating anyone.[54]

Patients began in the barracks at the top of the hill, and as their condition worsened, they were moved down the hill to the next hut. Zero Ward was the end of the line. Folks were hauled out of there to a mass grave. Guys who worked on burial detail have described how gross it was to carry men out to be dumped in a large pit dug in the rice fields. When they returned to bury more, arms and legs would be floating in the muck and they had to slush around in the putrid water, trying to dig and make room for more bodies.

\* \* \* \* \* \* \*

For a brief time, I gained enough strength to hobble outside for a bit of exercise. I heard someone call my name and looked around to see a bearded man sitting propped against a building. I didn't recognize him and, thinking he had mistaken me for someone else, kept walking.

A few steps further, he called my name again. The third time he called, "Chandler," I looked over and said, "Did you mean me?"

"Yes, but you don't know who I am, do you?" he said.

"Should I?" I answered, puzzled.

---

54      The "hospital" had 30 wards, made to hold 40 soldiers each, often holding up to 100 patients. In each ward were upper and lower decks made of bamboo slats. Each patient was allotted a two-by-six-foot space. The seriously ill were kept on the lower deck. "Camp Cabanatuan," Mansell.com

"I'm Elmore Rye," he explained.

We had known each other since childhood, back in Guin, Alabama. (My sister, Roberta, had married a Rye.) He was so emaciated; it was hard to believe he could still be alive. We chatted awhile, reminiscing old times and catching up on what had happened while we had lost track of one another.

Three days later, I managed to get outside again and went back to visit him. I couldn't find him and inquired as to his whereabouts. I was saddened to learn he had died in the interim.

I grew sicker and went down the hill, both literally and physically.

**Camp Cabanatuan - Giving a Sick Man a Drink, by artist, Ben Steele.** *Image courtesy Montana Museum of Art and Culture (All sketches are charcoal on paper.)*

\* \* \* \* \* \*

I got demoted to Zero Ward, the last place you stopped off before landing in the morgue.[55] Since the war had begun, my weight had progressively dropped from my average 180 pounds to around 108 pounds.

I knew I was in bad shape, but I didn't know how critical until Captain Burcham examined me with curious results. He touched my skin with a pin and I flinched, more as a reflex than from pain. He had me to roll over on my stomach and pricked me all over my back. I didn't jerk because I didn't feel it. As long as he stuck me when I was looking, I'd jump, but if I couldn't see what he was doing, I didn't know when he stuck me.

He rounded up two more doctors who repeated the same procedure. They backed off and conferred in whispered tones, then left, only to return with four more colleagues, including the ranking doctor in camp.

Those guys stuck me with enough pins that if I'd been a voodoo doll, somebody would have been in serious trouble. I felt like that *somebody* must be me. They said, "Son, you're not going to make it."

"Hell, yes I am. I've planned all along on going home!" I replied. I got up from the table and started to walk out. They went into another pow-wow. Directly, the head doctor came over and said, "Well, Chandler, the captain tells me you are a brave man."

"I don't know about being so brave, but if you're talking about making it, I am planning to go home," I said.

The doctor shook his head gravely and said, "If there's anything you think you need to take care of, you ought to do it."

"What are you talking about, Doc?"

"A man can't live long in your condition," he replied.

"Well, Doc, I'm bound to get better then," I concluded.

He stood there looking at me with a grim expression for a minute, shook his head, then turned and walked away. He didn't bother to tell me

---

55      Fenced off from the hospital was a quarantined area containing about ten wards, called the dysentery section. Within the dysentery section was a building missed when the wards were numbered. Later, it was called the "zero" ward, because the seriously ill or dying patients brought in there had "zero" chance of leaving it alive. Ibid.

their diagnosis of my mysterious ailment—just left me with his gloomy prognosis.[56]

\* \* \* \* \* \* \*

Five men were assigned to the bay each night, and for nine weeks I was the only one that woke up each morning. Not exactly an optimistic ward.

One morning I raised up, trying to get turned around to see what was going on.

"Good morning," a voice spoke behind me.

I almost jumped out of my skin! I thought the room was haunted. Misery loves company and I was glad to have some. However, he didn't last but a few days and then he gave up the ghost, also.

There seemed to be a never-ending supply of sick folks to restock the sick wards.[57]

\* \* \* \* \* \* \*

Sgt. Carl H. Price came into Zero Ward and remained with me while others went out to the morgue. I slowly resumed my ability to get out of bed, venturing out to get my own food. The sensation of feeling gradually crept back.

As far as I know, Carl and I were the first to come out of Zero Ward alive. We graduated barrack by barrack, moving back up the hill toward renewed activity. Somewhere along the way, I lost contact with him. Afterward, several more survived Zero Ward, including Bill Minnow, a good friend of mine.

---

56     During the first eight months of camp in Cabanatuan following the Death March, deaths totaled approximately 2,400. Approximately 30 to 50 skeletons, covered by leathery skin, were buried in common graves each day. Of the men who died during July, 1942, 85 percent were under 30. Mansell.com

57     Each day an attempt was made to clear each barrack of the dying. They were removed to "zero" ward, laid on the bare floor entirely naked. Report by Col. Webb E. Cooper's "Medical" Department activities in the Philippines from 1941 to May 1942. (Report courtesy of Jim Burnett, nephew to Camp 17 POW #195, Billy Alvin Ayers) Mansell.com

**Zero Ward. Sketch Drawn by Medical Officer Eugene C. Jacobs, this illustrates the place where dying POWs had a "zero chance" to survive.** *See many of Dr. Jacobs' drawings in a book called "Blood Brothers: A Medic's Sketchbook. Published c1985, by Carlton Press (NY). Library of Congress; Bos, Carole "Zero Ward at Cabanatuan" AwesomeStories.com. Oct 07, 2013. Sep 23, 2020. <http://www.awesomestories.com/asset/view/ Zero-Ward-at-Cabanatuan>.*

\* \* \* \* \* \* \*

After surviving Zero Ward, I still had to contend with a persistent scourge of diarrhea, which was not only annoying; it also prevented full recovery by keeping me weakened.

I was mulling over the problem one day when I remembered an incident that had happened to some of my relatives, before I went into service, and thought it might be the solution to my dilemma. Uncle John and Aunt Maude had three young children who contracted ulcerative colitis, and two of them died.

"I don't know but one drastic measure that might save your son," the doctor told them. They were willing to try anything, so he gave the boy a whole bottle of castor oil, and miraculously, he got well.

During my motor pool duty in Savannah, I was assigned to drive for officers, including a Jewish doctor. He and I didn't see eye to eye and, invariably, got into heated arguments while I was driving for him. As luck would have it, he was assigned to my ward and I became his patient in Cabanatuan; he seemed to enjoy being in the driver's seat.

One day I accosted him, "You call yourself a doctor but you ain't doing a thing for my dysentery. I think I can doctor myself and do some good."

"Just what kind of home remedy do you have in mind?" He asked.

"I want a bottle of castor oil," I said.

"We don't have any castor oil but we have some Epsom salt," he snorted.

"Bring me a dose," I instructed him.

"You think that'll help you?" He sneered.

"It's more than you're doing for me," I countered.

I guess it made him mad because I acted like I knew more than him and was telling him what to do. "I don't have to worry about you because you're not going to make it out of here, anyway," he huffed.

"I'll tell you something. If I get on the ship before you do, you better not start up that gang plank or I'll throw you to the sharks," I promised.

The next day he brought a canteen half full of Epsom salt. I got a spoon and started to get a dose out.

"You wanted it, now take it all," he grumped. "Kill or cure, one of us will be better off."

That infuriated me, adding fuel to the fire. "You're on," I replied as I poured water into the canteen, turned it up and chugged the foul-tasting stuff in a few gulps.

Sometimes I'd have to go to the latrine three or four times while eating my bowl of rice. On the third day, and this may sound indelicate but it's the gospel, I had a solid stool (bowel movement)—and from then on, the diarrhea was gone. That day, I left the relief station as a cured and proud man!

Soon afterward, that doctor was assigned to another ward. I don't know where he wound up or whether he made it home.

I sometimes wonder if he didn't use our personality conflict as a means to spur me on to live, just to spite him. Anger is good incentive when it motivates rather than immobilizes you.

When our buddies got lethargic or apathetic, as if they'd lost the will to live, we tried to stir them up about something, call their mothers names, etcetera, anything to snap them out of it. If we couldn't get them riled up, they were goners for sure.

* * * * * * *

Most of what I know about the Bible now, I learned during my convalescence because, as I was able, I read the New Testament extensively. Not because I was a Christian at that time, but because I was curious about what God had to say.

Bibles were easy to come by because most of the guys weren't using them. There wasn't anything else to read and when I got into it, I was captivated by the incredible stories. Its heroes were realistic. The scriptures exposed their frailties and didn't make any bones about their weaknesses and failures, as well as celebrating their strengths and victories. I could relate to the one and longed for the other. It came as a surprise to find that it was fascinating reading, although Chronicles and some of those books can bog you down with the "who begat who."

I had gone to church sporadically as a boy and knew right from wrong. In fact, I had made a confession of faith at the age of twelve. But I hadn't exactly lived up to the Good Book during the intervening years.

Back on the frontlines during heavy shelling, guys prayed so loud you couldn't pray for yourself for listening to them begging for mercy and making their promises to God about what they would do for Him if He got them out of that mess. Then, when there was cease-fire, they went on living like the devil, but I didn't believe in pretenses.

When I was first captured, I whispered a prayer of sorts and said, "Lord, if you take me through and get me home, I'll live for you." He brought me home. For a while, I went on my merry way as before, but one day He collected on my promise and said, "You have a choice to make." I've been serving Him ever since.

Back home, my folks were on their knees a lot, and I credit their prayers and God's protection for bringing me through the war in spite of the many times I popped off and brought trouble on myself through my cockiness. I've thanked Him for that plenty of times since then.

It's a good thing they were praying, because I didn't do much praying for myself. Whatever I am, I'm not hypocritical. Of course, I might have been hypocritical (untruthful, deceptive) with the Japs in some cases but, at the time, I called it survival.

I guess, without realizing it, while I was busy surviving, God was busy protecting me and fighting other battles on my behalf.

\* \* \* \* \* \* \*

One day a doctor said, "Chandler, you seem like a pretty determined man. You plan on going home, don't you?"

"If there's only ten men that can make it back, I want to know who the other nine are going to be!" I said. My mind was made up and, in part, contributed to my survival. I wasn't a psychologist, but I knew it was more what happened *inside* you than what happened *to* you that mattered.

While in Manila, I met a guy from Arizona who was of similar size, back when I was robust for my age. In fact, we resembled one another enough that people noticed and got our names mixed up. Malaria had knocked my weight down to around 108 pounds. Arizona came close to 180 pounds because he had been out on a detail where they worked hard but were well fed. However, he was sick with malaria.

I recognized him when he came into Cabanatuan and remembered him as the "real-live" cowboy who lassoed the carabao in Manila. I was able to move about at that time and visited him two or three barracks uphill from mine.

"Chandler," he said when he saw me one day, "tell my mother ... for me."

"If you want your mother told anything," I said, "you'll have to go tell her yourself because I'm not going to tell her anything."

"Oh," he said, "but I'm going to die."

"You will if you take that attitude," I scolded him. "Look at me and look at you. I've got the same thing you've got and had it a lot longer. And I'm going home. You can, if you want to."

"Oh," he moaned, "I'm not going to make it. You be sure to tell my mother ..."

"Anything you want your mother to know, you can tell her yourself," I insisted. "I'm not going to go tell her anything." I goaded him.

It was two or three days before I was able to get back up to see him. He was dead from malaria.

Dying was the easiest thing in the world to do. You just made up your mind you weren't going to make it and—kaput!—you were gone. You might make up your mind you were going to live and couldn't make it physically, but if you made up your mind to die, you did for sure.

I was determined from the first day I joined the service I was going home. In fact, when I was a kid, I had premonitions that I'd be in a war, but I felt deep inside I would come back. I never thought about getting killed or crippled up. In my mind, I always envisioned coming home whole.

*　*　*　*　*　*

Bouts of malaria plagued me relentlessly. I couldn't seem to shake it, although I did a lot of shaking myself from the feverish attacks.

Some people would take malaria and have chills for a week, then it would let up awhile, then they would start taking chills again. Not me. When I took it, it didn't let up. I had chills every day and nearly shook the house down. You could almost set your clock by it because every day at a certain time, chills would seize me.

For three weeks, my temperature didn't drop under 100 degrees and I never lost consciousness or threw up, although sometimes I wished I could because I nearly died before I threw up and got some relief. A lot of people got delirious and crazy as a bat, but I knew what was going on all the time because fever didn't affect me like it does some folks. That's the only reason I was able to help the others.

The doctors were lucky to get a hundred tablets of quinine at a time, then they dispensed one precious tablet per patient, as far as they'd go. This proved to be ineffectual in helping anyone.

Captain Burcham, a navy doctor assigned to our ward, told four of us patients, "The other doctors and I want to conduct an experiment. The skimpy rations of quinine we obtain only seem to aggravate the malaria. It doesn't knock it out for anyone because we don't get enough to really help. We're wondering what would happen if a few men took all of it. You four men have had malaria longer than anybody here. The next issue of quinine we receive, we'll count them out into four piles and give it to you men in one dose."

He let that sink in and warned, "We can't predict the outcome. It may kill you or it may cure you. You are a guinea pig. We won't force you to take it."

True to his word, the doctor came to us when he received the next supply of quinine, counted it out, and divided it equally among the four of us. There were forty-two 5-grain tablets each.

He reemphasized his concern. "This is strictly on a volunteer basis. We don't know what's going to happen. It may kill you."

"Hand me mine," I said. I took my canteen and started gulping them down, one right after the other, swallowing all forty-two tablets as fast as I could. The others dribbled them out over several hours, but each took all of his allotment of tablets.

The next morning, two of the guys were dead. The third man went blind. When we came back home, he was still blind; however, his malaria was cured.

I took a chill that lasted three days and nights, rattling the rafters and nearly shaking the rickety hut off its stilts. That was the last attack I suffered. I was cured!

When I came back to the States after the war, my blood was drawn at a blood bank and they said I didn't have malaria. It got rid of that bug!

Years later, a doctor tested my blood during a physical and exclaimed, "It's amazing that as long as you were in the Philippines you didn't have malaria!"

"I had malaria," I stated.

"There isn't a trace of it in your blood," he reported, astounded.

"Well, Doc, I had it. And I'll tell you what happened, but if you call me a liar, I'm going to throw you out the window," I declared. We were several stories up. "I took forty-two 5-grain tablets of quinine at one time and I had a chill that lasted three days and nights, but I haven't had it since."

He didn't say a word; just sat there looking out the window in disbelief.

**HOME SWEET HOME AT CABANATUAN**
A typical scene of the barracks, and barracks life of a Prisoner of War in Cabanatuan.
(This pencil drawing was found under the cat-walk of one of the barracks at Cabanatuan, by one of the Rangers who
went in to release the Prisoners of War there in early 1945. Artist Unknown.)

**Sketch of Cabanatuan Barracks – inside.** *Cabanatuan Barracks Drawing
Image online, courtesy NOAA (National Oceanic and Atmospheric
Administration) in an oral history story from a Cabanatuan POW,
Commander Ted Morris, Jr. PD View this asset at: http://www.awesomesto-
ries.com/asset/view/Cabanatuan-Barracks-Drawing. Bos,
Carole "Cabanatuan Barracks Drawing" AwesomeStories.com.
Oct 07, 2013. Sep 23, 2020.*

**Aerial photo Camp Cabanatuan.**
*Pinterest; ipinimg.com/originals. National Archives.*

134

# CHAPTER 15

## Mind Games

**Prison Hut at Cabanatuan.** *Wickimedia Commons–"Raid on Cabanatuan";*
*PD–USGOV-Army – alamoscouts.org/photo_archives/060_079;*
*Public Domain*

DURING my interminable hours of convalescence in the Cabanatuan prison camp hospital, from July to November 1942, I had visions of Americans coming in to rescue us. In my mind, they charged out of a building that resembled a barn, located approximately three hundred yards downhill from the hospital area. I used to lie on my rough timber cot and let my mind run wild, seeing it all as if it were a movie happening before my eyes. Imagining my rescue was a way of keeping my spirits up.

After the war, while reading about the liberation of Cabanatuan, it was exciting to learn that Alamo Scouts, dressed as locals, hid in that same abandoned shack for eighteen hours to watch the camp.[58] The actual raid occurred similar to my desired rescue, which I had envisioned.

\* \* \* \* \* \* \*

After the war, James Conley, from Anniston, North Carolina, who shot the lock off the gate at the Cabanatuan camp, gave a talk to us at a Second World War Veterans reunion. He told me that Guy Ford, a radio operator, was selected to go on the raid at the last minute when the guy who was originally scheduled to go suddenly became ill. I was acquainted with Guy because he bought a store next door to the building where Dad once had his mechanic shop in Detroit, Alabama. Two of my acquaintances were among those who were rescued. One man was blind and the other had been shot in the knee during the war.

A 1945 movie, *Back to Bataan*, starring John Wayne and Anthony Quinn, portrayed the raid on Cabanatuan, with a flashback of the Battle of Bataan. *The Great Raid* was later released in 2005. A documentary series, *Shoot Out!* was released in 2006, which also covered the raid in one of the episodes.

The site where the Cabanatuan prison once stood is now a park, and a memorial lists the two thousand six hundred and fifty-six names of the Americans who died there.[59,60]

\* \* \* \* \* \* \*

I have a lot of bad memories of suffering—both others' and my own—from inhumane treatment at that camp, but it is a comfort to know my

---

58       Jan. 29, 1945, known as The Great Raid: "While the 6th Ranger Battalion (total of 107 assisted and guided by guerrillas) rested at a village of Platero, the scouts conducted further reconnaissance from a nipa hut across the road from the camp." *http://www.army.mil*

59       "The 27th Bomb Group lost 236 men at Cabanatuan POW Camp." Ibid, "27th Bombardment Group—39th Anniversary Program and Memorial Service," Nov. 2–4, 1979.

60       Major Richard Gordon, who was there, estimated that 3,000 prisoners of war died at Cabanatuan during its existence from starvation, lack of medical supplies, mistreatment, poor sanitation and executions. "1931-1945 – Atrocities-Severe Mistreatment-Slave Labor", Edward Jackfert.

vision of rescue came true for those men. It was a mind game to keep my sanity intact.

I've often wondered whether my Japanese buddies—guys like Ching, with whom I later became good friends at that camp—got killed in the raid, or if they had already been moved out before then. Had it not been for some of the Japanese who were kind to me, I might not have survived. I hoped the good ones made it out safely.

\* \* \* \* \* \* \*

*Additional Information* - **January 30, 1945:** Lt. Col. Henry Mucci, led 133 U.S. Army soldiers from the all-volunteer 6th Ranger Battalion—trained for command-type missions, and Alamo Scouts—elite recon unit, and more than two hundred Filipino guerrillas. They traveled thirty miles, slipping behind heavily fortified Japanese lines to reach the camp.

The liberators divided into four groups to attack. Two groups of guerillas and Rangers were sent to hold the main road, one to the north and one to the south, near camp. Two other groups were assigned to attack the front and rear of the prison stockade.

Our troops were in touch with guerilla Capt. Pajota and his men, who waited at a town called Cabu, about a mile and a half away. They provided cover northeast of the camp as a first line of defense to guard the bridge from a force of more than a thousand Japanese soldiers camped across the Cabu River. A team of seventy-five Rangers and guerillas was posted eight hundred yards southwest of camp, down toward the city of Cabanatuan, which was nearly three miles away, to stop the enemy from that direction.

Mucci requested a fighter plane to provide distraction, from the air, for the Japanese guards in the towers, so that raiders could crawl unnoticed across the cleared area around the compound, which was surrounded by an eight-foot barbed wire fence. A P-61 Black Widow night fighter, named Hard to Get, performed an aerial act, flying dangerously close, making several loops, to keep the guards' eyes on the sky for twenty minutes.

They all moved into place from seven hundred yards out. At the appointed time of 19:40 (7:40 p.m.), a guy named Conley shot the lock off the prison gate. Certain men were assigned to shoot the lookout tower guards, and they all simultaneously fired on their specific targets.

Unfortunately, one of the Rangers moved too fast and got killed by friendly fire. Enemy fire within the compound wounded a medical officer in the stomach while attempting to rescue a prisoner; he later died on the journey to the American lines.

The liberators quickly evacuated the frail men who could walk out the gate. Other Rangers helped transport the sick and handicapped on stretchers, with some carrying the emaciated men on their backs across the compound. One Ranger was carrying a prisoner from the barracks toward the gate; the man died from an apparent heart attack, only yards from freedom. Evidently, the excitement was too much for him.

POWs were carried across the road, where they were placed in the twenty-six carabao-pulled carts driven by locals that the guerillas rounded up, as well as food contributed by them for the return trip. Rangers, Scouts, and guerillas escorted them to the American lines. By the end of the trip, a hundred and six carts had been accumulated along the route to transport weakened soldiers who could not endure the walk.[61]

During the raid, five hundred and fifty-two Allied prisoners of war were rescued, including five hundred and thirteen survivors of the Bataan Death March. An estimated seventy-three Japanese guards and a hundred and fifty soldiers who were stationed at the compound were slain. Between five hundred to more than a thousand Japanese were killed when they attacked the bridge that was guarded by the guerillas to the north of the camp. Four tanks were taken out of action. In all, two prisoners and two soldiers died; two Scouts, two Rangers, and nine guerillas were wounded in action.

After a headcount of POWs, one man was found to be missing; he was a deaf British soldier. Guerrillas went back to find him. It was discovered that he had gone to the latrine before the attack and fell asleep. When he woke up, all his fellow POWs were gone. He bathed, shaved, and dressed

---

61      Capt. Juan Pajota and his guerrillas continually sought out local villagers to provide additional carabao carts to transport the weakened prisoners. The majority of the prisoners had little or no clothing and shoes, and it became increasingly difficult for them to walk ... Despite the convenience of using the carts, the carabao travelled at a sluggish pace, only two miles per hour, which greatly reduced the speed of the return trip. By the time the group reached American lines, 106 carts were being used." Wikipedia: "Raid at Cabanatuan." http://wikipedia.org/wiki/Raid_at_Cabanatuan

in a set of clothes he had held onto for his release; he left the camp to find the rest of his comrades. Guerillas found him and got him to safety.

The freed four hundred and eighty-nine POW soldiers and thirty-three civilians were finally able to tell about their cruel captors and to relate stories of the atrocities of the Death March and harsh camp treatment. It heightened the determination of our nation to win the war against Japan."[62] Camp O'Donnell was liberated the same day in another raid. Bilibid was liberated on February 4. These and other raids were quickly planned to spare the prisoners of possible execution because the Japanese high command had given the order to kill POWs to keep them from being rescued by U.S. forces and returned to fight after their recovery.

**YP-61 Black Widow Night Fighter,**
*Source: United States Air Force; Public Domain.*

---

62      Prior to that timely rescue: "As the Americans consolidated their forces to prepare for the main invasion of Luzon, nearly 150 Americans were executed by their Japanese captors on December 14, 1944, at the Puerto Princesa Prison Camp on the island of Palawan. An air raid warning was sounded so that the inmates would enter slit-trench and log-and-earth covered air-raid shelters, and there doused with gasoline and burned alive." Wikipedia: "Raid at Cabanatuan."

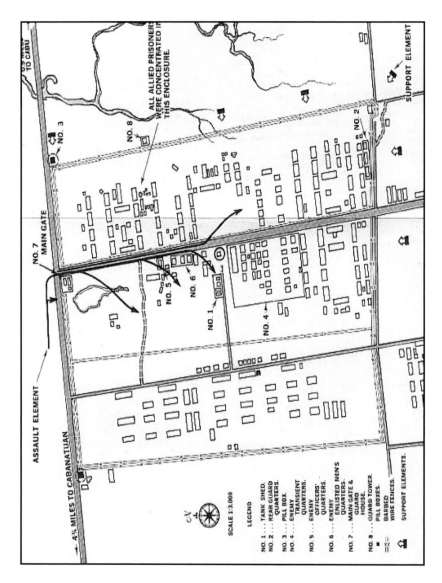

**Cabanatuan POW Camp layout.** *Michael J. King created this drawing—"Bird's eye view illustration of the actions taken by the US Rangers in their Raid at Cabanatuan". This provides an overview of the rescue plane undertaken on January 30, 1945. Bos, Carole "THE RESCUE PLAN" AwesomeStories.com. Aug 01, 2005. Sep 23, 2020. <http://www.awesomestories.com/asset/view/THE-RESCUE-PLAN-Great-Raid-The>.*

*"A number of the* **prisoners liberated at Cabanatuan** *were too weak to walk out of the prison under their own power. They were carried out by their liberators and helped onto carabao carts pulled by oxen." Great Raid on Cabanatuan by Charles W. Sasser, https://warfarehistorynetwork. com/2020/02/04/great-raid-on-cabanatuan/. Courtesy of Sovereign Publications.*

**Inside the camp, a prisoner walks past huts in this undated photo.**
*From https://warfarehistorynetwork.com/2020/02/04/great-raid-on-caba- natuan/. Courtesy of Sovereign Publications.*

**Henry Mucci on left and Rangers on right side, after "The Great Raid" at Cabanatuan.** *Image by Signal Corps. Public Domain*

**POWSs after rescue at Camp Cabanatuan,** *U.S. Army – http://www.alamoscouts.org/photoarchives/060 079.htm, Public Domain*

# CHAPTER 16

## BACK ON DUTY

AROUND November or December, I finally graduated to the last barrack uphill near the gate and was transferred to the duty side of the compound.

The next morning, Saturday, the Japs sent me out to work. Bolo in hand, I slashed and cut cattail grass, helping a work crew assigned to clear a thousand acres of land designated for an airfield.

Straight out of the hospital, my strength was not up to par and my hands trembled. The blisters on my palms and fingers became bloody pulp. I winced with pain each time I had to swing the blade. No slouching off was allowed, because a Jap guard stayed right with me, looking for any excuse to whack me in the head or back.

By high noon, my hands were bleeding profusely. When we stopped to eat a rice ball, I told the American sergeant who was in charge of the details not to send me back out to the farm any more.

"I don't plan to go back. I've made my first and last trip out there," I informed him.

"Yeah, you'll go back," he replied. "If you don't go to the farm, they'll shoot you."

"Well, I guess they're in for some target practice, cause I'm not going back to the farm," I said.

That afternoon they drew five men, out of seventeen hundred, to dig a sump for the kitchen. I was one of the lucky five. I started digging with my hands sore and still bleeding. Finally, I threw down the pick and fell out of rank.

"You'll have to get somebody else to work in my place, 'cause I don't aim to dig anymore," I told the guard. "There are too many men who are in better shape than me that you can draft." I marched back to the barracks, fully expecting a bullet in my back.

The next day, Sunday, was a rest day. I lay on my mat, overcome by exhaustion. The guy on the next mat, who had come over from the hospital at the same time I did, punched me, rousing me from my blissful nap.

"I just volunteered you to work in the Japanese kitchen with me," he said.

I jumped up and snorted, "I can't cook. I'm not interested and I'm not going."

He said, "OK!" and motioned for me to calm down. He notified the man who was scouting up kitchen help that we wouldn't be able to go.

I dropped back off to sleep. When I opened my eyes, the man who had been looking for help in the kitchen was hovering over me. "Let's go," he ordered.

"Go where?" I asked.

"I volunteered you for the kitchen again and this time you're going."

"I can't cook," I balked.

"You're already a cook—I volunteered you and I'll teach you." He had experience as a cook for both the Americans and the Japanese. I followed him to the kitchen and learned how to cook rice and soup as good as any Japanese momma-san.

That was shortly before Christmas.

# CHAPTER 17

## CHIEF COOK AND BOTTLE WASHER

MY duties included carrying buckets of rice to a bench at the back of the kitchen. In my frail state, I could manage half a bucket at a time when I first started working on kitchen duty. I had to sit down and rest on the way around the building from the front of the kitchen to the back.

Being "volunteered" to work in the kitchen proved to be a blessing in disguise; we had access to extra food. At that time, they were serving beef, so my buddy and I started holding out the liver for ourselves without the Japs knowing it. After a while, we tired of the liver but were afraid to put it back on the menu for fear they would realize what we had been doing. As much as I wanted to slip it out to other prisoners, I couldn't because of the guards' close checks.

I gained weight so fast it almost made me sick again. I had to stop working for a few days to get stamina enough to carry the added pounds. When I returned to duty in the Japanese kitchen, my strength built up rapidly. By the time I left that kitchen, I could tote a hundred kilos of rice.[63] I'd lug it all the way from the warehouse, where it was issued, across the compound.

\* \* \* \* \* \*

Rice, rice, rice. Rice with everything! It was a staple food served with every meal for the Japanese and Filipinos. For us in camp, it was the meal. Period.

We prepared the rice in fifty-gallon pots. It was unsalted, of course.

For years after I came home, rice was the last thing I wanted to see on the table. The memories and the taste made me want to puke!

---

63    Kilo = kilogram equals 1,000 grams (2.2046 lb.).

Eventually, I began eating it again and cooking batches for my family. I can cook the fluffiest rice ever by dumping it in an open boiler and turning the stove eye on high. Some folks turn the heat down when it begins to boil, and that's a mistake. I have to stay right there with it, so as not to burn it, but I boil it until it's the right texture, then cut it off and set it aside to dry out. I don't salt it beforehand. That cuts down the temperature. I salt it afterwards. I'd be proud to serve any Japanese my rice!

There were two kitchens at Cabanatuan: one on the Japanese side of the compound and one on the American side. Compared to my comrades, I ate well while working in the Jap kitchen, but when I had to work in the American kitchen, there wasn't much to brag about. Japanese officers were fed some tasty dishes, and their enlisted men were fed fairly well, but our menu was the pits.

Occasionally, farmers delivered potatoes from the market. When that happened, we made *hototay*—soup, a Filipino word—out of sweet potato leaves and vines.[64] The taste reminded me of spinach. If the Japs felt generous, they might add a few diced-up sweet potatoes in the soup. We called it "racehorse" soup: it would take a racehorse to catch anything that was in it because it was mostly water.

In the Philippines, a mango bean, about the size of dried lentils, is grown, which has a high protein content.[65] When we had money and a means to get them from outside the camp, we bought mango beans and boiled them to get the protein. I didn't ever have the money to buy any, but one of the guys who did would say, "I'll buy 'em if you'll cook 'em."

Our captors didn't worry about supplying us with enough protein and nourishment to provide energy for work. They knew how to get the work: they beat it out of you. When you did your quota, then you could call it a

---

64    Sweet potato leaves are very nutritious. They have a high amount of antioxidant for combating inflammatory problems like asthma, arthritis, gout, etc.; promote a healthy gut; regulate blood glucose levels; maintain heart health. Vitamin C fights free radicals, thus preventing premature aging and disease. Dietary fiber helps prevent colon cancer, contains components of natural painkillers, lowers blood pressure, and helps with anxiety and stress. Dietary fibers regulate flow of blood and prevent fat deposition in arteries and veins. According to https://www.onlymyheath, article by Amrita Kumari, 01-27-17.

65    The tropical, evergreen, Asiatic tree of the cashew family on which it grows. *Webster's New World Dictionary*. New York: Simon & Schuster, 1984.

shift. Thus, there was no problem with feeding you to get more work out of you.

The Japanese used a lot of seasonings made from soy sauce. "Miso," a paste made out of soybeans, was a popular seasoning. Radishes were canned similar to the way we can kraut with salt. It made a sour relish to eat with the rice, but anything was better than plain old rice.

We ate whatever we could get. They didn't have to doctor it for us; we were so starved that we weren't very choosey.

When I worked in the Jap kitchen, I had access to miso, which added much-needed protein. The corn, which they put in our soup, was hard enough to shell off the cob, not cut off like creamed corn. It went down like rocks.

They could fix some pretty tasteless soup by dicing up eggplants and boiling it in water, no salt, no nothing. The only way I can eat them now is to dice them like green tomato, soak in salt water, roll in batter, then pan-fry. I still don't have much of a yen for eggplants.

The Japanese had it figured out, or so they thought. They said there was enough protein for one day in a peanut for an American to live on. In one peanut! And that's about what they gave us! They called peanuts "beans" and cooked them as if they were beans. However, they served those *beans*, peanuts, to their men.

**"Protein"- POW commenting on why the man looks so sickly. By J. P. Bashleben.** *Courtesy of BataanProject.com; by permission from Bashleben Family.*

Many guys died of malnutrition. For the first two months in the Philippine camps, we buried approximately seventy a day at O'Donnell.

When the Japs started doling out plain (brown) rice, it didn't take long for what little vitamins we had left in us to evaporate. Later, when they used the polished (white) rice, there was barely any nutrition to be had at all. The main difference between these two types of rice is that in polished rice, the outer bran layer, which contains the majority of vitamins such as B complex, is removed, whereas it is present in the unpolished rice. Processing removes many of the nutrients and vitamins; lack of B vitamin causes beriberi. Also, unpolished rice has fibers that help in digestion; therefore, we should not eat polished rice.[66] Otherwise, every disease that comes along jumps on you, because you don't have any resistance.

*Chowline At Cabanatuan*

**Chowline at Cabanatuan, by Ben Steele.** *Image courtesy of Bataan Project, with permission of Montana Museum of Art and Culture (All sketches are charcoal on paper).*

---

66          https//www.Answers.com; also, "Medical tests have proved that consuming brown rice helps reduce the body's sugar and cholesterol levels." http://www.easyrambler.com/brown-rice-benefits.php

\* \* \* \* \* \* \*

One of the Japanese cooks, Big Ching, and I became good friends. He understood a smidgen of English, and combined with the brief tutoring on Japanese I had received from my captor, we managed some tolerable communication. He later proved his friendship, but initially, I almost severed our fragile Jap-American relationship.

I had been working in the kitchen a few days when a sumo-wrestling match was held for the Japs, that being one of their favorite pastimes.

Big Ching won the tournament for the day and stepped out of the ring as the champion wrestler. He returned to the kitchen, holding his hands over his head, boasting, "Ching Champ, Ching Champ!"

"No, not you, me," I teased him. We had kidded around some, so I felt safe joshing with him. He didn't seem to understand. I patted my hands together, patted my thighs, then said, "Sumo!" I knew that was the Japanese challenge to wrestle.

He took my challenge seriously and charged like a bull! He didn't understand enough English for me to be able to stop him. I tried to dodge him because I saw I was in trouble.

The windows were propped open inside the kitchen like those in a chicken house. By that time, Japs began to gather outside and peer through the opening. There was only one thing to do; pit my scrawny 108 pounds against my hefty 190-pound friend. I tried to hold him back and explain I was joking. It was futile and there was no way to back down. He lunged for me again.

Until this day, I don't know how it happened. Maybe the good Lord just helped me! Somehow, I used his weight against him and got the rotund Ching above my head, then dropped him to the concrete floor. His breath whooshed out from the jarring impact.

Japanese tradition doesn't count a man down until his shoulder is put flat three times. That was simple for me to do since Ching's wind had been knocked out of him.

Much to my dismay, the onlooking Japs began running around chanting "China Champ!" "China Champ!" They couldn't say Chandler, so they called me "China" instead.

Ching jumped up and stalked out in a huff. To understand the gravity of the event, one must understand the Japanese mentality of honor and shame.

Ching disappeared from kitchen duty for several days. I think that's the most antsy I have ever felt because I didn't know what to expect. When a Jap loses face, you don't want to be available to him any time soon.

At night, I cautiously returned to the American side of the compound to sleep. In the mornings, I dreaded walking through the gate to get back to the Japanese kitchen. My imagination went wild; I didn't know if he was planning to shoot me, bayonet me, or just plain pounce on me. None of the options seemed very healthy.

Three days later, he reappeared in the kitchen. Strangely, it was as if he had erased it from his memory and decided to remain on a friendly basis. I sure was relieved at that attitude because I didn't want to tangle with Ching any more. I became a dedicated "Ching Champ" fan from then on.

In spite of the little upset, Ching remained my friend and stood by me in some hairy moments to come.

* * * * * * *

One day I hid several potatoes under the pot and left them in the ashes to bake. My mouth watered at the thought of sinking my teeth into those tasty spuds.

I thought I got away with it, until Big Ching came to me and told me to get the potatoes out from under the pot. He must have had eyes in the back of his head.

I wasn't about to stick my neck out now by going to get the potatoes. Afraid another Jap would see me and not be as lenient, I stood there playing dumb.

Ching's eyes bore into me. He repeated, "Pull the potatoes out from under the pot. We are having *Emo* (inspection)."

I remained pegged to the spot, wearing my most innocent expression.

To my surprise, Ching ran to the pot, scratched around in the ashes, grabbed the potatoes and tossed them to me, yelling, "Get them out, get them out. Captain coming for inspection."

That was not my idea of the way to play the old game "hot potato." I whisked them out of the kitchen barely in the nick of time.[67]

**Reprimanded and Shakedown, 2010.06.57, Sketch by Ben Steele.**
*Image courtesy Montana Museum of Art and Culture*
*(All sketches are charcoal on paper).*

\* \* \* \* \* \* \*

Another day, several Americans came to me and said they were starving to death. Taking pity, I told a few of them to meet me at the fence. Our kitchen was straight across the road on the Jap side, and the fence was up the bank on the American side.

---

67        There was an organized underground system. Needed items were obtained, mainly by two American women (wives of soldiers who died there in 1942), who had avoided confinement at Santo Tomas, Manila. Food, medicines, notes were carried by a Filipino lady, Evangeline Neibert ("Sassie Suzie") by train to market in the town nearby. This loot was hidden in the bottom of sacks of rice slipped by Naomi Flores ("Looter"), a licensed vegetable peddler into camp to one of six officers ("helpers") who delivered the goods to prisoners. On May 3, 1944, the Japanese ended the operations by apprehending several of the "ring leaders" of the American sympathizers. They were severely beaten, imprisoned or executed for their participation. "Camp Cabanatuan", Mansell.com

"I'll give you a bag of rice," I promised them. Before daylight, they were eagerly waiting at the fence.

I glanced around, but didn't see any Japs in sight. I slipped the bag of rice from the kitchen, crossed the road to the fence, and then threw it over to them. The grateful Americans scurried away to their kitchen.

That time I was lucky.

* * * * * * *

I had a friend, Grady Palmatier, nicknamed "Shorty Red," with whom I recruited and later returned together on the same ship. He was sick with all kinds of ailments, as well as suffering from malnutrition.

"Will you eat some fish, if I can get it to you," I asked. I was worried we were going to lose him because he wouldn't eat anything. He agreed to try some.

"We're having fish in the kitchen today. Come down to the fence around 1:00 p.m. and I'll slip you one. Skedaddle as soon as I pass it to you," I warned.

After we ate, I hid one away for him. About 1:00 p.m., I looked out the window and saw him standing next to the fence waiting patiently. I eased the fish out of its hiding place and sauntered across the road. I passed the prized meat to him and told him to get out of sight.

The moment the fish touched his hand, a Japanese guard threw a shell in his gun and shouted, "Halt! What did you give him?"

"*Sakana* (fish), that's what!" I answered him. As he advanced menacingly toward me, the hair prickled on the back of my neck. I knew I was in a heap of trouble for stealing.

Big Ching stepped from the kitchen and yelled, "*Watashi wa kare ni sakana o ataemashita.*" (Japanese for "I gave him the fish.") I hadn't known Ching was aware of the theft.

A heated debate ensued. While the guard and the cook had a shouting match, I looked around and didn't see anybody to stop me; I made a bee-line for the American side of the compound. I couldn't understand enough Japanese to know what was being said, but when they got through arguing, I wasn't there to hear the outcome. I had disappeared like that fish!

\* \* \* \* \* \* \*

Big Ching was hoping to smuggle a Japanese Army blanket out of camp to sell. He feared when he got to the gate, the sadistic guards would catch him, and he would get beat up. Knowing my flare for connivery, he confided what he was trying to do.

"I can tell you how to get it out of the camp," I said.

"Oh, yeah. How?" He was skeptical.

"Pull your britches down," I instructed him. He wore big baggy pants tied around the waist with a rope. He was larger than the average Jap.

He shied away.

"Pull your britches down and I'll show you something," I repeated.

He reluctantly dropped his pants. I took the blanket and wrapped it around his big belly a couple of times, pulled his pants up over it, then tied the rope belt. He chuckled.

"Walk down to the gate like you normally do; they'll let you through." He had his doubts it would work.

"Well, I showed you how it can be done. If you haven't got enough nerve to take it out, that's your business," I goaded him.

He marched down to the gate and the guard nodded him through. He sold the blanket in town for a good price.

The next time he came in, he brought a bag of Filipino tobacco to me, wearing a Cheshire cat grin. He was so proud he had gotten away with the deception. I was proud, too, because I smoked at that time and tobacco was difficult to come by.

Thereafter, having given away a trade secret for smuggling, he made a show of patting suspiciously around my waist to see if he could catch me at his own scam.

"You know I'm smarter than to use that old trick," I'd say, and he'd give a hearty laugh. It's a good thing that big fellow liked me.

\* \* \* \* \* \* \*

Most of the Americans who worked in the kitchen returned to our side from about 1:00 p.m. to 3:00 or 4:00 p.m. for a rest break before cooking supper. The Japanese cooks usually went another place, which left the kitchen open.

The kitchen contained a dug-out space used as a firebox over which pots were placed for cooking. It stuck out enough on the sides to allow room to push firewood underneath the pots.

Behind the firebox was a small platform where the pots were washed and stored when not in use. They were rolled back in place over the firebox for cooking.

One day I carried my clothes to the kitchen to wash at the faucet on the platform out back.

Scarface, one of the Japanese cooks, had also stayed to wash his clothes. His nickname stemmed from the big ugly scar, perhaps a bayonet or knife wound, that slashed from his temple, down across his cheek into his chin. The beastly gash wasn't pretty to look at, and his temper wasn't a pretty sight either. I never learned whether an American had done that to him, but it might have explained why he was so mean to us.

Sidestepping him, I quietly began my chore, but Scarface decided I needed to do his washing for him and shoved them under my spigot for me to scrub.

I pushed them back to him.

He bulldozed them back over my way.

I angrily thrust them back to him.

The third time I slid his pile of clothes back, he dashed over and slapped me. The bad side of my nature showed its ugly face. I reared up and hit him square in the jaw, knocking him off the platform with one blow. He sprawled back on the ground in the firebox ashes.

I dove off the platform on top of him, determined to choke him to death. I knew I was already in trouble for hitting him. I figured I might as well finish the job.

He struggled loose and dashed out of the way. I didn't follow him, reconsidering that it might be best to let my temper cool down. I climbed back up on the platform where my clothes were strewn, unaware that he had gone for the rifle he kept stored in the kitchen. Leveling the rifle on me, I heard him cock the hammer.

If being ornery is a virtue, I was about to receive my reward! I figured, *"This is the end of the line, Chandler."*

Then Big Ching saved my bacon again!

Ching bellowed *"Ki-o-tsuke!"* (Japanese for "Attention!"). Big Ching, who was a sergeant, outranked Scarface, who was a corporal. Scarface stopped short of pulling the trigger. He brought the gun up and snapped to attention.

Ching took the gun and started whacking him with it.

That incident did not make points with Scarface for me. In fact, I was always leery of Scarface afterward, cautious not to be caught alone with him. I was sure he would get revenge on me the first opportune moment.

But I had my pride and refused to be a washwoman for anyone—until I got back to the States and got married, that is!

**Spitting Mad Reprimand with *Binto*,** *(real title uncertain),* **(2010.06.57),**
**by Ben Steele.** *Image courtesy Montana Museum of Art and Culture*
*(All sketches are charcoal on paper).*

\* \* \* \* \* \* \*

Salt and sugar were brought into camp in coal cars for the Japs. Prisoners who worked out in the fields had to cross the railroad tracks several times as they returned.

On the days the coal cars delivered salt or sugar, men broke ranks to climb the gondolas, eagerly grabbing handfuls to satisfy their craving for those precious minerals, which were sorely lacking in our diets.

Guards threatened to shoot prisoners who failed to obey and crawl down. But when you're hungry, threats fall on deaf ears. Being shot seems more humane than slowly starving to death.

As one of the few Americans who had access to the kitchen store-room, an idea struck me. We were permitted to carry tea back to the American side in a canteen. Since I had two water canteens, I cut the bottom out of one of them and left the other intact.

For a few days, I took the real canteen to the kitchen and filled it with tea. While passing through the guard checkpoints at the end of the day, I sloshed it around, making all the noise I could muster.

Alternately, I brought the bogus canteen to the kitchen, slipped into the supply room and turned it bottom-side up, filling it to the brim with salt or sugar. Then I stuck the aluminum cup back on and stuffed it into the canvas bag.

I walked past the guards without a hitch. I continued to rotate the bogey and the real canteen to keep anyone from catching onto my scheme.

Friends who were stricken with yellow jaundice were grateful to get the sugar and salt. I sold it to anyone else in the camp who had money (a full canteen was worth 100 dollars) and bought tobacco with the profits. Tobacco didn't come cheap either.

It's a wonder my little con game was never suspected; it could have been rough if I had been caught. But, like most things in life, if you don't take a gamble, you don't get anything. Like the turtle, if you don't stick your neck out, you can never move forward!

\* \* \* \* \* \* \*

There was little chance of escaping prison camps like Cabanatuan, especially after several men tried to escape. The Japs got wise and set up a system where, if one man escaped, nine other prisoners would die. The men were counted off into groups of ten; you kept your eye on the other nine in your group. In fact, since no one was allowed within ten feet of the fence, American officers set up the rule that no one could go within twenty feet of the fence; and had a number of people assigned to patrol the space to assure no one crossed it.

**Three POWs beaten by guards at Cabanatuan, suspected of trying to escape.** *Sketch, Artist unknown. Courtesy of Jim Opolony, bataanproject.org; National Archives; National Archives; P. M. Walton – http://www. wtv-zone.com/califPamela/beating.html.*

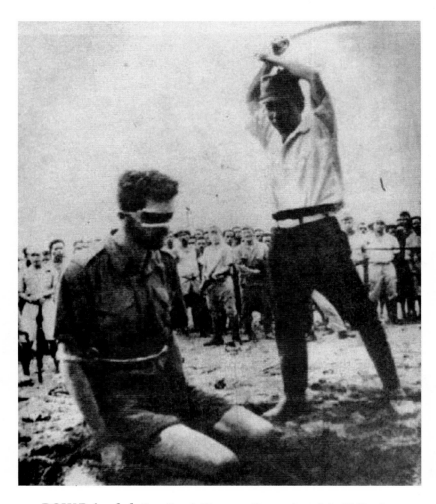

**POW Beheaded.** *Bos, Carole "Japanese Occupation of the Philippines - Beheadings" AwesomeStories.com. Oct 07, 2013. Sep 25, 2020. <http://www.awesomestories.com/asset/view/ Japanese-Occupation-of-the-Philippines-Beheadings>.*

# CHAPTER 18

## BAYONET BATTLE

IT infuriated me each time the Japanese mess sergeant boasted about how many Americans he had bayoneted during the capture of Corregidor. The more he talked, the madder I got, craving to avenge his victims. One day when he got cocky about it, I let my mouth override my brain.

"You're shooting a bunch of bull! Even I could whip you with a bayonet," I shot back at him.

"Prove it!" he snarled and went after the gear. It occurred to me I had gotten a little cocky myself, but fool or not, I didn't back down.

We slipped on the padded suits used to train the dogs. The Nips also used them like jousting knights to practice their bayonet skills. His compatriots gathered around, excited about the dueling match as we rigged up. He handed me a bayonet.

In basic training, all I learned to do was march, march, march. Combat know-how actually came from firsthand experience on the frontlines. After the war started, Colonel Mark Wohlfeld,[68] who brought our group overseas, taught us a few things about frontline bayonet fighting.

The Japanese seemed to be limited to an unimaginative single straight thrust and a *Banzai*[69] scream. They had to draw back to make a second lunge. Our officer had demonstrated a variety of strokes and said, "If you

---

68    Wohlfeld was a veteran Calvary man with fighting experience who later escaped with Jim Dyer after the Death March.

69    *"Banzai* (万歳 A war cry which meant "Long live the emperor! (Tennōheika Banzai!)—often just shortened to Banzai." Astrid Ingmarsdottir, DVM. "The banzai cheer is a common occurrence in today's Japan, meaning something like, 'Hurrah!' or 'Hip hooray!' Often repeated several times, each time raising their hands above their head, palms facing in toward each other." Quora.com, Sed Chapman. Banzai in modern Japanese culture basically means 'Yay! We did it! Quora.com, Alex Emerson, Half-Japanese, Half-American.

charge a man with a bayonet and miss, carry your gun on up and turn the butt down and split his head open, if you can." Armed with that knowledge, I hoped to outfox my opponent. The contest began.

The predictable straight thrust came slashing toward me. I blocked it with the length of my rifle.

I thrust at him in an upward motion, which he dodged.

Stepping forward, I pivoted and came back down, striking him in the head with the butt of my gun. The blow knocked him sprawling and defenseless to the ground.

Quickly, I plunged the point of the blade down at his throat and stopped short of terminating his boasting forever.

The mess sergeant lay there stunned and humiliated at the easy defeat, the jeers of the crowd ringing in his ears. He had lost face. I now had a dangerous enemy to guard my back against as I performed my kitchen duties. I obviously hadn't read *How to Win Friends and Influence People*[70] at that stage of my life!

* * * * * * *

A short time after that incident, my friend Shorty Red, who was still very ill and needed nourishment, asked for some food. I decided to take a chance on slipping one of the tomatoes, which we rarely served, out of the kitchen that day.

I usually went over to build a fire under the pot at about 4:00 a.m. to cook rice for the Japanese. I carried a jacket with me to conceal some food, more than to ward off the morning chill.

I got the best tomato I could find and slipped it into the coat pocket, then hid the coat. I was sure no one had seen me take it. I nervously kept my eye on it all day. Stealing anything, whether food, blankets, or clothing, carried a stiff penalty, possibly being shot on the spot.

Inspection wasn't pulled every day, but occasionally the guards searched through pockets, clothes, everything I had.

---

70      Written by Dale Carnegie.

The mess sergeant, with whom I had the bayonet tangle, waited until I picked up my coat to go back to the American side that evening before announcing, "Everybody fall in for inspection."

The incriminating evidence became a lead weight across my arm, but I couldn't put it down without being obvious. It dawned on me that he somehow knew I was up to something, even though he had kept mum all day. If the menu altered to stew for dinner, I was going to be the meat!

Big Ching, the sergeant in charge of the kitchen, looked at me. "China, go punch the teapot." Punch meant to fire up the teapot.

The 'teapot' was in another building. Chai, or tea, wasn't made by the jug; it was made by the vats. The teapot was fixed in a similar setup to the way we made sorghum in the country, with the vat sitting atop a firebox. Wood was shoved underneath to boil the tea.

The Japanese loved their tea as much or more than the British, and it is consumed in great quantities. Also, it is healthier than drinking contaminated water of that area. Thus, the tea vats were in constant need of being "punched" to keep them going.

I went on the double. Of course, at times like that, fast moves attracted unwanted attention, so I strolled out, carrying the jacket across my arm. The first thing that went under the teapot was the prized tomato! Then I fired the box.

Regretfully, my sick friend would have to get by on the meager rice ration for one more day, but my head was still on my shoulders. Breathing a sigh of relief, I hurried back. Inspection had been held up; he was waiting for me to come back to start the search.

The disgruntled mess sergeant barked at me, "Fall in for inspection." He grabbed the jacket, slung it up and down, and turned it inside out. He was so mad he couldn't see straight. I had gotten rid of the tomato, and he didn't have the evidence he suspected.

I'm convinced the only reason he had pulled inspection was because he thought my day of retribution had come.

\* \* \* \* \* \*

Shortly thereafter, I was working in the kitchen with Little Ching cutting up vegetables. There were two cooks named Ching in the kitchen: Little Ching, champion boxer, and Big Ching, sumo wrestler and friend.

Little Ching was standing near me, slicing the vegetables. Suddenly, he reached over with his butcher knife and chopped down at my hand. Taking it for a harmless game, I chopped back playfully at him with my butcher knife.

He struck back again, a little harder and a little too close for comfort. Things began to pick up speed and looked too serious to be labeled horseplay.

It occurred to me that getting beat up wouldn't be as bad as getting sliced to shreds, so I challenged Little Ching to box with me.

He halted slashing with the knife, his mouth dropping open in disbelief that I would challenge him, a champion boxer, to a fight.

I dared him again. He stood there a moment considering the situation. He had seen me wrestle with Big Ching and bayonet-whip the mess sergeant, so he hesitated awhile longer. Then he backed away. All the Japs in the kitchen started laughing and razzing him.

By the scowl on his face, I had just scored one more enemy. I now had so many to watch in the kitchen that I couldn't give much attention to developing my culinary skills.

Preferring to sweat out on the farm to sweating my fate out in the kitchen, I asked to be relieved from kitchen duty and reassigned to the farm.

Spring of 1943, I had gained to around 180 pounds because of my access to food. My strength was back and I felt much better than the first time I went to the farm in a weakened condition.

This old Alabama cotton picker would feel right at home in the fields!

**Rules and Regulations (2010.06.73), by Ben Steele.** *Image courtesy Montana Museum of Art and Culture (All sketches are charcoal on paper).*

# CHAPTER 19

## Donald Duck

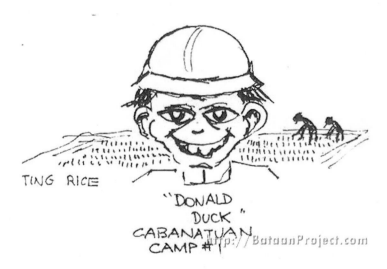

**"Donald Duck", cartoon by James P. Bashleben**, *courtesy of BataanProject.com, by permission of the Bashleben Family[71].*

DONALD Duck[72], one of the Japanese soldiers who stood guard on the bridges, became a good friend because I fed him well when he came in late from his post of duty. He transferred out to the farm, so when I returned

---

71        "Donald Duck was given the nickname because he reminded the POWs of the cartoon character. One day he found out who 'Donald Duck' was." Cartoonist J. P. Bashleben was in the Death March, and POW at O'Donnell, Cabanatuan, transported to Japan on the Canadian Inventor, then placed in Camp 17, the same camp where Drolan was sent.

72        The cartoon character Donald Duck is copyrighted by The Disney Group. However, this is the guard's nickname.

to work there, he always tried to draw my number to work in his group. He liked me and remembered how well I treated him.

On the occasions that he drew my number, life was almost bearable because he didn't work me as hard. Life wasn't as easy when it happened that someone else drew my number to work in the fields, in the scorching 100-degree heat.

We planted tomatoes, potatoes, pumpkins, squash, and watermelons. No, I never tried to steal one of those watermelons!

One day, while working with Donald Duck[73], we were given potato plants to set out. A deluge of rain hit as soon as we got to the fields. Rain was no excuse to stop working; we worked all day drenched from head to toe. By the time we were supposed to go back in, I was in a mood to rival the thundercloud.

A feisty little Jap named Little Speedo, who had been kicked around by his superiors and others, was one of two main guards—Big Speedo and Little Speedo—at the narrow gate leading back into the compound. We called them that because if you were slow while doing your work, they'd holler, "Speedo!" Big Speedo was not as harsh as Little Speedo, who used foul language and vented his frustrations on the weary prisoners as they passed through the gate by jabbing them in the side with his bayonet. He didn't mind beating up on them if he was in a bad mood.

Deciding not to be used as his whipping post of the day, I looked him straight in the eye and swore that if he laid a hand or bayonet on me, I'd choke him to death.

Little Speedo reared back and hollered *"Yameru!"* which meant, "Stop!"

I balked and repeated my intentions as to what I would do if he punched me with his gun.

Donald Duck, who was standing beside him at the gate, spoke decent English and translated what I said. Aware of my skirmishes in the kitchen,

---

73    "The prisoners had many 'affectionate' nicknames for their guards: Big Stoop, Little Speedo, Big Speedo, Air Raid, Laughing Boy, Donald Duck, Many Many, Beetle Brain, Fish Eyes, Web Foot, Hammer Head, and Hog Jaw were just a few names known to most prisoners at Cabanatuan." *Report on American Prisoners of War Interned by the Japanese in the Philippines*, Prepared by the Office of the Provost Marshal General, November 19, 1945.

he added, "You better not hit him. He will do what he said and choke you to death."

The little Jap considered the advice a few seconds, then reluctantly stepped back while I walked through the gate. He didn't touch me, but he was angry about pacifying me and took it out on the next unfortunate prisoner by raising a nasty stripe on him.

Typically, I made one less friend and one more enemy that day.

\* \* \* \* \* \* \*

I was not always lucky enough to be drawn by Donald Duck. Some of the other guards weren't as favorable toward me. We had several guards, like One Armed Bandit and Sailor who enjoyed slapping prisoners savagely. I can verify their cruelty personally from a few run-ins with them; they were only two on the list of least-liked guards.

We were hauling vegetables from the field one day, using platforms, called *butai*. Wiley Smith from Shreveport, Louisiana, and I were fooling around. Wiley was a friend I had known since enlisting in the service, back at boot camp.

Smoking was prohibited on the farm, but by hook or crook—more likely by crook—we had gotten hold of some tobacco. We sneaked behind the building, like adolescent boys, for a smoke.

One of the guards, dubbed "Air Raid," was a mean rascal to deal with if he caught someone fooling around. Nobody wanted to mess with him or the big stick he always carried, so we had a lookout that was supposed to call "Air Raid!" if he came around.

Thinking I'd pull a fast one on my buddy, I stuck my head around the corner and hollered "Air Raid!" I had no idea he was actually standing back there.

When I stuck my head out to yell "Air Raid!" he saw me and walloped me sharply across the head, busting the new Filipino coconut fiber shell helmet I had just been issued.

Wiley heard the commotion and, curious to see what was happening, stuck his head around the corner, too. Air Raid used his big stick to bust another coconut helmet, nearly cracking our skulls underneath!

We grabbed our *butais* and charged back for another load of vegetables from the prisoners who were busy washing them.

I won't say we didn't goof off any more after that. We just made dog-gone sure we stayed out of Air Raid's big stick's swinging distance as much as possible.

Air Raid remembered the incident and kept a slanted, hawk-eyed watch for me.

\* \* \* \* \* \* \*

One day I was out in the field smoking a cigarette when a guard spied the puffs of smoke. I saw him coming, so I quickly chewed it up and swallowed it. He stomped out there—ready to tan some hide—and looked around where I was standing. He bent down and scratched up the dirt all around, mumbling, *"Sore wa doko ni aru?"* ("Where is it?")

With a puzzled expression, he looked at my hands and searched through my clothes. Scratching his head, he poked around some more. He knew he had seen the smoke, but he couldn't find a trace of the cigarette.

*"Sore wa doko ni aru?"* he said and walked off, bewildered.

\* \* \* \* \* \* \*

Another day I was working—really working, that time—with two Jewish guys who were goofing off. Air Raid spied them, but they saw him edging down for a closer look.

I was stooped over working, minding my own business for a change, and didn't see him approaching. By the time Air Raid got near, they were busy as beavers and I happened to raise up to catch my breath. Air Raid motioned for me to come to him.

I obeyed and when I got within arm's length, he drew back and hit me with his fist, square in the face, as hard as he could swing. He was a big Jap and his surprise punch almost knocked me off my feet. My legs went weak and almost went out from under me.

Most of the men fell down on their knees and started begging him to stop hitting them if he struck them one time, to avoid a beating. That's what he expected me to do. But something, whether it was the devil or insanity I don't know, just surged through me. I braced myself and stood there, obstinately looking him in the eye. It had the same effect that trying to stare a dog down has—it made even him madder. He drew back and plastered me again and again, but failed to knock me down. All I could do was clench my fist and lock my jaw, because he wore a pistol. If I had dared to return the punches, he would have an excuse to shoot me. My face was beaten to a bloodied pulp by the time he worked through his frenzy. However, I toughed it out and he gave up first.

I had to keep a keen watch for old Air Raid after that, because he hadn't gotten full satisfaction off me.

I might have been better off if I had known the saying, "To get rid of an enemy, make him your friend!" But neither of us were very friendly chaps anyway.

* * * * * * *

When I returned to camp, one of the prison groups had begun digging postholes to install a power line for a pump to irrigate the pond for the farm. I volunteered for that detail, rather than go back to the farm. I decided I had rather dig postholes than risk another face off with Air Raid—the next time he might finish taking my face off!

One guard was assigned to each American while digging the postholes. The guard who drew my name was eager to learn English; thus, we didn't get much digging done. I was one of the best English teachers he ever had; in fact, he was learning it with an authentic Southern accent!

**Punching a Prisoner for not following Orders, by Ben Steele.** *Image courtesy BataanProject.com; permission for Ben Steele images granted by Montana Museum of Art and Culture (All sketches are charcoal on paper).*

**Carrying Cut Rice, by Ben Steele.** *Courtesy of Bataan Project.com; permission for Ben Steele sketches and paintings granted by Montana Museum of Art and Culture (All sketches are charcoal on paper).*

| Name | Rank | Serial # | Destination | Boarded Hellship / Ship Name | | Primary Philippine Camp |
|------|------|----------|-------------|------------------------------|--|-------------------------|

DRAFT ROSTERS OF ARMY POW'S SHOWING TRANSFERS FROM BILIBID PRISON TO OTHER

INFORMATION EXTRACTED FROM NATIONAL ARCHIVES IN COLLEGE PARK, MARYLAND, OCTOB

Last revision - May 27, 2014◆◆ ◆◆◆◆◆◆◆◆◆◆◆◆◆◆◆◆◆◆◆◆◆◆◆◆◆◆◆◆◆◆◆◆◆◆◆◆◆◆

**CAMPS IN 1944 OR EARLIER**
OCTOBER 2008 & MARCH 2009

**Robert Logan Hudson**

| Chandler, Drolan | Pvt | | | 14026383 | Western | 7/23/1943◆◆◆ Clyde Maru Cabanatuan |
| Harp, Robert | Pfc | 14011927 | | | Western | 7/23/1943◆◆◆ Clyde Maru Cabanatuan |
| Demers, Raymond A | | Pfc | | 11017288 | Japan | 8/25/1944◆◆◆ Noto Maru Cabanatuan |

https://www.west-point.org/family/japanese-pow/HudsonFast/BilibidObf.htm

**Draft Roster with Drolan Chandler, Robert Harp and Raymond A Demers listed.** *Due to the size, width and length, of the Roster, these particular names were cut and pasted. This shows their transfer from Camp Cabanatuan to the ship, Clyde Maru. Draft Roster of Army POW's Transfers, National Archives.gov*

# CHAPTER 20

## HELL SHIP

**Hell Ship –** *Clyde Maru, Image courtesy of Fumio Nagasawa, mansell.com.*

**JULY 8, 1943:** The Japanese assembled all of the prisoners together. The men were deathly sick from malnutrition; it resembled a death convention of emaciated skeletons. I had fared better than most because of my kitchen duties.

While the doctors examined us, we were kept in the dark as to the purpose of the proceedings. Five hundred of the fittest men were selected, and I was one of "the chosen," along with Bob Harp. We were wondering if it was good or bad news to be chosen.

We were informed that we would be shipped to Japan, and to the best of my knowledge, we were the first group to be transferred from the camps.[74]

**July 23, 1943:** We were transported on one of the "hell ships" or "death ships," as they later became notoriously known. Ironically, I was fortunate to be on one of the first ships to Japan, because many Americans lost their lives during later transfers due to bombings by our own forces who were trying to shut down Japanese operations, unaware that POWs were on board those ships.

"Hell" is a descriptive word for the intolerable conditions we experienced. Filth and stench filled the hold where we were packed in wooden kennel-like structures like Vienna sausages. Food was served in buckets handed down the hold on ropes. We were not allowed on deck for exercise or fresh air.

Down below, the conditions were so cramped, we had to take turns sleeping. There wasn't enough floor space for all to lie on; one guy stretched out long enough to work the kinks out and the other sat or stood.

Diarrhea was prevalent among our men; thus, human defecation, in addition to vomit, permeated the airless quarters in the bowels, appropriately termed, of the ship. No sanitary facilities existed; therefore, the holds served as a toilet and we wallowed in filth. There was a bucket on deck and one man at a time was allowed to go up topside. Most of the hundred men had dysentery, so chances were not in their favor to make it topside in time to avoid embarrassment. Most were too sick to be aware or care anyway.

Before leaving the Philippines, our ship stopped at Santa Cruz port for approximately a week to load iron ore. We stayed onboard, while it was loaded, until the ship sailed for Japan.

The manganese iron ore had to be brought down through our hold, and they shifted us to another part of the ship where they had hauled the

---

74        The first five hundred POWs arrived at Camp #17 on August 10, 1943, after a fifteen-day journey that left Manila on July 23, 1943, to Moji aboard the *Clyde Maru* (known to the men as the *Mate Maru*). No POWs died aboard the *Clyde Maru*, but several died during the following months due to the atrocious conditions on the ship. Clyde Maru was torpedoed and sunk on January 29, 1945, by the submarine USS *Picuda*. Mansell.com, "Movement of POW Into Omuta." Source: Research by Jim Erickson, Texas A&M University. See Drolan Chandler 258 on Clyde Maru Roster at masell.com, which is an excellent site to also see his name on POW Camp 17 roster. Roger Mansell (www.roger-mansell.com) was a great military historian.

cavalry horses. Acrid, urine-smelling water sloshed on the floor. When we lay down, the water came up to our ears. When the ship rolled, it sloshed over us. It was unsanitary and hardly fit for animals, but we were treated like that's what we were and had to live with it.

John R. Mamerow, an American major (later, colonel), nicknamed Honest John, was in charge of the first five hundred men. On many occasions during the trip, John stood up to the Japanese officers and pled for more rations for our men. He and the other officers distributed buckets so everyone would get a little.

"You've got to feed them properly," he insisted. He was beaten until he'd fall because of his vocally adamant demands.

During the passage, the ship made another stop on the China coast and picked up a bunch of rice and pork. Most of the men were already seasick from the rocking and rolling of the ship during the trip, unable to eat the meager rations, and were getting progressively worse. The Japs started boiling that pork in the soup they served to us. Here we were crowded in the airless, stinking hold, and they hauled down buckets of greasy soup for our meals. Some of the guys just couldn't take it. Most of the men almost died when they started eating that greasy pork.

For some reason, it didn't bother me. Men who were nauseated at the sight of it passed their share to me. That meant there was more soup left over for me to eat, which was a tremendous benefit and boost to my physical condition. That greasy pork soup tasted good to me, and it didn't affect me any more than sitting down and eating a good sandwich here. I almost got fat on the trip over to Japan!

\* \* \* \* \* \* \*

**July 31, 1943**: The ship docked at Formosa to load tobacco. As we arrived, one of the men, Jerry—Jerome E. Okonski—a good friend of mine, was stricken with appendicitis. The Japs refused to take him to the hospital, so one of the American doctors, Dr. Hewlett, performed his operation out on the deck of the ship. Using a hatch cover table and dental Novocain in the spine, Dr. Hewlett removed his ruptured appendix.[75]

I smoked at the time and got a hankering for a taste of the tobacco that we knew was stowed away down in the hold below us.

When dinner was called, the Jap guards all left. Some of the men began to slide down in the hold after the tobacco, and I was right behind them.

Climbing back up the ladder with a handful, I looked up to see a Jap guard standing at the top of the ladder glaring down at me. I was sure it was the end of the line and he had the cure for my habit, all in one shot.

I froze in place and stared up at the Jap, eyeball to eyeball. He hesitated as if trying to decide my fate, then made the sign of the cross over his heart, wheeled around, and walked away. I knew by the hand sign he made that he was a Christian or believer and did not relish the idea of killing me.

Needless to say, I got back where I belonged and put my tobacco craving on a back burner. Strangely, I didn't see that particular guard again on the trip. After the tobacco was loaded, we sailed on for Japan.

My memories of the trip are vague and sketchy, similar to others I have talked to who made the trip over with me or on other ships. I don't know if it is the mind's way of blocking out unpleasant memories or if the fever had me dazed. Some say the flies were swarming like a plague. I can't remember very much about most of the trip, whether they fed us or what they gave us.

The interminable, nightmarish trip took from July 23 to August 10, 1943, to cross over to Japan.

---

75      Our only available anesthesia consisted of several vials of dental Novocain tablets. Two of these tablets dissolved in a small amount of the patient's spinal fluid and injected into the spine gave about forty-five minutes of anesthesia, giving us time to perform most operations that had to be done. *The Hewlett Report* by Thomas H. Hewlett, M.D.

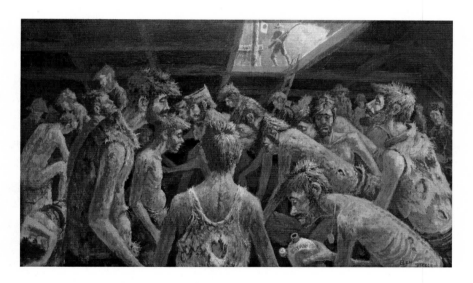

**The Hold of a Hell Ship** *(2010.06.07) Painting of deplorable conditions while transported to Japan by Ben Steele, artist. Image courtesy Montana Museum of Art and Culture (All paintings are oil on panel.)*

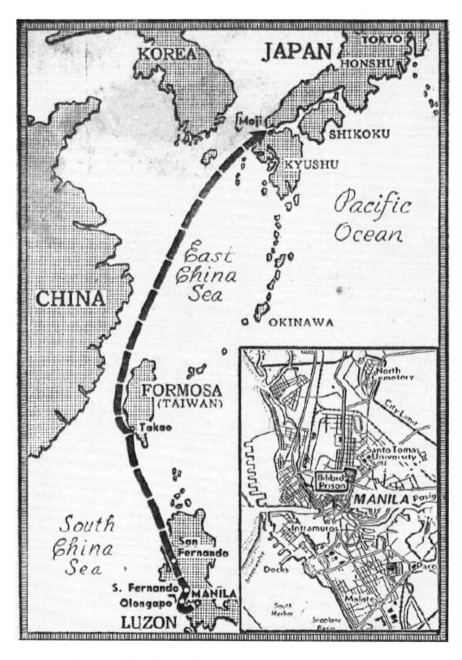

**Cruise of Death - Hell Ship Route,** *Courtesy of Mansell.com*

*Clyde Maru* **POW roster** (complete 500/500) Copyright 2009 by James W. Erickson
This roster contains the names of the 500 Americans sent from Manila to Moji, Japan, aboard the *Clyde Maru* from 23 July to 9 August 1943. The men were transported by train from Moji station to camp Fukuoka 17 at Omuta, Kyushu, arriving on 10 Aug 1943.

Many sources were used in recreating this roster, but the most important were records of POWs imprisoned at Fukuoka #17 obtained from Wes Injerd. These included documents originally from the US National Archives (probably RG 407 Box 22) and others provided to Wes by former camp 17 POW, Cecil Parrott. Additional information was obtained from a partial *Clyde Maru* roster unearthed at US National Archives (RG 407, Box 80, File 501-1-1), camp 17 records from the US National Archives (RG 407 Box 187) provided by Roger Mansell, the Fukuoka camp 17 webpages developed by Linda Dahl ( http://www.lindavdahl.com/ ), and transcripts of the court martial of Lt. Edward N. Little provided by Richard Szczepanski. The late Roger Mansell generously provided additional information from his POW database.

The file is in delimited format, divided by semicolons. It is sorted alphabetically. "Fk-17 camp #" refers to the number assigned to the prisoner upon arrival at camp 17. This number may also represent their position on the *Clyde Maru* roster. Numerous POWs were later moved from Camp 17 to other locations. Where known, such movements are listed in the Notes. No POWs died aboard the *Clyde Maru*, but the names of the 22 men who died in Japan are marked in dark red. Newly added names (16 Nov 2010) are marked in blue. 12 Aug 2019 update: I may have additional information about these men. Contact me if there is a particular POW you are interested in.

**Name;Rank;Svc #;Branch;Subsidiary unit;Assigned Unit;Parent Unit;Fk-17 camp#;death date;death place;Notes**

BYARS WILLIAM RAYNARD;Pvt;17017126;CAC;E Btry;60th CA Regt (AA);HDM&SB;299;;;

CARRINGER WAYNE;Pfc;6972776;AC;Hq & Hq Sqdn;27th Bomb Gp (L);V Bomb Cmd;399;;;

CHANDLER DROLAN;Pvt;14026383;AC;Hq & Hq Sqdn;27th Bomb Gp (L);V Bomb Cmd;258;;;

CHUMLY GEORGE E (Chumley?);Pvt;20523452;INF;D Co;194th Tank Bn;Prov Tank Gp;269;;;

DAUBENSPECK CLARENCE;Cpl;6921015;INF;H Co;31st Inf Regt (US);Phil Div;87;;;

HARP ROBERT R;Sgt;14011927;AC;Hq & Hq Sqdn;27th Bomb Gp (L);V Bomb Cmd;156;;;

LEE WILLIAM D;Pfc;14011931;AC ;Hq & Hq Sqdn;27th Bomb Gp (L);V Bomb Cmd;158;;;transferred to another camp then back

MAMEROW JOHN R;Capt;O&276134;AGD;Hq;Phil Dept;;1;;;to Mukden 25 Apr 45 nickname "Honest John"

MC CLINTOCK DOMONY (Dominick?);Pvt;18048999;INF;E Co;31st Inf Regt (US);Phil Div;178;;;

OKONSKI JEROME E;Pvt;15017273;CAC;B Btry;60th CA Regt (AA);HDM&SB;498;;;appendectomy on Clyde Maru

PRICE CARL H;Sgt;6380394;AC;21st Purs Sqdn;24th Purs Gp;V Intcp Cmd;65;;;

ZIMMERMANN WILLIAM E JR;Sgt;6973893;MD;;Hosp #2;;83;;;

*Cut and paste (of particular names used in roster) was used due to size of document. Mgj. West–Point.org*

# CHAPTER 21

## CAMP 17

**Fukuoka Camp 17-Main Entrance,**
*National Archives Catalog ID 2143324*

AMAZINGLY, all five hundred prisoners survived the rigorous trip to Japan, although the first two deaths among those who came over on the ship occurred in late December 1943, after leaving Manila.[76] We left Manila on July 23, 1943, and arrived in Japan on August 10, 1943.

After docking on the island of Kyushu, at the northern Port of Moji near Omuta, a small town thirty-five air miles from Nagasaki, we were

---

76    Unfortunately, nineteen more deaths would follow due to the hellish conditions in the Mitsui company coal mine, where the men toiled as slave laborers until the war's end, and to the terrible conditions of Camp #17, widely considered to have been the most brutal in Japan. Mansell.com

quarantined briefly. Afterward, we were transported from Omuta by train to camp. The guards kept the shades down on the train car windows so that we could not see landmarks and get our bearings.

When we went into Fukuoka Camp 17 (forty miles from city of Fukuoka), we were all strip-searched. They turned everything inside out and upside down, searching through our meager stash, before taking us into camp.

Six weeks later they pulled a surprise inspection. After shaking down the camp, they came up with three tow sacks full of razors, knives, and more. I've never figured out how guys got them in there.

\* \* \* \* \* \* \*

*Additional Information:* "Camp 17 was opened August 7, 1943 and gradually populated 1,857 prisoners of war of mixed nationalities, mostly Australian, American, British, and Dutch.

The site was originally the laborers' quarters built by The Mitsui Coal Mining Company owned by Baron Mitsui, a 1919 Dartmouth graduate. Mitsui's company leased the POWs from the Imperial Army, who received payment from the Company of about 20 yen per day.[77]

The camp's twelve-foot wooden fence, fixed with heavy-gauge electric wire, enclosed the 600 by 3000 feet area of land. There were thirty-three barracks, all one-story buildings 120 by 16 feet with ten rooms to a barrack. British, Dutch, Americans, etcetera, were in separate barracks and areas. They were constructed of wood with tight tar paper ceilings and windows with panes and corrugated iron roofs.

Officers quartered three or four per room, measuring 9 by 10 feet, with four to six enlisted men accommodated in rooms of the same size. Each room had one fifteen-watt light bulb.

There was no heat, which was a problem in the winter as men lived on starvation diets. There were two meals served daily, one cup of rice and one cup of radish soup."[78]

---

77    That's what they claimed, but we never saw the pay! I assume the Japanese Army collected all our bonuses.

78    Wikipedia: "Fukuoka 17."

**Aerial View of Fukuoka Camp 17 in Omuta Japan.**
*Photograph courtesy of Mansell.com*

**Map of Japan - Kyushu, Fukuoka. Notice the outline of Japan vaguely
resembles a dragon breathing fire. Japan is located off the coasts of
South and North Korea, China, and Russia.** *Map from Mansell.com/
lindavdahl/omuta17/fukuoka17_description.html*

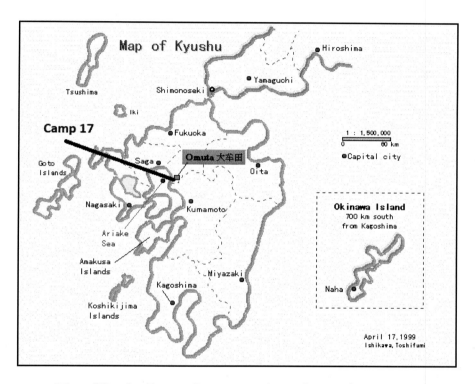

**Map of Kyushu, Japan - Camp 17 was located near Omuta, Japan.**
*Courtesy of Linda V. Dahl, Mansell.com,*
http://www.mansell.com/lindavdahl/omuta17/fukuoka17_description.html

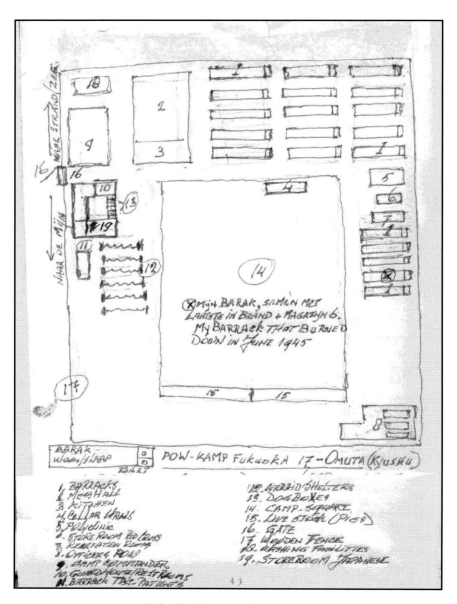

**Fukuoka Camp 17 layout map.**
*Mansall.com/lindavdahl/Omuta17/photo_gallery/*

\* \* \* \* \* \* \*

The rough clapboard barracks accommodated fifty men. We were assigned rooms and I looked for mine in the third barrack, room number nine. The room had Japanese style sliding doors with windows made of rice paper, and the walls were nearly as thin, made of wood with no insulation. The lights in the hallway stayed on day and night. Mats served as our plush, comfy beds. The facility was actually clean.

After checking it out, I came back down the hall, toward the front, when I saw a guy sitting in room number one.

I overheard him say, "It's amazing. Another guy and I were the first to come out of Zero Ward, but I lost track of him. Here I am, having lived through Zero, and I've been brought here with this group that's supposed to be the healthiest five hundred of all the prisoners. I wonder what happened to that other guy."

I let him finish talking and, when he paused to take a breath, I stepped up and said, "What's your name?"

"Carl Price," he replied.

"I'm Drolan Chandler. I'm the other guy who came out of Zero ward with you." Now, we had both made the first five hundred coming over and survived the death ship. I guess we were just lucky all around!

\* \* \* \* \* \* \*

A day consisted of pretty much the same routine from the time we got up: we had roll call inspection, ate breakfast - usually one cup of rice, packed a lunch (rice with salted radishes and several strips of soy-soaked seaweed, if we were fortunate), walked more than a mile to the mines from the prison camp, pulled a day's work—ten, but often as much as thirteen hours in the mines, or until quota could be reached. After working in the mines, we came up top and took a bath, walked back to camp, went through roll call procedure again, then went to our barracks and passed out from exhaustion on the floor mattress.

The lunch we packed was a variety of either a cup of rice or a ball of rice (which averaged seven hundred calories/day) for working in the mines.[79] As far as something to drink, we had our own canteens that most of us had hung onto when we were captured. The only water we had in the mines was what we carried down in the canteen. If you didn't have a canteen, you just didn't get any water.

Each man had a bed, which consisted of tissue paper and cotton batting covered with a cotton pad 5'8" long and 2'6" wide, and a cotton blanket and a comforter made of tissue paper, scrap rags and scrap cotton.[80]

When it got frost-bite cold, Bob Harp and I would sleep together on one of our mattresses and blanket, and covered up with the other guy's blanket and mattress on top. Body heat helped keep us from freezing to death. Anybody that didn't have a buddy to sleep next to just shook, bones rattling and teeth chattering, until he got warm.

It snowed in the winter. In fact, there was a snow-capped mountain in view from the camp all year round. We were also near the ocean, and the wind could get awfully frisky.

No heat was provided in the barracks. The Japanese were afraid of anything that might set off a fire in the tinderbox buildings. A small clay pot was issued for each room, along with a few pieces of charcoal. We were happy until we figured out it took so much stuff wrapped under and around it to protect the room from catching on fire that all it did was produce smoke. Smoke didn't provide warmth. Disgusted, we chucked the miserable little pots outside and suffered for two years from the lack of any heat in the barracks. So much for a warm and toasty "home sweet home" barracks!

Generally, it was warm in the mines, even in the coldest part of winter. We were glad to get down there in the winter, so we could thaw out and warm up. In the summer we were glad to get down there to cool off. Generally, a cave stays at a constant 55 to 57 degrees and it stayed that temperature in the mines, except in the main lateral, where the wind would

---

79     Later, barley was used with the rice, which filled it out and gave us a bigger amount, and we thought we were eating grapes nearly; but they were cutting the rice and blowing us up with barley. Soybeans, so called pigeon weed (small grains half white, half red) which have Vitamin B, were also used or potatoes (spoonful only). Occasionally, a treat of pickled vegetables or seaweed was granted but, again, no more than a spoonful. All prisoners lost weight at an average of 60 pounds per man. *Mansell.com*

80     *Mansell.com*

nearly cut a person in half while walking down the tunnel. However, there were certain sections of the mine that were tremendously hot to walk through or work in. We would get wet with sweat just walking by the coal wall, not even exerting effort, in those areas.

It's a miracle our guys didn't contract pneumonia more than they did, because some of the places where we worked were so hot the sweat would be sloshing in our shoes, then we would enter the main tunnel and our teeth chattered, as we came out of the mines, to a temperature of 15 to 20 degrees. We'd go to the bathhouse and jump in the tub of hot water to warm up. There were buckets of cold water around the room to use to wash off, but it was best to get in the hot tub water.

As we returned to topside from the mines, the difference in the air pressure coming up from 500 feet below to ground level in a matter of minutes caused men to black out. The Jap workers told us to fill our canteens and drink as much water, as warm as we could tolerate it, as quick as we could gulp it down, to prevent blackouts from happening. The first thing we did when we came out of the chute was to head for the hot and cold spigots. We'd put some cold water in the canteen then, test it until we got it as hot as we could drink it, and turn it up. If a guy didn't do that, he was just liable to be standing there, knees hitting together a couple of times and down he'd sink when they missed each other.

Bath time consisted of a Japanese custom, family soaking tub, *furo oke* or *yubune* (*yu* is hot; and *bune* is tub) as big as the room, four to five feet high, almost full of water, about as hot as we could stand, heated by boilers at the mines. Everybody jumped in the tub, as quickly as they could, after coming out of the mines. It was stagnated water with no circulation to it. They gave us very little soap, but the hot water would help take the coal dust off, or at least the top layers.

We had one old boy, nearly 6'3", who wouldn't take a bath. We got tired of smelling him and gave him a GI bath—with a stiff brush we had used for cleaning—and soap. He glowed a healthy red color when we let him up. He got the message.

They didn't issue clean clothes at bath time. If we had a clean set, we put them on and threw our dirty ones across our back for the return hike to camp, to be scrubbed by hand later. Most times we didn't have an extra set of clothes. Some of the time I did, sometimes I didn't. At least I had a pair of tennis shoes to wear, which was better than some had, which was nothing.

Year-round attire consisted of short-legged pants, short-sleeved shirts and an overcoat, which we wore all the time in the winter to keep us warm. We had leggings but didn't wear them all the time. Later, I used them to hide contraband when I wanted to smuggle something in and out of the mines and camp.

We kept our hair short, not only to prevent lice, but because the Japs threatened to pull your hair out with pliers; they proved they meant it by demonstrating on several of the boys. We had a pair of hand clippers in the barracks that we used to cut each other's hair. I wasn't about to let them pull my hair out!

We had a dentist in the camp, but nobody gave him their business unless they were dying with pain. He used pliers to get the job done.

**Fukuoka Camp 17 - 75-man bath tubs.**
*Photo from Omuta Coal Industry & Science Museum*

* * * * * * *

We had ten-hour shifts, but with continual roll-calls and endless counting procedures, it tended to be twelve to thirteen-hour days. We had a ten-day week before shift change, then we were supposed to have a day off, but it only worked out to once-a-month rest days. We laid around as much as we could to recoup.

One of the days off, the Japanese had us dress up in our heavy old suits and walk three miles to see the cherry trees in blossom. The Japs prayed to old Buddha. They felt they were doing us a favor.

In the morning they had us bow to the rising sun because, according to their beliefs, it was the strongest element they knew. They believed that the Emperor was a descendant of the rising sun goddess. That's where they got the red sun for their flag.

Before going into the mines, we were required to stop at a building located at the mines, where a statue of Buddha was displayed in a box on the wall. We were to bow and pray to him for safety in the mines and, coming back out, to bow and thank him for taking care of us. Unless they cheated in their prayer devotion to look around to see if we were complying with orders, they didn't realize that we just stood there and told old Buddha off under our breath.

**Sitting Buddha statue**

**Example of Shrine of Buddha platform at the coal mines where prisoners were forced to pay homage before and after every shift.**
*Courtesy of Kroger, Sept. 15, 1945, at Mansell.com*

**Imperial Japanese war flag with red sun and rays**[81]

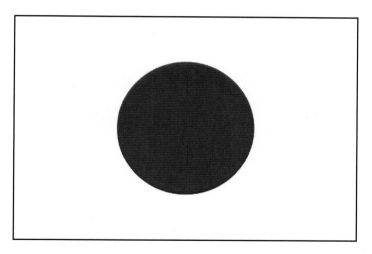

**National flag of Japan with red sun.**[82]

---

81          **Imperial Japanese war flag,** with red disc and rays, used by military in WWII. It is considered to be offensive in East Asia, referred to as "war crime" flag, used to invade neighboring countries especially if used during fleet reviews involving East Asisa, South Korea. Maritine used 16 rays; Army used 8 rays. *Wikipedia.org*

82          **National flag of Japan,** white banner with crimson-red disc, officially called Hinomaru – "circle of the sun" which is the country's sobriquet: Land of the Rising Sun. Emperor is said to be the direct descendant and divine appointment from sun goddess Amaterasu in Shinto religion. Wikipedia.org

**Tubs at Bathhouse.** *Photo courtesy of Linda V Dahl, Mansell.com.*[83]

---

83      Bathing facilities were in a separate building equipped with two tanks, approximately 30' x 10' x 4' deep, with hot, steam-heated water. A preliminary bath was required before entering the tubs. Men had to watch each other to see that no one passed out, because of the heat and their weakened condition. The men filled their canteens with the hot water to put in the bed with them. Also, the mining-compound had two large tanks to wash the coal dust off. "Fukuoka POW Camp 17," Mansell.com/ pow_resources/camp-pics/fukuoka

**Camp View** – *from www.mansell.com*

**Camp 17 Barracks.** *From Mansell.com*

**Barrack inside walkway / hallway.** *Ibid.*

**Inside typical barrack room of 8-10 men; sliding doors, windows made of paper. (Fuk#2, Sept 14, 1948)** *from Mansell.com/pow_resource/ camppics/*

**Laundry.** *From Mansell.com[84]*

CAMP 17 - OMUTA, JAPAN--OVER 1700 POWS INTERNED HERE

**Camp 17 Omuta Japan, 1700 POWs interned here.** *(see benjo/latrine midway of buildings and entrance to air raid shelter in lower left area). Mansell.com*

---

84   Every two barracks had an outside wash rack, 16 cold water faucets and 16 wood tubs with drain boards. POWs washed their clothes by scrubbing with brushes on the drain board and rinsing them in the tubs. There was a constant shortage of soap.

**Camp *Benjo* – latrines**[85] [86] *Mansell.com/pow_resources/camplists/fukuoka/ Fuku_17/Fuk-17_Photos-s.pdf*

---

85          "Japanese women came into camp with 'honey carts' to carry bucket loads of offal out from latrines to be used by farmers in gardens for fertilizer. They carried two buckets, one on each end of the end 'yohoo' poles, to dump in the cart. They carried such heavy loads that many were hump-backed from years of work. A Japanese man often followed to tap them and keep them moving. They also carried coal in that way." - Bob Harp

86          Latrines were located in each of the barracks, and at the end thereof, were three stools covered with a wood seat and one urinal. A concrete tank was underneath each stool. The prisoners made wood covers for each of the stools, thereby reducing the fly nuisance. The offal in the tanks were removed by Japanese laborers each week. By Mansell.

**Fukuoka Camp 17 Roster: See Drolan Chandler, second name from top. From February 16, 1946.** *From Mansell.com*

# CHAPTER 22

## The Coal Mines

**Camp View.** *Mansell.com/pow_resources/camplists/fukuoka/Fuku_17/ FUK-17_Photos-s.pdf*

UPON arriving at Camp 17, each man was assigned a number from 1 to 500. My lucky number was 258. Bob Harp's was 158. They were put on our caps and on blocks, called a *'ban'*, which were to be hung up anywhere a POW was at the moment, whether at the bathhouse, mines, barracks, *banjo* (bathroom), mess hall, etcetera. This helped the Japanese keep up with everyone.

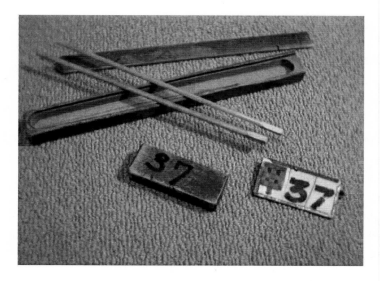

**Example of a "Ban" Block & Chopsticks.**
*HIR-06-OmineCamp-D E Groen photo. Mansell.com*

Three shifts per day, 100 men per shift, comprised the mining crews for the coal mines and zinc smelters. The Americans worked the coal mines; Australian and British prisoners worked the smelters. We labored 12 hours per day, with a 30-minute lunch break.

Bob and I were assigned to the coal mines. The first group was designated to blast the coal out of the mines. The second group was to prepare the supporting *eumacks* (stone or timber support pillars - also referred to as curb wells).[87] The third group shoveled coal. They counted down the line, rotating the duties.

Each day numbers were drawn within the groups to determine which Jap would be the work leader. Some were good to work for, but some were

---

87        The terms *eumacks* /pillar (curb wells) and *narrubes/*timber is the phonetic spelling of the words Drolan used when describing his work in the mines. I was unable to locate the words in a Japanese dictionary. They may have been colloquial terms. The 'well curbs' or pillars were made with stone or *hari/*timbers crisscrossed in a square design filled with stones or slag, which supports the narrubes or beams of the mine.

cruel. Each day, we crossed our fingers while the numbers were drawn in hopes of a favorable work leader.[88]

I was in the alternating construction group, called "preparation group," although duties changed from time to time depending on what needed to be done.

Bob was in preparation, too, but we weren't often in the same work group. We were to build new eumacks to brace the roof where the coal wall had been moved back, or blasted out, approximately eight feet during the day. The coal had been dug out and shoveled into coal cars, which were in turn pushed out and loaded onto the conveyor belts and sent to topside.

Most American prisoners practiced sabotage whenever the opportunity arose. While building the eumacks, we were supposed to fill them up with rocks, dirt, and/or sand, but when we could catch a Jap not looking, we filled them with coal. They weren't very amiable if they caught us; we were reported and a beating ensued.

The preparation crew also put up *narrubes* (*hari*/timbers) for *biimu* (beams). The eumacks were erected eight to ten feet apart, extending over each side where it had been blasted. The narrubes, four to six feet long, were wedged against the roof by driving smaller ones, about the size of your arm, in between to tighten it against the roof so there wasn't any slack. If the ceiling started settling down, that would hold it. If there was too much space between the biimu and the top, the momentum would build and it would just keep coming down from the force. It was important to drive the wedges tight underneath it to hold it against the ceiling.

It required four or five men to work a eumack. We usually built three reinforcing eumacks in the coal shaft, called lateral, during a shift.

The group drilled holes in the roof to get rock with which to build the eumacks. Another group bored the coal wall using a drill bigger than a jack hammer so the next shift could shovel coal. I usually helped build the eumacks.

---

88      "Very few of the Japanese guards spoke English and internees were forced to learn Japanese in order to understand commands they were given. Failure to comply with instructions would merit a beating. *Tenko* was the name given to the daily roll-call and prisoners had to call out their prisoner number in Japanese." Warren Kozak, *Curtis LeMay: Strategist and Tactician*, Washington, D.C.: Regenery Publishing, 2014. by. From "Japanese POW Camps During WWII," *History on the Net website.*

Typically, my job was to bore into a coal wall or overhead with a jack-hammer. Looking up, dust showered down into my face. About all you could make out was my eyes and mouth.

I guess that's one reason I have so much trouble with my lungs from breathing in that coal dust coming down in my face. In fact, I didn't shovel much coal. I built those eumacks, but I dynamited, bored rock and coal walls, and busted up rock for the pillars. I guess I qualified for that job because of my size. It took a pretty big man to hold a jackhammer, and I was bigger than a lot of them, especially the Japs.

Any work our captors demanded previously was child's play compared to the strenuous task of mining. All work was done by hand. Working conditions were hazardous; safety for prisoners was low on the priority list. There were no protective glasses, or masks, or safety equipment. Japs didn't worry about safety in the mines. Prisoners were expendable.

You lived—if you could—one day at a time.

**Omine-Machi Prison Camp – Japanese in coal mine** (*2010.06.68*), *Ben Steele. Image courtesy Montana Museum of Art and Culture (All paintings are oil on panel).*

\* \* \* \* \* \* \*

# COAL MINE WORK SCHEDULE

## *(As supplied to Linda Dahl, Mansell.com by POWs)*

"There were elaborate discussions on the work schedule presented to the camp and what the schedule actually turned out to be. The work schedule presented for the first shift was as follows:

6:00 AM – Leave camp to go to mine.

7:00 AM – On the job at the mine

12:00 PM – Lunch time

5:00 PM – Leave mine for camp.

Every other Sunday a day of rest

### *A typical time table for the day shift was as follows:*

4:00 AM – Wake-up call by a guard pounding on the catwalk with a rifle butt. Most of the time it was near 3:30 AM. About an hour to get ready to leave.

4:45 – Escorted by a guard to the main gate, where we were to be counted and recounted, before leaving.[89] Wait twenty to thirty minutes for the escort guards to get ready. A hard slap, kick or a chopping blow to the kidney for not being in a straight enough line, according to the guard.

5:00 AM – Thirty to forty-five minute-walk to the mine depending on the mood of the escort guards. Their mood was always bad.

6:00 AM – Ten minutes to an hour wait for the overseers to arrive. There was usually a meeting of all overseers before entering the mine. The coal and rock miners were assigned first.

6:30 AM – The remaining overseers would present their work orders to the shift superintendent for the remaining POWs to be called for a detail. Maintenance workers and general flunkies were last to be assigned. Usually it was between 7:30 and 8:00 before getting assigned to a detail.

---

89    "The men were forced to count off in Japanese and beaten if they did not. Many told me they were beaten early on as they tried to learn the more complicated number "vocal" system of counting that the Japanese have. One man tells of refusing to count off in Japanese for Lt. Little (see Chapter 40 Post War – Tribunal Verdicts for War Crimes) at the chow line, and Lt. Little took his food rations away for it!" *Linda V. Dahl, Mansell.com*

These details were to do repair work in the mine and odd jobs in and around the buildings at ground level.

7:00 AM – Visit shrine, then sign out tools needed for the day's work.

7:30 AM – Into the mine. The job site could be anywhere in the mine. Sometimes walk down, sometimes ride down, then walk up to job.

8:00 AM – Assemble air drills, check ceiling supports, continue the assembly of the conveyor, finish cleanup left by previous shift. Get timber for ceiling support after a blast.

10:15 AM – Fifteen to twenty-minute rest.

1:00 PM – Lunch hour. Move into a side tunnel to get out of the way, eat, then a short rest. Lunch time was thirty minutes to two hours depending on the job and the time required and the mood of the overseer. Coal workers seldom had more than thirty minutes.

3:15 PM – A short rest. Fifteen to twenty minutes.

5:00 PM – Stop work, collect tools, start for topside. Time varied from 4:30 to 6:00 PM, depending on the importance of the job and the difficulty in doing the job. The job was always important. The cable train made trips every twenty minutes.

4 to 6:00 PM – The Japanese and Koreans had priority on seats on the cable train, depending on the arrogance of the overseer.

5:30 PM – Tools turned in, a visit to the hot tub, IF you got to top side early enough. Check with the guard for permission to enter the bath house. Everyone washed and rinsed off before climbing into the tub to relax in the hot water twenty to thirty minutes. A concrete tub three-foot deep, about thirty foot across, steam heated. A guard would tell those in the tub when it was time to go.

6:30 PM – Go to assembly room and wait. Some of the men are still in the mine. Workers in coal section. Cleanup and timber supports must be in place before leaving work area. All work delays and causes are discussed with the shift superintendent. Comment: "They should have done better in a shorter time." The last men up usually did not get to use the hot tub. Sometimes the guards would wait for the last group to use the hot tub long enough to cleanup. This depended on the mood of the guards.

7:00 PM – Leave the mine for return to camp. This time varied with time the last man got out of the mine. Once the march started, the guards were always in a hurry to get back to camp. In the evenings the march was brisk.

7:30 PM – All stop inside the main gate. Everyone lay their possessions on the ground at their feet. Everyone stepped forward several steps for the guards to have easy access to search the belongings. Not moving at the instant that the command was given, it was a hard slap, kick or hit with a rifle butt. The rifle butt was their favorite. The searches ranged from no search to an hour of searching especially if it was raining or extremely cold. Months later it was a look in the lunch boxes. This type of search some of the men liked. They did not have to be magicians when they brought something into camp from the mine to make the camp lifestyle a little more comfortable.

8:00 PM – Marched to the parade ground for dismissal. It was to the dispensary for sick call or to the barracks to put things in the sleeping area, get the mess kit, head to the mess hall for the evening meal. After the meal, those who were not too tired joined a bull session. Those who needed to wash clothing that could not wait until a Sunday, headed for the wash racks. Some did not bother to get their meal; they were tired enough to lay down without changing their clothes and to heck with everything else.

The work schedule as presented was not followed. A work day was fifteen to sixteen hours a day most of the time. The work schedule was the same for all shifts, only the hours were different. The cable train was for the workers to ride in and out of the mine, making five trips for each shift. There was no problem getting down into the mine, it was coming out that was the problem. Everyone wanted to get out at the same time when there were not enough seats for everyone. Being tired, it took almost an hour to walk from the bottom, all up a steep hill, to top side. The guards were upset when we had to walk out."

*(end – Coal Mine Work Schedule)*

# CHAPTER 23

## Mining Episodes

**Camp 17 mines – cave-in where roof collapsed.** *Courtesy of Mansell.com*

BOB Harp was fortunate on one particular occasion, when his preparation group was working in an area approximately five hundred feet under the bay behind the camp. Someone noticed the pump, which worked steadily to keep the water pumped out, had shut off. Water was coming in and filling the lateral. Bob's crew came close to getting pinned on the other side of the pump and drowning, but the alarm was sounded in time and they were rescued.

\* \* \* \* \* \* \*

One day, as I worked in the back of a lateral, a stream of sand cascaded down on my back. I looked up in time to see a crack stretching across the roof like a streak of lightning. It got bigger with every second I watched. I made a mad dash through the lateral.

As I raced by, shouting, "Cave-in!" everyone frantically joined the race for safety, except one Japanese work leader who restrained his group from leaving. They were working close to the motor pulley that hauls out the coal. He was more concerned about losing it than the men.

The roof thundered down at the back. By the time we all got out, it was crashing in toward the front. The men near the motor pulley were trapped, but luckily the ceiling held up long enough and no one was crushed.

When the dust settled, we rushed back in to rescue the stranded men. The unstable ceiling began to collapse again. We swarmed out as quickly as our legs would carry us, leaving the Jap who had refused to release his workers abandoned in that section.

When the cave-in settled that time, we went back to dig through the rubble for him. He was really screaming for help by then. As soon as we got him out, the crumbling ceiling began closing up the lateral. We barely saved his Tojo hide and ours.

Jap guards hurried down from topside to see why the men were coming out in such a panic. The engineers also came down to check it out. It was closed up so tight you couldn't have stuck your hand back in the area where we had been working.

After every cave-in, regardless of the risk, crews were sent back in to dig out the electric motors. Japs considered them more valuable than humans. The antiquated conveyor belts couldn't be replaced, and parts for the motors were scarce. The motors were no longer being manufactured, thus each one had to be retrieved at all cost.

We figured everything we put out of commission would cause less coal to be produced for the steam ships supporting their war efforts.

Conveyor belts ran over a *sao* (pole) instead of metal rollers of the modern-day standard. A *sao* was placed at strategic points wider than the belt, for support, and nailed to two posts on either side. Americans tried to gain access to nails and hammers when they got the chance. Prisoners would drive a nail up from the bottom side of those poles, tapped it up until it just barely came through the end of the *sao*, on the underside of the belt. Naturally, that would start wearing on the belt.

Usually, more than one guy was in on it. After it ran a little while, someone else would come by and tap the nail up a little bit more. Soon, the belt would rip apart. The Japs would go crazy. The penalty for sabotage was facing the firing squad, if you got caught. So, our men had to be pretty slick about it. Fortunately, none of my crew ever got caught.

Occasionally, a big nail was dropped accidentally on purpose down through a hole in the top of an electrical motor. Sparks flew and everything came to a halt. Of course, the culprit was nowhere around by the time Jap leaders assembled to investigate.

Japanese civilians were the *hanchou* (foremen) and "overmen" or work leaders and did not carry weapons other than tools. They, along with the other Japanese workers, were hired hands from the community. But the guards, on topside, had weapons because they were military personnel. If we were reported for transgressing during the day, we met swift retribution when we came out. There were no courts to appeal your case. The Japs were final, unmerciful judge and jury.

The leaders had a quota to meet every day, except when we were going in after buried equipment from a cave-in. A quota couldn't be set because they didn't know how far we would have to go or how long it would take to bring it out. Otherwise, unmet quotas resulted in beatings and other ingenuous methods of torture as means to motivate us to submit.

One old Jap, dubbed "Zombie," was usually assigned to work with us when we went in after those motors. I don't know whether they sent him because he was old and more expendable or because he was so experienced at it. I knew my loss wouldn't cause any grief either. I worked with him numerous times in such rescue attempts. We worked in places where the coal wall had to be mined to get a single motor out.

Some of those places were extremely hot and we wore only a G-string, instead of the olive drab uniforms they issued when we first came into camp. I worked in one of the sweltering areas and sweated so profusely that when I started out, at the end of the day, I had to drag myself along on the cable because I was in such a weakened condition.

Zombie and I were working in a place one night when it caved in at the front, blocking our escape. We had to get out of there quick because it was so hot. I didn't see an open blaze anywhere, but the heat blistered our skin as we pushed through. We could have been mining into hell for all I could imagine.

Zombie knew the mines like the back of his hand. He moved back a short way and knocked a hole in the wall, and we came out through another section that was blocked off. It always amazed me that he knew where escape routes were that nobody else would have known. There were a couple of times we'd have been in deep trouble and unable to get out, if it hadn't been for Zombie.

He knew the mines so well that he didn't bother to draw tools at the tool house. If a guy needed a shovel, he would scratch around in the dirt a few minutes and hand him one. If someone else needed a pick, he'd dig around the wall down the line somewhere and hand the guy a pick. He had them hidden out everywhere and didn't bother to take one back to the tool house, either. He'd bury them like bones to be dug up when needed. Pretty smart, because it saved hauling heavy tools any more than necessary.

I was always glad to be with him. We never had any trouble and got along fine together. When old Zombie gave out, he didn't work or push us as hard as others. He led the way in and we led the way out.

\* \* \* \* \* \* \*

Bob Harp came back to the barracks with food, like a piece of fish or potato, from time to time that Zombie slipped to him in the mines. He hid it in his mess kit and brought it in to divide with me. Zombie was good to me, but he especially liked Bob; there's no telling how many times he smuggled something to eat to him. That suited me fine because we both benefitted from his kindness.

\* \* \* \* \* \* \*

We labored in one place where the air was so stale that if a person stopped moving, he'd fall asleep. During the time I worked in that location, we came out of the lateral for a blast. I eased down a little further than some of the others, selected a remote cleft in the wall, and flopped down for a quick shuteye. I snoozed like a baby, unaware that the rest of the men had gone back to work.

Termite, our Jap leader of the day, missed me and came looking for me. He had a maddening habit of sticking his finger in your side and gouging you, trying to rush you. That annoying gesture made me furious. After he jabbed me in that manner a few times, I told him not to ever do it again.

So, Termite came out to wake me. Fuming, he tried to hurry me back to work in the lateral. He stuck his thumb in my side, purposely provoking me, *"Isogu!"* (hurry).[90] That's all it took for me to lose my cool. I automatically swung around and hit him.

There was a conveyor belt running close by that hauled coal out. I ran behind the small space between the belt and the coal car and knocked him across the belt. After I hit him, it occurred to me I might as well do a good job considering the expected consequences, so I hopped on the belt coming down by him. I reached down, grabbed him, and slammed him down. Then pulling him up again, across the belt, I stepped off and held him up so I could throw a square punch at his ugly face. I drew my arm back for the deadly blow, but a hand clamped tightly around my wrist, halting me in mid-swing. I spun my head around to see who had intercepted. A high-ranking Jap who spoke English stood behind me.

"Don't hit him," he ordered.

"I might as well. I've already hit him. I'm in for it anyway so I might as well finish him off," I said.

"Yes, I saw it all, but it was his fault. If you won't bother him, I'll go to the topside and tell the guards not to punish you when you come out," he promised.

"OK," I agreed. "I'll back off if you'll do that." I let him go and stepped back.

---

90      *Isogu* means "hurry up; rush; get a move on". WordHippo

Old Termite was infuriated by the turn of events. He returned to the lateral while the big-shot Jap went on his way.

When I came to the front part of the lateral, he greeted me with a hatchet, determined to reap revenge by cutting me apart. Desperate, I snatched up a nasty-looking jagged rock and drew back. "Put the hatchet down," I roared.

We commenced a brief shouting match while I inched toward him and began to poke him with the rock. Finally, he dropped his arm down that held the lethal hatchet. In an unguarded moment, I grabbed it from his hand. I worked the rest of the day with that hatchet in my hand. He took the hint and stayed well out of reach.

Subsequent to our little brawl, Termite always traded me to someone else if he drew my number for his work group. I guess he didn't appreciate a hard worker, like me.

After Termite and I had the run-in, I was assigned to a Jap we called "Dick." He was the greatest person in the world to work with. The men talked in front of him as if he were deaf, calling him all kinds of names, cussing him to his face. He just laughed and shrugged his shoulders. All the men thought he was really dumb, but I worked with him enough to suspect differently. I was pretty sure he wasn't deaf or dumb.

"Ya'll be careful!" I warned them. "Don't talk like that around him. He isn't a moron."

They brushed my concern off with a chuckle and said, "Dick's a dumb ass and can't help it."

After the war, we found out Dick was an American sympathizer who understood English. We were very fortunate he was on our side, because it was a common practice to plant spies among the Americans to watch and listen, then report any infractions of the rules to the officers.

\* \* \* \* \* \* \*

I operated a jackhammer, blasting rock out of the tunnel. My work group, at that time, consisted of Lewis A. Hazel from Illinois,[91] Dick, and

---

91     Lewis had moved to Savannah, Georgia, by the time we had our first 27th Bomb Reunion.

another Jap, dubbed "Green Eyes." The four of us worked close together, using dynamite.

Hazel and I became very adept in handling dynamite. Sometimes they had us bore a coal wall and we learned how to set a charge at precise amounts so as to blow down a whole load of coal or a small amount, whatever the leader specified.

One day the two Japs left us to bore the coal by ourselves. Just to be contrary, we decided we wouldn't knock down much coal. We goofed off awhile, then heard them coming. We knew they would catch onto the fact we were deliberately blasting less than our quota of coal. We shouted for them to stay back because we were setting off the charge, so they wouldn't come in.

When we quit blasting that day, we should have knocked down about hundred cars of coal; however, when the air cleared, we had only brought down about ten cars' worth.

Dick was hopping mad when he discovered our hoax and flew into a rage. We saw we were in big trouble when Green Eyes started going berserk with fury.

Dick, realizing that Green Eyes was becoming uncontrollable, backed off and began to laugh. He accused us of not being any good and not knowing what we were doing. He acted as if we were idiots. Green Eyes quieted down and also began ridiculing us. Instead of Dick being dumb, as the others had accused, it was our dumb asses he had saved.

Dick's actions that day confirmed to Lewis and me that he was an American sympathizer. We still couldn't convince the others. But we knew Dick could have cooked our goose for dinner, had he not been for us.

**Dangerous, unsupported roof in a Camp 17 lateral.** *Mansell.com.*

**Inside Camp 17 coal mine.** *Kroger, Mansell.com*

**Loading chutes being operated by prisoners. American POWs had to fill 5-8 of the chutes per shift.** *Mansell.com*

**Mine workers drilling holes to set explosives.** *Mansell.com*

人車ゲージ（2段式エレベータ）で地底へ
（常磐炭礦西部礦業所・いわき市渡辺町
泉田）
　斜坑による入坑時間を短縮するため、竪坑
人道が開削された。緊張が高まっていくなか、
今日の作業を思いやる。昭和40年（1965）に開
削された。

**Japanese mine elevator or lift cages.** *From Mansell.com*

The following photographs were graciously supplied by the Omuta Coal Industry and Science Museum. The museum photographs display illustrated phases of mining operations.

**Replica of Conveyor Belt.**
*Illustrated replica display. From Omuta Coal Industry and Science Museum*

**'Curb well' full of stones (or filled with coal when POWs could slip them by Japanese work leader).** *"Coal Mine Terms," Yoshiya Sakai, Director, Omuta Coal Industry and Science Museum.*

**Lift cages on various levels of mine,**
*illustrated display in Omuta Coal Industry and Science Museum.*

# CHAPTER 24

## MUMPS!

MUMPS! Who would believe that a grown man, in the middle of Japan, in the throes of winter, would contract a childhood illness like mumps! Well, this old country boy managed that feat, somehow.

Growing up, I had been around folks who had mumps, but I never contracted them. Then, Bang! I came down with mumps where nobody else around had them.

My jaws were swollen to double the normal size; it appeared that I didn't have a neck. I ached all over and worked for three days in that wretched shape. Finally, I couldn't take it anymore.

By the fourth day of misery, I went to the American doctor to get sick leave to keep from working in the mines. Doc said, "There are men in worse shape than you are. Get back to work. I have to put a certain number of men on the work list and you're one of them. You're in pretty good shape."

According to that doctor's diagnosis, cardiac arrest was about the only thing that excused anyone from work.[92]

"I'm going to see what the Japanese doctor has to say," I fumed and stomped out the door. The doctor scowled and told the other guys, "We've seen the last of him."

Entering the Japanese side of the compound was strictly forbidden and was punishable by getting shot. Of course, that wasn't anything new,

---

[92]    The medical section of the infirmary had ten rooms each with a capacity for 30 men. The isolation ward would accommodate 15 men. American officers, mostly Navy personnel, did daily medical and dental inspections, but had scarcely any medical supplies. April 1944, ten men were added to the hospital corps with two doctors and one dentist. After October, 1944, medical supplies were provided and an operating room installed. On the Japanese side of the compound, the doctors had medicines and supplies, but were not interested in the American needs. *Mansell.com*

because it seemed everything else was punishable in the same manner. In fact, at the moment, being shot seemed a welcome relief to the way I felt. I thought I'd take a shot at getting shot or not!

I crunched across the snow in my thin tennis shoes over to their compound, determined to see the Japanese doctor, and trudged into the hospital. The doctor started jabbering and flailing his arms around in the air.

"What's he saying?" I asked another Jap who was in the room.

"He said to get you out of here. You have the mumps!" He immediately took me off that shift.

Several days later, eight out of our crew of fifty were the only ones who were able to go into the mines to work. The rest of my group had mumps! I ended up wading back and forth through the snow to the kitchen for food and water to help feed them.

"Oh, I had the mumps so long ago I had forgotten about it. I'm not worried," boasted William (Raynard) Byars, a tall guy from a wheat farm in Fairdale, North Dakota. He came down with a case of them that took him three weeks to get over. He almost died.

All five guys in my room, and most of the barracks, contracted the mumps, too. Bob Harp got them in a most inconvenient spot; they fell on him!

In fact, before it was all over, just about everyone in the whole camp passed them around.

They sure couldn't say I never gave them anything!

**Inside typical hospital room. Fukuoka 1-B hospital.** *Mansell.com*

15105 Army doctors who cared for POW's interned with them at Omuta prison camp #17, Kyushu Japan. L. to R., Lt. Harold F. Proff, Capt. Thoams H. Hewlett and Lt. Theodore Bronk. 45/09/15

**Army doctors who cared for POWs interned with them: Lt. Harold P Prof, Capt. Thomas H. Hewlett, Lt.** *(see Hewlett report of medical cases at Mansell),* **Theodore Bronk.** *Photographer: Kroger, Sept. 15, 1945, Mansell.com*

# CHAPTER 25

## Thief!

ONE day I went to the mess hall to collect my food before going to work, but the guys dishing out food balked.

"You've already got your rations," they snapped.

Not being a Christian at that time, I didn't use the best language to inform them, "I have not gotten my food."

"You have, because there is a nail in the holes, one for lunch and one supper. You don't get any more," said the servers.

Food was drawn by the number on your cap. A board listed each prisoner's number, with three holes punched out to the side, one for each meal. As you proceeded through the line to collect the skimpy meal and pick up the meager ration to carry into the mines, they'd drop a nail in the hole for each meal. When you got off your shift the next morning and came to receive your breakfast, they'd drop a nail in the third slot.

Obviously, some lousy thief had stolen my meals, which meant I'd get nothing to eat before going into the mines and have nothing but hunger pangs for supper while working.

By the time I came out of the mines the next morning, I was tired and cranky as a bear, hungry for food, as well as to find my thief. My stomach was hugging my backbone, and I was in no mood to be denied my rations. But again, I was informed that my meal had already been drawn.

I tried arguing, pleading, demanding, and even threatening, but my tirade fell on deaf ears. They wouldn't budge so much as a spoonful because there was a nail in my third slot.

Recently, I had been issued a new cap because the numbers on my old cap had gotten worn and dim. The Japanese guard was supposed to destroy the old one, but I knew that someone had gotten hold of it, by hook or crook. He had drawn my food while I was asleep and again while I was in the mines. Then he put on his own cap to go draw his food, spacing it out so they wouldn't catch onto his scam.

Anybody could stand to eat two rations at a time because we were all starving.

Hiding so that I could observe the culprit, but he couldn't see me, I waited until cap number 258 came masquerading through the mess line on the head of a guy named Domony McClintock who lived three doors down from my room in our barracks. We were in the same work group and had labored together in the mines from time to time, but he had been on sick leave for a few days.

You realize what hunger is when it makes you want to grab someone and choke the life out of them. I exploded after him, but he saw me coming and bolted for the door. I would have taken him in the mess hall, but fighting was forbidden. We had an air raid shelter, and the Americans slipped down there occasionally to settle disputes so as not to stir up the Japs.

He tore out across the compound on the run, headed for his room at the barracks with me fast on his heels.

I stopped outside his door because that area was strictly off limits to fights. "Come on out McClintock and get what's coming to you," I ordered.

"I'm not coming out," he retorted.

"Either you're coming out or I'm coming in after you," I bellowed.

"I'm not coming out," he repeated.

The fellow was about my size, around 120 pounds, except taller. Charging into his room, I grabbed him by the nape of his neck and hauled him roughly out to the platform that ran the length of the building in front of the rooms. We stumbled into the enclosed walkway, where siding was nailed to exposed two-by-four studs in the aisle.

With the force of hunger, anger, and betrayal, my first blow was devastating. That punch knocked him from his feet, ramming his head into a support post with a sickening thud, nearly splitting his skull open. He sprawled out, blood gushing everywhere. It's a wonder it didn't killed him.

Others heard the commotion and came rushing into the hall. To my dismay, I didn't get to hit him again. He was promptly hauled away to the hospital to stitch up the gash.

The Japs said I caused his problem; therefore, I had to do his job quota, in addition to mine, before I could come out of the mines. Jap leaders in each work group kept up with what you were doing and kept score. The soldiers didn't go down in the mines with us. Usually, five Americans worked for one Jap who served as leader. On some jobs, and blasting was one of them, one American was assigned to a Jap; the American actually did the work with the Jap overseeing it.

Besides having lost my meals, I didn't get the satisfaction of really whipping him because I couldn't get in but one lick. And then I had to do his work while he laid up in the hospital.

But he didn't dare to draw my food ever again!

I've never run into him since Camp 17.

# CHAPTER 26

## A Close Call

FLANGE Face, one of our Jap guards, had a ferocious temper coupled with the unfriendly habit of grabbing a hammer to knock his offender in the head. The unlucky prisoner who happened to be within arm's length caught the brunt of his rage. He knocked quite a few heads under the guise of letting off steam.

Of course, when his good humor returned, he apologized for flying off the handle, but the victim still had a bump on his head. He claimed he went crazy and couldn't control himself.

One day Flange Face and I were assigned to work together down on the eighth level. The rest of the crew was working up on the fourth level.

As Flange Face and I were descending in the cable car to our designated area, I turned the hatchet I was carrying to work toward him and said, "When you get mad and go crazy, you use that hammer. When I get mad and go crazy, I use this hatchet."

I kept that hatchet in view so he understood that this American boy might go nuts, too.

When the cable car rattled to a stop, he informed me that we had to place a metal trough into operation to pull coal out. We worked together, moving the trough over and setting it into place.

"Go work the controls," he ordered when everything was ready to try it out. He walked back to the end of the conveyor belt to see if it was in working order.

"No, you go push the buttons and I'll go watch the back," I said. I knew that was usually when he knocked folks in the head. As soon as the troughs started folding up, he ran over and whopped the guy upside the head with his hammer; it wasn't a love tap, either.

The proper signal for trouble was to wave the lamp on your cap in a circle above your head to alert the man on the switch to shut it off. He never took time to wave his *"anzen-toh"* (cap lamp or light);[93] instead, you got the message when he charged in your direction waving his hammer for a signal.

Flange Face objected to my plan and sent me up front to the controls. I pushed the button, and predictably, something went wrong. The troughs started folding up like an accordion.

As expected, I saw his light coming, so I stopped the motor. Here he came, stomping down the side of the trough, yelling as he stormed toward me. I could see that hammer pass through the light from the lamp on his hat as he swung it over his head. I knew I was a prime candidate for a potential head-knocking!

Having learned from high school football that a good offense is better than defense, I met him halfway with full intention of winning the game.

The trough was about waist high where we met. He ran up one side and I ran up the other. Waving his trusty old hammer in a cursing fit, he shouted, "You crazy!"

"If you come on this side of the trough, you're going to see how crazy I am," I countered.

He hurtled over the trough. I cut down at him with my hatchet. He dodged as I slashed at him, ripping a hole through the trough. He backed off and started to run. I jumped across and shot after him in hot pursuit.

Alternately walking or running, we moved up two laterals, with him in the lead and me closing in, recklessly waving my hatchet.

*"Matte, matte!"* (Wait!) he called back breathlessly. *"Hanashi o shi-mashou!"* (Let's talk!)

He stopped and I did, too. "Let's get back and fix that trough, then we'll be done," Flange Face pleaded with me.

We called a truce and retraced our steps.

---

93        *anzen-toh:* Cap lamp/light attached to cap or helmet, which used batteries. WWII mining terms from Omuta Coal Mine Museum, as translated by Taeko Sasasmoto.

"You get the switch this time," I ordered, shaking my weapon. He got on the controls and I went to the back to straighten out the trough. He watched me like a hawk, and, likewise, I kept a cautious eye on him, knowing each of us was as mean and crazy as the other.

For the remainder of the day, I was in charge. I performed my duties, working close to him. When an opportunity arose to loosen a *narrube* (*hari*/timber)[94] for an apparent accident to befall my adversary, I took the chance, allowing it to topple toward him.

Alert to my intentions without giving a hint of knowing my moves, Flange Face stepped aside each time; the *narrube* fell in the trough, missing him by a close shave. I could not catch him off guard.

Armed with the knowledge that my temper matched his, Flange Face made sure this wild hatchet man didn't work for him again. I have to admit that I didn't volunteer to work with that crazy hammerhead either.

\* \* \* \* \* \* \*

Big Stoop was a large guy compared to most Japs. He was good to me and often shared his dinner with me, cutting his rice portion by half.

But Big Stoop had a big flaw as far as I was concerned. He loved to work as though he believed he had to win the war single-handedly for Japan by digging coal to supply the ships. His devotion was admirable; however, he expected us to work with the same fervor.

The Americans weren't so gung-ho in the mines, knowing the end result. The majority of the coal was used to fire steam ships for the war. Conversely, our goal was to slow the pace or sabotage equipment every chance possible.

The Japanese knew our ulterior motive; however, they prevailed upon our natural instinct to stay alive by cooking little sourdough biscuits to reward a man when he worked extra hard. That was good incentive for starving POWs.

---

94        *Hari* / timber: It supported the mine roof horizontally. Both wooden and iron *hari* were used. Yoshiya Sakai, director of Omuta Coal Industry and Science Museum. Drolan used the word *narrarube*.

"I'm going to have to kill old Big Stoop because he is working us to death," I mouthed off to some of my buddies. "That's about the only way I can stop that fanatic."

"Naw, you ain't got guts enough to bother Big Stoop," they taunted me.

At that time, I was assigned to getting rocks to build eumack pillars. The usual procedure was to blast between the pillars, then blow the top. Sometimes it shattered into rocks, which were the proper size for building the pillars. More frequently, though, the boulders had to be busted down to the right size.

Some guys took the sledgehammer and nearly pounded themselves to death, trying to break up the boulders. I had learned to walk around and look at the rock, find the right niche, and hit a lick or two with a hammer to break it. My talent, which might have come from pre-war training, namely splitting logs for firewood, won me the job of busting up the boulders.

One day we blasted between two pillars and the rocks fell in a pile about six or eight feet high toward the front, leaving a hole big enough for a man to wedge through. I squeezed in there with my hammer and looked around.

I shoved the busted rock down through the opening to Big Stoop. He was so busy building a rock pillar he didn't have time to look up. I'd hand a rock down to him, and with great zeal, he practically ran to put it in place, hastening back for another.

I decided to cool his fever a bit. I found a sizable rock that barely fit through the opening. After gathering a pile of smaller rocks, I began pushing them quickly through the hole to him, working him back and forth like a shuttle.

Expecting more of the same, Big Stoop rushed back for another rock without looking up. I gave the big boulder a nudge and let it roll. Just before it hit him, I yelled, "Get out of the way!" seconds before it flattened him to the ground.

I knew it wouldn't be smart to stay up there, so I jumped down as if shocked and concerned about his injury.

*"Gomen-nasai!"* (I'm sorry!) I said while heaving the rock off of him. *"Gomen-nasai, gomen-nasai!"*

"Hush, hush," he groaned, "It's OK. It was only an accident."

As the guards carried him out, he adamantly confirmed, for my sake, that it was unintentional. All of the Americans were standing around chuckling because they suspected what had happened.

It temporarily crippled Big Stoop, taking him out of the mines for about two weeks. We sure missed Big Stoop. Come to think of it, some Japanese steam ships out in the Pacific Ocean probably missed Big Stoop, too.

\* \* \* \* \* \* \*

In the meantime, I guess I got what was coming to me for my cruel prank.

Some places in the mines had so much pressure that you could take a pick, stick it in the coal wall, and nearly pull down enough to fill a coal car. Several days prior, the engineers had been working in that area and we asked them our location.

"Approximately 500 feet down, a mile from land under the sea," they said. That was an uncomfortable thought, and it explained the tremendous pressure.

As a rule, five men had to fill thirty cars of coal, which was approximately sixty tons, around twelve tons per man. That particular vein had so much pressure you could stick the pick in the wall and coal gushed down.

The five of us filled our thirty cars and pushed them out, figuring we had earned a rest.

"More five, more five," the Japanese leader shouted, demanding another five tons above quota.

"We've done what we were supposed to do. I'm not going to fill anymore," I fumed to my group. I stubbornly ignored him and found a place to sit down and rest my weary bones.

"Come on and help us. We'll fill five more, then we can quit," urged the other Americans.

I remained seated while the others pushed another five cars in and started loading them. When our guys had filled those five and pushed them out, the leader said, "More, more."

"See," I sneered, rubbing it in, "as long as you keep filling them up, he'll keep pushing them in. We already have our quota."

The Jap leader stomped back and shouted, "More two, more two," while pushing in two more cars. The rest of the Americans sat down, joining the protest.

That happened on the weekend. The cable car was sent down a certain number of times and then it was shut down. Anyone left in the laterals had to walk out, which was an unbearably long way to the top after an exhausting day, not including the one-mile walk back to camp on topside.

Working alone, the Jap leader obstinately shoveled and filled the empty cars, making us wait for him to finish. He was mad as a hornet, and we weren't too happy at the thought of walking all the way to the top since we had missed the last car.

Finally, he dismissed us, and the other guys made a quick dash for the light tools. Crippled from a previous leg injury, I hobbled over to get a tool and found I had been left with a jackhammer, weighing 80 or 90 pounds. I cursed under my breath, because the others had left me the heaviest piece to carry, knowing I had a bum foot.

The ceiling was so low in some areas of the mines that a man had to crawl through, so I dragged the jackhammer behind, muttering and cursing and crawling. When I finally got to a place high enough to stand up, I put a pole about three or four feet long through the handle and propped it like a yoke across my shoulders.

As I plodded up through the lateral with the pole balanced on my shoulders, I had plenty of time to think. The more I thought, the madder I got. *Great buddies they are, taking off and leaving me to carry this heavy jackhammer,* I seethed to myself. *The guards won't let them out at the topside until I come up, so I'm going to sit down and let all of them sweat it out for a while.*

I plopped down to stew about my misfortune. Shortly, the Jap leader came back down to see what had happened to me. I saw the pinpoint of light on his cap bobbing up and down, advancing at a fast pace toward me.

The only light we had in the back of the laterals was the one on our heads. Electrical lights ran along the ceiling closer to topside. My resting area was pitch black except for my small helmet light.

He came charging up, panting, and none too happy he had to come looking for me. "Why you waiting? How come you here?" he shouted.

"My foot is hurting and I had to rest," I moaned.

"Let me see it," he said.

Like a fool, I stuck my foot out. Wham! He hit it with his walking stick. Pain shot through my body and I reacted instinctively. I whopped him over the head with the pole I had across my shoulders. He returned the blow with one across my head. We knocked each other's lights out and fought blindly in the dark. Both of us went for blood.

He broke away and fled, leaving me to limp awkwardly after him. He made it to the lighted lateral first. I couldn't catch him because of my sore, throbbing foot.

*Well,* I reasoned, *I'm not going to be in any hurry for sure now because he will turn me in when he reaches topside. I won't get a good breath of fresh air before the guards shoot me. I'll just take my own sweet time 'cause all I've got left is a little time.*

I discarded the jackhammer and started my slow death march. *I may not even get to see daylight again if they send a search party after me,* I thought.

Dreading the consequences, I prepared myself mentally for the firing squad reception awaiting me. I sweated it out, step by step, the last few yards. I could see my coworkers' lights. They were all mad because the shuttle left them stranded. The guards had refused to let them start the hike back to the camp until I showed up. The delay was cutting into their valued time off.

To exit out of the mines, we had to walk up a cattle chute with a gate at the end of it. The guards shut the gates between loads and were the only ones who could open them.

There I went, moping, bloody, and anticipating my fate. My adversary, the Jap leader, was waiting with them. He had cleaned up the blood on him and was standing at the front of the gate. I sweated out those last few steps up the chute. I figured he had informed the guards, who were waiting beside him, and knew my hour of reckoning was coming to a close.

As I stepped up to the gate, to my astonishment, the Jap leader said, "Number 258 worked extra hard today. Here are two biscuits."

You never knew how those foreigners were thinking. He was obviously scared I would get him back while we were alone in the laterals. He couldn't shoot me because he didn't have a gun down in the mines. Only the guards were allowed to have them at topside. Whenever the Japanese workers had a grievance against the prisoners, they reported it to the guards. We were not allowed to fight the Japanese workers. Of course, they were really like us. They were practically slaves, too. But, in addition to getting paid, they did have more motive than us. They earnestly believed they were helping win the war for Japan.

The rest of the group had hurried out the gate, leaving the two of us to walk the mile back to camp together. He kept some distance between us. We were late, which took away from the rest time that remained. My buddies were so furious at me; it had infringed on their precious few hours left to gather enough strength for the next shift. Can't say I blame them. I was pretty beat, too!

15038 Mine at Orio, Kyushu, Japan, where prisoners of war were made to work. How POW's were searched coming into mine entrance. 45/09/15

**Example of chutes where POWs were inspected as they were going into the mines and upon exiting them at the end of a shift.** *Photo courtesy of Linda Dahl, Mansell.com.*

**Example of loading coal cars** *(photo taken at another Japanese mine).*
*The Truth of Hashima, Photo by Airang. Courtesy of Mansell.com*

# CHAPTER 27

## PREMONITION

ONE day the Japanese leader sent me after a jackhammer that had been left in the back of a lateral.

I had never been in that lateral and was amazed to come to an area with a 25-foot coal wall. I had never seen or heard of one that high. Pressure on the roof of a four-foot wall sometimes caused it to burst; therefore, the 25-foot wall would be under considerably more pressure.

As I was walking along the side of the coal wall, a disturbing thought flashed through my mind. *If that coal wall decided to burst right now, it would bury me and no one would know where I am.*

Uneasy about that idea, I crossed to the other side away from it. No sooner had I moved than it exploded, spewing out coal with such force that it knocked me down and buried me. I had no protective clothing on my body because I was wearing a G-string like Indians wore, which was the usual attire in the hotter areas of the mines. I struggled out from under it, cut from head to toe, bruised and bleeding, but still breathing. I found the jackhammer and rushed out of there, thankful to be alive.

I don't know whether it was a premonition, a nudge from God, or what. Anyway, I made up my mind that I was never going anywhere in the mines by myself again.

I figured God helps those who help themselves, and from then on, I'd help him out a little by staying out of tight places.

* * * * * * *

We were busy building a rock pillar in the mines, and a Japanese worker was rolling large rocks down to us from an area of the wall that had been blasted. Unintentionally, he hit an American prisoner, and the guy's hand was smashed pretty badly. He shoved his hand down between his legs

231

and hopped around groaning. The Jap came down to see what happened and said, "Let me see it, let me see it."

The guy held out his hand. It was badly bruised, but not bleeding. If Japs didn't see blood, they didn't think you were hurt, so he said, *"Oh, it didn't hurt bad. Sukoshi"* (a little bit).

That made the prisoner real mad. Sometime later, the Jap worker bent down to place a rock and the injured man picked up a rock and let it fly. Blood splattered from where it busted the Jap worker's hand. The Jap crammed his hand down between his knees and danced a jig. The prisoner came running over and said, "Let me see it, let me see it."

The Jap held his hand out.

*"Aw, sukoshi, sukoshi,"* the American said.

The Jap grabbed up a pick and started beating him and would have killed him if we hadn't pulled him off of the old boy. The Jap knew he had been hit accidentally on purpose.

\* \* \* \* \* \* \*

Cave-ins were frequent in the mines.

One such disaster involved approximately one hundred and thirty-five to one hundred and seventy-five Japanese who worked on a coal wall in one of the laterals. We never could get the whole scoop on the exact number. Fortunately, no Americans were working in that area at the time of the disaster.

It was a freak accident. As the cable car was let down, it somehow struck a spark and set off the accumulated gas in the area. When it blew the lateral, the ceiling crashed down, trapping the men inside. The Japanese decided not to expend the effort to dig them out and merely sealed up each end of the lateral. It's eerie to think there might have been some workers alive for a while, waiting for rescue; however, it became their tomb.

It wasn't an encouraging thought to know they had buried their own in a cave-in and didn't bother with preferential treatment. We Americans knew not to expect any consideration if the same thing happened to us. That's why cave-ins were so frightening and why we really scrambled to help each other escape.

* * * * * *

Another curious accident occurred when one of our guys was walking along the coal wall and a rock the size of your fist popped out of the wall from the pressure. It hit him so hard he died instantly. He never even knew what hit him. It made me grateful for my own premonition.

* * * * * *

The main danger and fear of working in the mines was losing an arm or leg, or getting otherwise maimed. Several men lost limbs.

Four or five guys lost legs when they were smashed during cave-ins. It's a miracle that more limbs weren't severed from cave-ins.

The Good Lord was watching after us, that's all. Some guys were killed in the mines, but they were on different shifts from me, so I didn't know the details of what happened. Japs didn't post or inform us of the news events of the day, and we learned things only by chance or word of mouth. It was hard to keep track of everybody because we worked on different shifts in various areas of the mines.

# CHAPTER 28

## WELCOME NEWS

THERE were five hundred of us who went into Camp 17 together, but the number climbed to seventeen hundred later when they brought more prisoners into camp at intervals.

A lot of the ships were destroyed by our planes on the way over. One ship bringing American prisoners to Japan was sunk; only one of the American prisoners, named Ayers, survived. A guy out of my original outfit, named Ayers (Pvt. Billy Alvin Ayers, 19th Bomb), came into Camp 17. He was the old boy who loved whippoorwill peas so good and stuttered when he talked.

Sometime in 1944, another load of prisoners was brought into our camp. One of the guys looked me up with some good news. Jim Dyer, my childhood buddy and comrade in arms, had escaped and hooked up with Filipino guerrillas.

Later, when I got home, Jim told me his dramatic story of escape (see Chapter 39).

Good news of that sort was welcome and lifted our sagging spirits immensely.

# CHAPTER 29

## BLACK MARKET

BOB Harp and I got to dealing in the black market. Anything we could buy, sell, or exchange. It was a risky business with grievous consequences if caught: beatings, food ration cutoff, possibly facing a gun barrel.

Communications with the outside world were very skimpy, and you never knew just what to believe. There were some sympathizers among the Japanese. They helped us to obtain food and traded with us on the black market. That's how we were able to earn money.[95]

Prisoners were searched as we left camp to walk to the mines and again coming back in. We weren't allowed to have more than ten dollars on us.

Managing to smuggle something like a blanket out of camp was one dilemma, while slipping the money, or whatever was obtained in exchange—food, cigarettes, etcetera—back into camp became another. It took a lot of imagination and guts for anyone to attempt it.

Blankets, issued by the Japs, mysteriously went missing when we learned that we could sell them for 1,000 dollars. If we had not been liberated at the time we were, the following winter would have caught us without adequate cover, and we might have frozen to death because we sold all of them.

A package of Japanese cigarettes could be bought for forty cents. The Japanese mine workers who didn't smoke purchased their ration of tobacco; every two or three days they could get ten cigarettes to sell to the Americans. They brought them to work and weren't scrutinized as closely as we were. It was up to us to sneak them out of the mines and back into camp. We

---

95      Quoted from an article, "Prisoner of War Medal Awarded to Droland [misspelled in title] Chandler," in the *Lamar Democrat* newspaper interview with Drolan. Date of xeroxed clipping is unknown.

could swap one American cigarette for salt with the Koreans in the mine, when they were able to traffic it to us. I bought cigarettes every chance I got, then sold them for a dollar apiece at ten dollars a pack. That was a moneymaking deal! The only drawback was that the consequences might not be too profitable to my well-being.

**"Cigarettes" - POW attempting to barter cigarettes for another POW's food. Cartoon by Bashleben.** *Courtesy of BataanProject.com. By Permission of the Bashleben Family.*

We wore brown khaki canvas lace-up leggings similar to those worn by the First World War infantry. I finagled a pair and it became the perfect place to cache the loot. I just prayed mighty hard nobody checked me.

I got bold about bringing out cigarettes. I stuffed them down the leggings and laced them up. One day I got twelve packs of cigarettes from a Jap and laced them up in my leggings. It was scary to think about when a guy could be shot for having one cigarette. Smoking was dangerous in the mines due to possible explosions from gas fumes.

As I exited the mines up the chute, I saw that the Jap guard at the top was permitting only one man through at a time. He conducted a closer inspection than was usual of each one.

It was too late to turn around. I couldn't climb over the railing. I couldn't go back. There were three or four men ahead of me. One of them wore a pair of leggings, which the guard checked.

My heart galloped so hard it was pounding in my ears. It raced with nowhere to run. I felt it was going to burst out of my chest. I knew I was in a tight place. My boldness turned to mush, along with my knees.

All I could think about were those twelve packs of cigarettes hugging my leg. *Chandler, keep your wits together,* I chided myself. *This is one time when there's nothing you can do but bluff your way through.*

The man in front of me was waved past without being stopped. He wasn't wearing leggings.

As soon as they got ready for me, I went running up the ramp and reached down to untie my leggings. The guard impatiently motioned me on through without checking. I nearly passed out with relief and disbelief.

A hungry man will do a lot of crazy things to get enough money to buy extra rations!

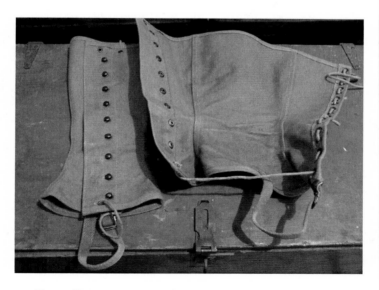

**Typical Vintage WWII Army Leggings (reproduction).**
*Photograph courtesy of Taylor D. Dewey, http://wwiimedic.com/*

\* \* \* \* \* \* \*

Bob and I accumulated a nice little nest egg from our racketeering. Together, we stashed back 10,000 dollars, over time. Some people in camp always had money from gambling, black market dealings, or whatever, and others knew who they were.

A guy came through the barracks peddling a can of salmon. How he got it, I don't know. It's not smart to ask too many questions about things like that. But it was up for grabs from the fist with the most money.

He sidled up to one of the guys who always seemed to have cash and said, "I have a can of salmon. I want 100 dollars for it."

The second guy said, "I will give you 75 dollars."

"No, I've got to have a hundred or no deal," the first guy repeated.

Well, I'll only give you seventy-five." The guy walked by me and winked. "Let him sweat awhile," he whispered, "he'll take the seventy-five."

I was standing there with 100 dollars in my pocket and a mighty empty, growling stomach. At that point, Bob and I had hoarded back nearly 1,000 dollars. I wasn't going to interfere with his trade right then, but I waited for him to finish his bargaining and make his best bid before leaving the room.

After he got out of earshot, I asked, "You still want 100 dollars for that can of salmon?"

"I sure do. And I won't take no 75 dollars either," he replied firmly.

"Well, ole Buddy, you've got a deal." I slipped the 100 dollars to him and grabbed the prized can of salmon. It was going to be a real delicacy to spice up the tasteless rice rations!

I went scouting for Bob Harp. "I've got a can of salmon. Came a little high, though," I teased.

"How much?" he asked.

"A hundred bucks," I grinned.

"What's money, anyway? Money ain't nothing but a means of exchange," he replied. I liked his attitude.

That rice was tasty with the can of salmon that night. We feasted like kings!

* * * * * * *

"Number 258, over here." My number was drawn and I was put in with a bunch of Japs I hadn't seen before. That didn't happen very often. I went to work with them in an unfamiliar, obscure section of the mines.

The two Japs to whom I was assigned started talking among themselves. By that time, I was adequately fluent in their language and could understand the gist of what they were saying. I couldn't talk it so fast, but as a Southern country boy, I haven't been accused of speaking English too fast, either.

I grasped enough to learn those guys were going to have a rest day in two or three days. They were planning a trip to the country to buy vegetables, which was forbidden and carried grave penalties, because food was so scarce and strictly rationed. They had decided to chance it to buy extra food for their families.

I spoke up. "Boys, when you go out there, what about getting me something to eat?"

Initially, it frightened them out of their gourds because they suspected I had been put down there to spy on them. It was a tough job convincing them I was just starving and honestly wanted something to eat. I didn't intend to get them in trouble any more than I wanted them to report me. It was chancy on both sides. It was very likely that they could have been sent down to spy on me, as well, to see if I had money or contraband.

I finally succeeded in gaining their confidence. They said, "OK, you bring us money and we will get you food."

When I got back to camp, I told Bob about the deal. I wanted 100 dollars out of our mutual pile of cash.

"No," he warned. "You stay away from them. You'll get killed. I ain't having nothing to do with it. You'll get shot for sure."

My belly won out over my brains. I got the 100 dollars and laced it securely inside my leggings. They searched us as we went out and I tried my bluff again of reaching for the leggings before they could order me to unlace them. They motioned for me to move on through. I went back to work and gave the money to the two Japs.

They had their rest day. Several days passed and I didn't run across them. Bob began ribbing me about donating that 100 dollars to those two Japs.

"You'll never see it again," he chuckled.

* * * * * * *

One day as I was getting ready to come up out of the mines, another company came down in the cable car. Two Japs began to frantically wave and shout. I didn't recognize them. I walked down to see who they were and why they had signaled me. It dawned on me they were the two Japs I had trusted with the 100 dollars.

They explained that they had changed shifts and had been looking for me ever since their rest day. They had hidden some food out for me.

"Well, great! Where is it?" My mouth was already watering at the prospect of something besides rice to sink my teeth into.

"It's under the lumber pile stacked by the guardhouse at the entrance to the mines." That was the only place they knew to hide it.

The car shuddered to a stop and they got off. I didn't have time to find out what they bought, but I didn't care as long as it was edible. I worked my shift, anxious to get it over; my stomach rumbled for hours in anticipation.

Murphy's Law: When you look forward to something, minutes yawn and stretch themselves into hours, taking their lazy time. It was a long day. I was in the first group leaving for the bathhouse on topside.

When I got to the lumber pile, I looked to the left and right, but didn't see anyone watching. I furtively reached under the boards and nervously rummaged around. My fingers found a sack and dragged it out.

I saw Bob. "My two Jap buddies came through with the deal. We've got some food."

"Yeah? What is it?" He looked incredulous.

"A bushel of onions." I grinned.

"You're crazy. How are you gonna get a bushel of onions into camp? I ain't having nothin' to do with it. You are on your own. You're gonna get shot yet!"

They called us out, counted us off, and lined us up for the march back to camp. I reached down, got the bag of onions and slung it across my shoulder, grasping the strap in my fingers. One of the guards walked right beside me the whole mile back to camp. It was as if he was blind to that bag!

When we arrived at the guardhouse entering camp, they said, "Turn your pockets inside-out."

Several rows up from me, ten or twelve Japs were at attention facing our lines. I took the strap of the bag in my left hand and turned my right pocket inside out. The guard inspecting the line looked at it, said, "OK."

I reached up like I was scratching my neck, shifted the bag to my right hand, reached down with my left hand and turned the pocket inside out. "OK," he nodded and moved on to the next guy.

Sweat trickled down my back. I rolled the bag around my shoulder, eased it down my side, and dropped it on the ground in front of me, never veering my eyes, always looking straight ahead.

He started down the next row to check our back pockets and, simultaneously, checking the front pockets of the guys in the row behind us. After searching my back pockets, he proceeded to the next guy. I bent down slightly, wishing my arm could automatically stretch a couple of inches, grasped the strap, and eased the bag up and around my shoulder to the back with the strap across my shoulder again.

Satisfied he had made a thorough inspection, he walked back to the front and barked, "Dismissed!"

It was an exercise in composure. I wanted to break and run, but I strolled along to the corner of a building, looked back over my shoulder, then struck out running.

Once inside the barracks, I grabbed the mattress and stuffed the onions inside, tied the ends, and put it back in place on the floor. I think I breathed for the first time in an hour or so and wiped the perspiration off my brow.

In the meantime, I couldn't resist pulling out one of those onions. I was sitting there chomping on it like an apple, tears pouring down my face, when Bob came in.

"What are you eating?" he asked.

I ignored him.

"Give me a bite," he pled.

"Don't aim to do it," I said.

"What you got there?" he persisted.

"Onion, you fool. I told you coming to camp I had 'em. You said, "'Boy I ain't having nothing to do with it.'"

"Give me an onion," he demanded.

"Ain't gonna do it. Like little Red Hen, you didn't help me out so you needn't expect any!"

# CHAPTER 30

## RED CROSS

14034 Yokohama Camp - Christmas dinner. Some food from red Cross packages - A portion of this food was collected by Japanese staff after photo session.

**Red Cross visits Yokohama POW camp.**
*Staged publicity photo by Japanese. Courtesy of Mansell.com*

**CHRISTMAS Day, 1944:** A group of four or five Red Cross workers from Switzerland were permitted into camp to survey treatment and feeding of prisoners. We weren't allowed any contact with them, but the Japanese put on an elaborate show for their benefit.

The representatives attempted to talk to some of the men, but the Japs kept too close a guard and cautiously intervened. Regardless, we couldn't complain because it was the most humane treatment we had received since being captured.

The representatives brought boxes which contained medicines, surgical instruments and other supplies, such as YMCA items. The Japanese refused to make these available to the Americans after their departure, but they did give out the British overcoats.

Their appearance, at least, helped us for a day because we got a tiny bit of wine, along with a pretty good feeding, including some pig to flavor our rice meal, which amounted to about a two days' ration of food. It was purely for photograph purposes; a publicity ploy, staged to impress the Red Cross workers with our menu.

We got worried we were going to stretch our stomachs and get spoiled!

* * * * * * *

Sometime in 1945 I got a card from home. A single line read, "Jim is home and well." There was no Jim in my family. I understood the code and knew it meant that my friend Jim Dyer had made it home alive!

I got four or five postcards, since letters weren't allowed, in the two years of my visit in Japan. The Japs obligingly sent a couple of them to our families toward the end of the war. I still have three. A line or two said that we were doing well and received pay for work—what a laugh![96] We were merely allowed to sign our names. It was the first word that our families knew we were still alive. My family had not known my fate for three years.

News circulated through the mines that packages had been brought in for the prisoners. This is the only time I can recall that they actually distributed our packages to us.

The Imperial Japanese Army deemed it best to store Red Cross supplies and packages in a building on the compound and often referred to it as a work incentive, promising to award extra food or supplies if we increased our quotas. Somehow, they never got around to fulfilling the promises, and the building only served as a sore spot to remind us there

---

96      Men were supposed to receive five cigarettes per day, but they actually received one pack of ten cigarettes for one ten-days' shift. Cigarettes were used to barter for other items. Two cigarettes were worth a half bowl of rice. They received toothpowder and a small soap with the cigarettes, when available. *Mansell.com*

was food within reach; spitefully, they used what they needed or wanted from it. It also served as a provocative temptation. Several guys through those lean years couldn't withstand the lure of food to soothe their gnawing hunger and attempted to steal food from it, only to be caught and tortured for their efforts.[97]

Mother and Daddy were barely scraping a living for the family and I didn't expect a package. I knew they cared, but really didn't think they would know how to get it to me. Bob was sure that his folks had sent one and was full of expectation.

The Japanese called us out to the parade ground where they had set up six tables full of stacked, brown packages. An officer opened each package and took out anything he wanted, then called out the name of the man it belonged to and gave him the remaining contents.

Bob and I were standing near a table watching the proceedings. He was straining to see if his name was on any of the packages nearby.

"I'm not expecting anything," I whispered, "but if I get one, those slant eyes won't have the chance to put their hands on it. They aren't going to open my package and raffle through it."

The Jap opened another one and took most of it out for himself. My temper flared.

"I'm telling you, Bob," I huffed, "if one of those blockheads tries to put their syrupy paws on a package of mine, I won't stand for it."

"Hush, they'll hear you," he whispered.

"I mean it. They ain't opening it as long as I'm breathing," I bristled.

"I guess they will or they'll shoot you," he whispered.

"Well, they're in for target practice," I concluded.

More packages were piled on the table.

Low and behold! One of the labels read *Drolan Chandler* as plain as my hand that reached out to snatch it.

---

97    The Greek "Pavalakos" was starved to death in the guardhouse for buying two bowls from a Jap and selling one to another prisoner. It took them 38 days to accomplish this execution by slowly reducing ration; benefit of trial was denied. *The Hewlett Report*, by Thomas H. Hewlett, M.D.

Bob grabbed my arm in a panic and cautioned, "Don't touch that, Chandler. Just take what they leave or you'll get shot!"

"They'll just have to shoot then," I said, easing my package off the stack and down by my side. I waited a minute or so, then turned and casually strolled away from the excited crowd of guys.

I slipped to my room and ripped it open. Mom and Dad had paid for a pre-assembled Red Cross Care Package and I was delighted to find a small bag with square blocks of Domino sugar lumps—sugar was a premium treat. There was a bar of soap, a toothbrush and toothpaste, powdered coffee, cigarettes, a pack of playing cards, and a shaving kit.

At yearly POW reunions, a buddy of mine still laughs about the tie that was in my package. I don't remember it, but he says I put it on and kept saying, "Wonder what they'll think about this down in the mines?"

Just think, if I hadn't grabbed the package, one of those Tojos might have stolen my one and only Sunday go-to-meeting tie! It was just the accessory I needed to go with my G-string!

**Outside of Red Cross box.** *Photo courtesy of Mansell.com*

**Example of Prepackaged 11-pound Red Cross box contents.**
*Mansell.com /pow_resources/red_cross_bullletins/ ANRC_bulletins.html*

**The Freedom statement was removed from Old Gold package before Japanese would distribute in POW camps in Philippines during WWII.** *Photograph courtesy of WWIISoldier.com.*

* * * * * * *

I guess Schick ought to pay me big bucks for a commercial at this point. Right after the first day or two that I was captured, I found a Schick razor and a full pack of twenty blades in the road. I managed to hold onto it all the way through the war. Bob and I, and no telling how many other guys, had used that same razor and pack of blades for three and one-half years! We'd take a piece of glass and strap them, then use them again. I kept them until the barracks were burned during a bombing raid toward the end of the war.

During those years, I kept my hair cut with the razor and used the skin for the pattern. Lice would eat you up if you didn't keep it shaved, so I kept my head slick as a cue ball in camp.

We wore a cap all the time with our number on it for identification and to draw our food. The cap had a battery light attached to be able to see it in the mines.

* * * * * * *

Considering the lack of toothbrushes during imprisonment, I only had one or two cavities when they examined me at the end of the war. I was cutting my wisdom teeth when I went overseas and they were still under the skin when I came out. Those things hurt me all that time, but I didn't dare mention it to one of the Japanese dentists. I'd rather have had a crane operator pull my teeth. When I got back home, I had those four teeth jerked out.

After I'd been home a year or so, I went to Sulligent to get a cavity filled, but the dentist said it was too far gone and wanted to pull it. While extracting it, he broke it off, and probed it out. I squirmed under his hands and he said, "You must be allergic to pain."

When I got out of his chair, I never went back to him. I hated to tell the fellow I'd had better treatment under the hands of the Japanese!

* * * * * * *

The lights never went out in the barracks' hallways so that the Japanese guards could keep an eye on all our activities.

Sometimes I had periods of restlessness, probably due to nerves, and was plagued with insomnia for a week at a time, in spite of the exhausting hours in the mines. I couldn't go to sleep because I felt as though I was smothering. By the end of a sleepless week, still working the eighteen-hour shifts, I finally crashed and slept through the night.

One night after a long shift, I couldn't fall asleep, so I pulled out my new pack of playing cards to enjoy a game of Solitaire. The guard discovered what I was doing and took the deck away from me because they disapproved of gambling and thought all card games were gambling. I told him that he wasn't allowed to do that. He said I could get them back at the guardhouse in the morning.

When daylight came, I was at the guardhouse ready to collect my cards. The night guard had gone off of his shift. I caused such a ruckus that they stirred him from his sleep and made him come to the guardhouse.

"Did you tell this prisoner he could have his cards back today?" they asked him. He couldn't deny it with me staring him down. They returned my pack to me and I stalked back to the barracks. The guys couldn't believe I made a big issue over such a small thing.

When you lose your freedom, your rights, and everything else is taken from you, you have to maintain your dignity in some manner. It seems right to stick to your guns, even if it is being possessive over a silly pack of cards.

**Guardhouse.**
**This is where the dreaded beatings and torture took place, both inside and out front of the building.** *Photos courtesy of Mansell.com/pow_resources/ camplists/fukuoka/Fuku_17/*

**Japanese prison guards.** *Mansell.com*[98]

---

98        Several pseudo names were given by the POW's for the Japanese Guards: Sailor, One-armed Bandit, Pig, Smiley, Long Beach, Riverside (the Japanese Interpreter), Yotojisa also called Flangeface, Fox, Screamer, Devil, Wolf, Sikimato San – called Blinkey, Mouse, Big Stoop, Gold teeth, Turtle, Devil, Toko-San – called Billy Goat, Rat, Greyhound, Wingy, Pretty Boy and The Bull. Mansell.com

**Entertainment Show "The Great Zigfield" by POWs at Camp 17, August, 1944.** *Photo Credit: Lester (Tenney) Tennenberg at Mansell.com/ lindavdahl/omuta17/*

*Additional Information:* Lester Tennenberg said, "I was asked by Major Mamerow to be in charge of the little entertainment we could have, and "The GREAT ZIGFIELD" was the culmination of my effort... a musical comedy was the result. The Japanese allowed this show, and Baron Mitsui (Mitsue, Baron Mitsui, Coal Mining Company) came for the opening night." August or September 1944. *mansell.com/lindadahl/omuta17/photo_gallery/entertainment_show*[99]

\* \* \* \* \* \* \*

---

99 *Note:* The YMCA provided equipment for games i.e. football, volleyball and tennis, but prisoners were too tired to play. The YMCA also provided a library of about 300 volumes. The prisoners planted and maintained a vegetable garden in an attempt to supplement rations. They raised livestock, too, but the Japanese helped themselves to the livestock when they got the right size for eating. Entertainment was allowed, but rare. Mansell.com

Drolan did not mention attending any shows and may have been on a work shift in the mines. When I interviewed Bob Harp and asked him about recreation or exercise in sports, he dryly commented, "We got enough exercise in the mines."

# CHAPTER 31

## MASS PUNISHMENT

EXHAUSTED and hungry, my group came dragging out of the mines at the end of our shift around midnight. We walked back to camp and were ordered to stand at attention with the rest of camp. Normally, we were fed supper when we got back from the mines, but that particular night, no one was eating.

Mass punishment was nothing unusual and that appeared to be the case, although no explanation was offered. We were left to wonder what and who the alleged offense was against.

We stood at attention all night and into the following morning. Finally, we were told we would remain standing until the culprit confessed his crime. Someone had broken into the Red Cross building and stolen food. It didn't matter that we had been pulling our shift down in the mines.

By daylight, half of my fellow shift workers had passed out from exhaustion and hunger, littering the parade ground like swatted flies. We remained at attention until time to go back into the mines for the next shift without being fed or having any rest.

During the following shift, men were still falling out in the mines from having stood at attention the previous night and day, and from food deprivation.

I managed to stay on my feet. Others feebly crumpled to the floor for a while, and when they revived, they got up and worked as much as they were able.

Work had to go on and quotas had to be met, whether all hands were present or not. A guy from Savannah, Georgia, and I covered for three to four men's work each. Many of the stronger prisoners who could endure the grueling hours and backbreaking work had to cover for the weaker ones. Everyone suffered mass punishment by not being able to leave the mines until all quotas were filled.

Whether anyone confessed or not, I do not know. The Japanese ultimately relented and began our rations again. Otherwise, their mining operations might have ceased. It was in their best interest to feed us.

\* \* \* \* \* \* \* \*

Beatings and torture were a daily part of camp life.

Bob said he heard that a guy who had broken a rule—someone said he had the nerve to wear his US Army cap—and got such a bad beating with a rod that he died the next day. It happened in front of the guardhouse where most infractions were punished for all to see.

It didn't take much to set the guards off; they used fists, rods, clubs, or whatever they could get their hands on to beat up the offender. One man was tortured by making him kneel in front of the guardhouse all night during the winter. Both of the poor guy's legs had to amputated to the knees, but he lived through it.

We saw another POW punished by being forced to get on all fours while the Jap guards put a board across his back and made a sport of see-sawing back and forth. It ruined his back.

Although most punishment was administered in front of everyone for an example, rumors circulated that one guy was taken out back of the barracks and used for bayonet practice. We never could find out who the guy's identity, since the British, Dutch and Australians were in separate barracks. [100]

\* \* \* \* \* \* \*

Harold Feiner, a friend of mine, killed one of the Japanese in self-defense. He was brutally tortured, but they didn't execute him because it was

100    Among the long list of men who were tortured in this fashion, David Runge – lost both feet, William H. Knight - died, Walter R. Johnson – died. These men were listed among multitudes in the War Crimes evidence as prisoners who had tortured in sadistic ways, resulting in loss of limbs and lives. This often took place in the guardhouse or in front of it, for an example. Guards Matsukichi Muta and Sadamu Takeda, One-Armed Bandit, were among those hanged for such crimes. (See Chapter 40- Post War – Tribunal Verdicts for War Crimes). Info from Linda Dahl, Mansel.com.

near the end of the war and the Japanese knew they would have to account for the POWs.

We got away with more things toward the end of our imprisonment than at the beginning for that reason.

**Prisoner used for bayonet practice by Japanese soldier.**
*US National Archives – WWII Japanese Atrocities to POWs*

# CHAPTER 32

## FINE CUISINE

OCCASIONALLY, I was pulled from the mines to work in the kitchen because of my cooking experience at Cabanatuan. I'd gain a few pounds, only to sweat it off in the mines.

One of the times they pulled me out to work in the kitchen, a load of whale meat had been delivered. We were close to the ocean which sloshed on shore approximately two hundred yards from the fence at the mines. We could see ships come in loading coal within sight of our camp; we figured one of them must have brought it in with them.

I cut that meat all day, anywhere from 500 to 1,000 pounds of whale meat. Even before I went in service, back home, when we dressed out hogs and I cut up meat, I couldn't eat it the same day. So, by the time they served it, I just said, "No, thank you. I don't want any." And I didn't touch it.

It hadn't been under any kind of refrigeration and it gave most of the camp, several hundred men, ptomaine poisoning. Everybody was sick with it, doctors included. There was no medication to treat it. Talk about a stinking place! All that diarrhea and vomiting all over the place. I did what I could to help folks, but they mostly had to suffer through it themselves.

Bob Harp was one of the unlucky ones. He nearly died from the meat. It didn't matter to the Japanese; he had to go back to work the next shift.

Besides me, there might have been as many as ten others who didn't get it because they hadn't eaten any either. I was mighty glad that, for one time, I had been finicky about my eating habits. I haven't looked for whale meat on any menus since then.

\* \* \* \* \* \* \*

During the last three or four months of captivity, rations got slimmer than slim.

Another fellow and I were walking alongside the Jap kitchen going toward the door. He glanced into the window and spied some meat lying on the table.

"Oh, boy, we're going to have some sheep meat to eat," he observed.

I looked in, too, curious about such a change in menu. "Sheep, my eye. Where do you see any sheep?"

"Look in there," he said, pointing out the slab of raw flesh. "Ain't that sheep?"

I chuckled and said, "Nope, that's German shepherd dogs." I could see them stretched across the table, dressed for cooking.

"Can't be!" he gasped.

"Go up and look again," I argued.

He went back and peered inside. When he came back, he shook his head in disbelief. "You're right. Those are German shepherds and I don't aim to eat it."

"Fine," I said. "You stay right there in front of me in line and when you draw your portion, turn around and pour it into my mess kit."

"OK," he agreed, "but I can't stomach dog meat."

He drew his and I drew mine, then he turned around and poured it into my container. I poured the doggy stew over my rice and dug in.

The only way I can describe it is that it tasted like dog—a different flavor from anything you've ever eaten—sort of a slick taste. The Filipinos and Chinese, maybe the Japanese, dressed them, stuffed with rice, and considered it a great delicacy. But, if I hadn't been mighty hungry, it might not have gone down as well.

Just like the worms and roaches I had eaten. Stirred it all together with the rice and didn't look too closely or think about it. Survival was more important than satisfying taste buds.

The next meal, I followed that old boy through the line and scooped up his serving again. I hunted him down every time the line formed. About the third time, I held out my mess kit for his share he said, "It hasn't hurt you, so I'm eating it this time."

It sure does help to change your mind about being a picky eater when your stomach's growling like a dog!

**Camp 17 - Kitchen / Mess Hall - fed 1735 men. Rice pots under the window. Work table and water tank is in the center. American officers' private office is in the upper left of picture.** *Photo courtesy of Mansell.com/lindavdahl/omuta17/fukuoka17_description.html* [101]

**Kettles used for cooking rice in the kitchen.**
*Photographer: Kroger, Dec. 16, 1945, Mansell.com*

---

101     The kitchen was ruled by Lieutenant Little (See: Chapter 40 - Post War – Tribunal Verdicts for War Crimes). Little ingeniously constructed scales to make sure the POWs did not get an extra grain of rice. Cooking was done by 15 prisoners of war, 7 of whom were professional cooks. The kitchen had 11 cauldrons, 2 electric cooking ovens for baking bread, 2 kitchen ranges, 4 store rooms and 1 ice box. Mansell.com

# CHAPTER 33

## Happy Birthday to Me

ONE day, down in the mines, one of the *eumacks* (pillars) was close to where we were building and hadn't been knocked down during the dynamiting. That area was about 12 to 15 feet high.

After the coal wall was blasted and moved over eight feet, I grunted and strained to lift a large rock and climbed up to place it on the eumack to build it up. I leaned back against a *narrube* (post) to get in a better position to handle it, shifting it around, and began to wedge it into place on top.

While attempting to level it, I lost my footing and fell back against a supporting narrube. I lost my grip on the rock and it rolled back against my chest, crushing me against the eumack. It took several guys to get it off of me, leaving me with permanent injuries.

The next day, I could barely move or breathe because of the broken and bruised ribs, but I was forced to go back to work. Our captors figured if you could draw a breath and had two functioning arms and legs, you were good to go. Sick leave wasn't granted for little injuries like that.

If I hadn't gone in, some other poor guy would have been required to do my work in addition to his. They didn't miss a man. He might not go to work, but they didn't miss him because somebody else had to take up the slack.

\* \* \* \* \* \* \*

Sometime later, after surviving another mine cave-in, I got it in my head that I didn't intend to work on my birthday and began saying the same.

Around the tenth of June, while being examined in the hospital, the doctor asked, "When is your birthday, Chandler?"

"June 15th."

"What are you going to do? Escape? You know we never quit work for any reason---Emperor's birthday, holidays, or anything else," he joked.

I shrugged my shoulders and said, "I don't know, but I don't aim to be working that day."

As the days ticked by, the guys really began to rib me about it. I stuck to my guns. I swore I'd take a beating before I'd budge.

June 13th arrived. Hazel Lewis and I were blasting in a short lateral that extended back about fifty feet. Three or four men had already gotten injured in that area from cave-ins.

"This damn hole has been hurting men ever since it was opened up. Let's just close it down so that it won't happen again," one of us suggested, and the other agreed.

Our two Japanese co-workers had slipped off somewhere to grab a few minutes of sleep. Between the American airplanes dropping bombs on Japan above ground and being alert inside the mines for dynamiting and cave-ins, undisturbed rest was virtually impossible.

Hazel and I got the fuses ready, but to our alarm, we heard them coming back before we had the chance to blast. We knew they could look at the number and arrangement of charges and discover what we were planning to do. In desperation, we shouted "Dynamite!" to keep them out so that they wouldn't foul up our scheme.

Supporting narrube posts throughout the lateral propped up biimu (beams) that crisscrossed the ceiling to brace the roof. While scrambling out after setting off the dynamite, I glimpsed a post that looked as if it might prevent the explosion from doing the extensive damage we had calculated on. I frantically tried to knock the post out just as the dynamite began to ignite. The dynamite closest to me exploded, blowing the end of that post back into me, knocking me down, and plunging a pick (work tool) into the calf of my left leg.

I frantically crawled and clawed my way toward the opening on my hands and knees, dragging the pick in my leg, before the rest of the charges surrounding me could go off.

Hazel barely escaped. The Japs were standing outside the lateral and saw my head appear at the opening when the rocks crashed down, covering me up. We had achieved the complete cave-in which we had planned, except I hadn't planned to be under it.

As soon as the rocks quit falling and the dust cleared, the crew started digging to find me.

After unburying me, they helped me stand up. The pressure had been so immense that I was numb all over.

One of the Americans and a Jap each put an arm around my shoulder to help carry, or rather drag, me out. The other Jap followed behind us, shouting, "*Chi, chi!*" (blood), pointing at the blood gushing down my leg, filling up and pouring out the top of the shoe. We paused to examine my leg and could see the ugly gash where the pick had stuck into my flesh.

Bit by bit, they struggled to work me to the top. It took several hours to get me out of the mines.

Fortunately, my blood coagulated and the bleeding became a trickle, assisted by a crude bandage tourniquet, before we reached topside.

The guys carried me to the American hospital where the wound was cleaned and bandaged. My back, badly injured for a second time, had taken a terrible beating, so I was confined to bed.

That was on the 13th of June, 1945. It was getting closer to my birthday, but they soon sent me back to the barracks. The next day some of the guys helped me hobble back over to the hospital because the leg looked angry with infection.

"Something's got to be done about that leg," the doctor announced as he examined it. "All I can do is go in and scrape the bone and, hopefully, that will stop the progression of infection. At least it hasn't set up gangrene or erysipelas,[102]" he surmised.

"I'll get some of the men to hold you down so I can scrape it," Doc suggested. No morphine or painkiller was available to dull the excruciating ordeal.

---

102    Erysipelas—an acute, sometimes recurrent disease caused by a bacterial infection. It is characterized by large, raised red patches on the skin, especially that of the face and legs, with fever and several general illnesses. *Oxford Dictionary.*

"Doc, if you just let me lay up there on the table by myself, I think I can hold still for you to scrape it."

"I don't believe you can, Chandler." He shook his head doubtfully.

"Let's try it. I don't need anybody to hold me down." I thought I was pretty tough, so I crawled onto the table face down and gripped the legs on each side. Sweat beaded across my face and I was soon drenched with perspiration as he opened the wound and scraped the lacerated skin. I ground my teeth so hard my jaws ached. It seemed every nerve in my body was screaming.

Surely those table legs carried the imprint of my hands! I know the experience is indelibly imprinted on my mind.

Come June 15th, I celebrated my birthday in the hospital. It was a real party, I can tell you, and I had taken my beating. Sometimes it takes a lot of work to get out of a little bit of work!

**Camp 17 Hospital Zone.**
*Photographer: Kroger, December, 1945, Mansell.com*

# CHAPTER 34

## FIRE!

AROUND the 16th or 17th of June, 1945, a rumor rumbled through the camp that the Americans were going to bomb us at midnight. The bombings had started up toward the end of 1944 and intensified in 1945. However, there had been false alarms before. Someone had a radio in camp—although it was kept strictly undercover—and leaked out information. I never could find out who had it.

I was still laid up in the hospital recovering from my leg and back injury. Doc came in around 4:00 p.m. and confirmed the rumor.

"When the air raid signal sounds, get to the air raid shelter, because this isn't going to be a dry run. It will be the real thing," he warned the other patient, then turned to me. "Chandler, you can't walk, so stay put."

A rope was wrapped around my leg and attached to a pulley at the ceiling, then pulled over to the corner out of my reach. My leg was swollen and tender from the surgery.

We were on Navy time and could keep up with the hour by the beat of the gong heard throughout camp. While they were clanging the time at midnight, the air raid signal blared. The rumor proved correct.

Everyone jumped up and dashed for the door. My fellow patient joined the stampede. "Give me your pillow so I can have two to lie on," I told him before he left. Pillows had become a forgotten luxury and somehow the hospital had acquired a few. If it was my time to go, I wanted to go in plush comfort!

He tossed it my way and I plumped it, raising my head to a level that enabled me to view the commotion that was taking place outside the window.

I spotted Zimmermann—Sgt. William E. Zimmermann, Jr.—a medic corpsman and friend of mine, scurrying down the hall.

"Come here and untie this rope," I pled, hoping to be liberated from the imposed restraints. I felt like a wild animal caught in a trap.

"I'm not going to do it. You can't walk anyway," he chided.

"Well, I just might get to where I can walk if you untie this rope," I raved.

"I'm not tied up and I have to stay here," he countered. "They won't let me go to the air raid shelter, so you can keep me company." What a friend!

Resigned to my imposed leash, I faced the window and saw that my comrades had narrowly cleared the building before the first bomb dropped. In the distance, incendiary bombs appeared as small matches being struck. Etching a trail like a string of white Christmas lights, one followed after another, getting brighter as they approached the compound.

One wave of planes swooped down low, dropping their lethal cargo, then took off into the horizon, followed by another wave in their wake. They kept striking those matches and advancing toward the hospital. I could see they were targeting the mines where we worked, burning them out.

I lay there and watched helplessly as they closed in. The explosions were deafening. I strained on the rope, testing to see if it could be broken. It wouldn't give.

Another plane dived down and three incendiary bombs lighted up inside the fence, approximately fifty feet from the hospital.

I held my breath and thought, *the next one's going to be in my lap!* I could hear another plane approach. My nerves were as taut as the rope strung up to the ceiling.

I let out my breath. It was a Japanese plane "plugging" over. Zimmermann and I both sighed and whooped from relief, "Thank the good Lord!" I was never so glad to hear a Japanese plane because that meant the Americans were gone or it wouldn't be up there.

It was a stroke of luck that they didn't hit our guys who were escaping from the grounds and no one was hurt in the mines that I know about. The building where we sat while waiting to go down for our shifts was burned out, along with a number of other buildings at the mines. It made charcoal out of everything as far as you could see.

* * * * * * *

Work didn't stop because of the bombings. The Japs wanted their last pound of flesh, so we were sent back into the mines.

The Japanese had installed a battery of anti-aircraft guns inside our camp at each corner, directly over the fence, and one in the center.

Around the 24th of July, we were all getting ready to go down to work. American planes came over swooping so low that you could read the insignia. The anti-aircraft guns opened up on them, knocking one of the planes out of the air. It went down smoking. We couldn't see where it crashed and didn't know whether the pilot parachuted to safety or went down with his plane. We knew they would come back soon.

My shift returned from work at midnight. It was hot, so I went to the barracks and pulled off my shoes and shirt, but left my pants on. Grabbing my mess kit, I headed across the parade grounds to the mess hall to get a bite to eat, which was about what the ration was down to—a bite!

As we crossed the parade grounds, we heard the drone of American planes advancing toward us. Everyone fell out in place; there was no time to race to the air raid shelter located near the parade grounds.

Another fellow and I hugged the dirt, close to the back of the parade grounds, about fifty yards away from the building where the Japs stored our Red Cross food. It was well-stocked because they had recently received a shipment. Of course, they used what they wanted and allowed the rest to accumulate.

When we heard the planes, the old boy next to me said, "I hope they burn that place to the ground." He wasn't the only one who resented food being so near and yet denied. It was a raw nerve for the Americans.

"You must be crazy," I said. "All we're going to have left to eat, when this thing comes down to the wire, is what's stored over there. If they burn it out, we're going to be mighty hungry by the time our boys get in here to rescue us." I weighed around 118 pounds, down from my original 185 to 190 pounds, although my weight had fluctuated during those years.

The first plane came along and peeled off. He hit the anti-aircraft gun on the right. The next one flew over, peeling off to the left and taking out that gun. The third one came over the center and lifted off a little too early, producing a different sound.

"Get a hold, good buddy. I think you're gonna get what you asked for!" I yelled.

The misplaced bomb struck the Red Cross building and flames shot into the air. Fire whipped from building to building within moments, setting them off like matchboxes.

We jumped up and took about three steps to where the first bomb crater was hewn out of the ground.

I charged back to the barracks, but couldn't get in due to the flames leaping out of the doors and windows. The intense heat was unbearable. What few belongings I had accumulated, my shoes, shirt, etcetera, were feeding the ravenous flames. Mostly I was frantic to get to a bunch of money Bob and I had squirreled away under our mattresses. We had removed some floor matting and created a private safe for our black-market dealings.

It was useless. Everything was going up in smoke, with the walls caving in. That's when they burned my sweet, happy home and all my worldly goods, including my hard-earned savings.

I turned and started back toward the mess hall, but saw that the hospital caught fire. While racing to the back door, I screamed for the others to come help. Those within hearing range, amid all the tumult, joined the frenzied efforts to get the patients out before the flimsy building collapsed. Just as we carried the last of the patients out the front door, the hospital crumbled behind us.

The whole area of the compound where I lived was burned out that night, in spite of our futile attempts to fight the fires with hoses from the water tanks.

Bob and I moved into the recently constructed barracks, built in anticipation of a new load of prisoners.

\* \* \* \* \* \* \*

The Japs put us right back into the mines. Those of us who had lost everything in the fire worked barefooted and barebacked.

Before the bombings, Duck Hunter, one of the Japanese mine foremen, had befriended me, slipping me salt, hidden in a little container the size of an aspirin box, from time to time. He spoke a good deal of English and we got along well. But after the air raids began, he seemed to turn on the prisoners, exhibiting a latent mean streak.

One day as I walked past Duck Hunter at the guardhouse with guards nearby, he ordered us to salute. I wasn't in my most amiable mood at the moment and walked on by, looking the other way.

He called me to come back. "How come you didn't salute?"

"I didn't see anything to salute." I replied curtly. He was a foreman, not a soldier.

That didn't suit him too well. He told me to go back and see if I could march correctly. We called it goose stepping---a straight-legged, stiff-kneed step used by the troops of some armies when passing in review. I retraced my steps, turned my head the other way, and shuffled past him again with my farm boy walk. He ordered the soldier to beat me with the butt of a rifle.

"Go back again!" he ordered, determined to draw some respect out of me if it meant drawing blood first. He wanted me to goose step like a regular soldier, with a sharp salute.

I backed up and bounced by, imitating my sloppiest plow-jockey stroll, for a third time. I didn't high step or salute. He evidently decided I was a lost cause and ignored the slight, allowing me to pass.

I guess my stubborn streak matched his mean streak after he rubbed me the wrong way. Thinking back, it was a real miracle—probably some of those prayers being offered up on my behalf back home—I didn't lose my head or my life before the Americans had time to liberate us.

\* \* \* \* \* \* \*

The last day we worked, I backed up at the loading trough with a pick and announced, "I'm not working any more. My feet are too sore." They were still cut and blistered from the fire and I had no shoes to wear.

"Yes, you'll work," one of the Japs demanded.

"If you want me to work, come and get me," I retorted smartly.

No one came in after me because I had that pick handy.

When we returned to topside that evening, one of the Japs, who was mad because I had refused to work, grasped a saw by the blade and walloped me over the back of my head with the handle.

There was nothing I could do but clench my teeth and take it, because a guard was standing nearby. But I tucked it away in my memory. Not being a Christian at the time, I wasn't concerned about vengeance belonging to the Lord.

"You've hit me and got away with it," I vowed, "but your day is coming." He probably figured I'd come after him first chance I got and he had it figured right!

\* \* \* \* \* \* \*

Approximately six months before the end of the war, Bob was in a cave-in that hurt his back and took him out of work for six weeks. He could barely walk before then from a rock that fell and broke his foot. With the combined injuries, he worked very little those last months.

"Bombing News" - Two POWs discussing the latest bombing news at Fukuoka Camp 17. Cartoon by J. P. Bashleben. *Courtesy of BataanProject.com; with permission of the Bashleben Family.*

**Camp 17 after Americans bombed. Hospital Zone.**
*Photos from Mansell.com/pow_resources/camppics/fukuoka*

**Camp 17 Hospital Zone.** *After the bombings.*

**View of building bombed out at Camp 17.**
*Photos from Mansell.com/pow_resources/camppics/fukuoka*

# CHAPTER 35

## Pay Back Time

**Nagasaki Atomic Bomb. August 9, 1945: The second atomic bomb dropped at Nagasaki, on the island of Kyushu, Japan.** *Wikipedia.org. Public Domain*

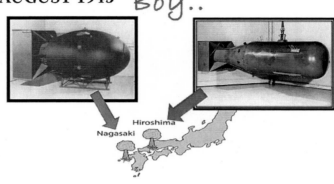

# Fat Man and Little
## AUGUST 1945 Boy..

**Fat Man & Little Boy.** *Photograph courtesy of Jeff Aydelette,*
*The County Compass, NC, August 8, 2016 article by Gordon Allison.*

Bob and I heard a loud boom and saw a great flash of light. A bizarre mushroom cloud arose to the sky as we were going into the mines. We had seen so much bombing, we didn't think much of it. It did seem to be a little brighter than usual. We speculated that the apparition had something to do with ending our ordeal. We didn't realize we had witnessed one of the most catastrophic events of the Second World War, the bombing of Nagasaki.[103]

When our group came out of the mines, the relief shift went in; however, before their shift was completed, the Japanese brought them back out and dismissed them. Something news-breaking had to have happened for

---

103 'Little Boy' weighed as much as a car and exploded with the force of 15,000 tons of TNT over Hiroshima on August 6, 1945, killing 80,000 people almost instantly." Article by Marco Margaritoff, "Inside the Creation and Detonation of 'Little Boy', the First Atomic Bomb Used in Warfare" published April 9, 2018, Updated July 27, 2020, at *https://allthatsinteresting.com/little-boy-bomb*

"The second atomic bomb (22-kiloton *Fat Man* kills 70,000—See Defeat of Japan 1945, was dropped from a B-29 flown by Major Charles W. Sweeney, at 11:02 a.m., Aug. 9, 1945. *http://history.acusd.edu/gen/WW2Timeline/Pacific08.html*

The Japanese estimated 44 percent of the city was destroyed." The History Place, p. 7 of 8, *http://www.historyplace.com/unitedstates/pacificwar.html*.

the Japanese to prematurely end a work shift. It had never happened before.

Work came to a halt for three days, but nobody dared ask questions for fear of provoking the Japanese. It was evident the war was over, because they didn't stop work for anything. But the Japanese refused to believe or accept the inevitable. Camp 17 mutely waited to see what would happen next and to receive official word.

On August 18th, Camp Commandant Asao Fukuhara called the prisoners to assemble on the parade ground. Standing atop a table for added height, he somberly announced, "The war is over. America has won."

A dazed, almost reverent, silence spoke for the depth of our emotions as he told us about the atomic bomb and Japan's surrender.

"We will maintain our guards here in camp in order to keep the civilians out, but they won't bother you. You will be free to go around the camp anywhere you please."

How did we react? Did we whoop and holler or throw a party? No. It's strange, but we merely wondered around in a daze or sat and looked at one another. After all that time, it seemed surreal. I suppose we were numb with shock. The full impact of regaining our freedom took time to register.

Several of the Japanese asked, "What are you going to do to us?" They had beaten, bashed, slapped, and kicked us around for years. They expected like treatment.

"We're going to leave you here and let you eat that damn rice, that's what!" I quipped. It was about seven years after I got home before I could even look at it, much less eat it.

Soon after the commandant made his speech, Japanese mine foremen began bringing gifts to throw over the tall wood fence surrounding the compound to those whom they had mistreated. They'd call out a number; word was passed to the fellow, who would go to the fence and say, "I'm number so-and-so." The Jap then tossed a *saki* (Japanese rice wine) peace offering over to him. Most of the gifts were for the original five hundred POWs who came into Camp 17. They had always maintained control of the camp, as far as the Americans were concerned.

One foreman came to the wall and shouted, "Number 258." I ambled over to the wall and caught a gallon of *saki* that sailed over the top. I carried it to my room to share with Bob.

Shortly, someone called Bob's number, and he came back with a bottle of *saki*. It was coming over the fence at regular intervals; a number of humbled, and frightened, guards were making penitence.

Whether it was the *saki* or the idea finally sank in that we were truly free men, someone suggested, "We don't need those Japs to guard us to protect us from civilians. I believe we can take care of ourselves."

Taking heart, or emboldened with inebriated courage, we trooped over to the guardhouse.

A bunch of the original five hundred told the Jap officers and guards, "Just leave your guns and get out."

The second day after we heard the good news, we woke up and the camp was unguarded. There were no Japanese in sight. Two guys in the room next to mine got all *sakied* up and boldly took off downtown. The Japanese had ordered their troops to assemble at a certain place to turn in their guns and ammunition since the war was declared over.

The two roommates walked down to the train depot at Omuta, boarded a car loaded with Japanese soldiers, marched them all off the train, and ordered them to stack their weapons on the platform. The Japs did as they were told and got back on the train. One of the guys stayed to guard the guns while the other sped back to camp.

"Boys, if anyone doesn't have a gun and wants one, there's plenty down at the train platform." Everyone was armed after that.

\* \* \* \* \* \* \*

Many of the Jap workers had refused to be paired with me in the mines because of my quick temper and tendency to swat them if things didn't go to suit me. When they drew my number for their work group, they traded me for someone else.

Termite, the first Jap I punched in the mines after I got to Japan, called my number at the fence and invited me to his house for a meal as soon as the war was over, trying to buddy up to me. He was the one who had the annoying habit of poking a guy in the side and yelling, *"Isogu!"* (hurry). The first time he punched me in the side, I punched him. Actually, outside of the time we had that fight, we didn't have any more problems, mainly because he wouldn't work with me. I wasn't overly fond of him either.

When he asked me over, I told him I didn't know, but then he called another guy's number and invited him, also. We talked it over and decided to go. For the last two months of captivity, we lived off rice and boiled sweet potato leaves stripped from the vines. We had starved so long that our stomachs weren't choosey about the company they kept.

We weren't afraid to go outside the compound, but Termite walked the short distance to camp and escorted us to his home to eat supper.

He and his wife didn't have children and lived in a barrack-type building crowded with other tenants. Each family was allotted a room or two. The housing project was similar to lumber camp housing, provided in close proximity to the mines for the civilian workers.

Termite's wife prepared a good meal, and it was pleasant to see the hospitality side of the Japanese for which they are so famous. Afterward, he walked us back to camp.

\* \* \* \* \* \* \*

We lost two or three men in camp after the war was over. One of the original five hundred who had shipped over, an Aztec Indian whom we called Chief, died of tuberculosis.

As was the common practice in Japan, the body was cremated by a local crematorium and placed in the Fukuoka Camp 17 Crematorium burial ground, which had an underground vault where urns containing the ashes were stored.

**Inside Crematorium at Moji Kyusha where POWs from camps were cremated.** *Photographer: Kroger, Sept. 15, 1945, Mansell.com.*

**Fukuoka Camp 17 Crematorium burial ground.** *Ashes were kept in boxes on a table inside the underground vault. Ibid.*

**Liberated POWs address boxes containing ashes of deceased com-
rades.** (*Notice type of sandals worn at camp.*) *Photographer: Kroger.
Courtesy of Mansell.com*

\* \* \* \* \* \* \*

**American B-29s airdrop supplies to POW camps.**
*US Military archives; Public Domain*

American airplanes began dropping care packages to us by parachute. Each one contained food and supplies packed in six-gallon sealed drums with handles welded on them so they could be attached to parachutes. At first, they caused as much excitement as Santa Claus, to see the parachutes flutter open, with the suspended drums swinging back and forth, promising items we had only known in our dreams for all those years. Many of the parachutes of varied colors were taken to the tailor in camp who made flags from the parachutes.

The barrels were stuffed with C-rations, corned beef hash, salmon, fruit cocktail, cigarettes, soap, underwear, sugar, instant coffee, bars of candy and other canned goods.

Unfortunately, a case of fruit cocktail broke loose from a parachute during one of the drops. It plummeted down and hit a guy's left leg and severed it. Gangrene set up and he died at camp before the Americans arrived with medicine.[104]

One day Bob and I were sitting in the barracks, taking life easy. We had scavenged all the cases being dropped and had stored away all we could eat. We heard the planes making passes overhead. They made two or three drops, but we didn't care because we had plenty.

We could hear a bunch of ruckuses erupting outside; guys were hooting and carrying on like the planes had dropped a load of gold. We decided to go out and watch the free-for-all.

Just as we stepped outside, another plane came over and dropped a fifty-five-gallon drum loaded with supplies. It pulled loose from its parachute, sailed through the roof of the barracks, special delivery, and crashed into our bedroom where we had been sitting only minutes before. My guardian angel was surely on duty that day!

Nearly everyone got a new set of clothes and shoes among the barrels. So much food was dropped that folks didn't bother to go outside to pick it up.

The office safe was opened that had held our valuables since capture. My high school class ring was still there with my name on the tag. It was the only thing I carried through the war.

\* \* \* \* \* \* \*

One day a parachute dropped a barrel close by and I took out after it. When I got close enough to try to grab the barrel, the inflated parachute decided to continue on its journey in spite of my tugging and trying to wrestle the barrel to a stop. My legs got tangled in the strings and I thought I was going to be carried away with the parachute. The strings tightened around my legs and I was in jeopardy of having one or both of them cut off by the tension in the strings.

---

104       The Hewlett Report – Fukuoka #17, Omuta, Japan, "Nightmare Revisited," by Thomas H. Hewlett, M.D., F.A.C.S., COL. U.S.A., Dec. 1978, reported the following facts. MORTALITY: One hundred twenty-six men died in the 2-year period; 48 deaths attributed to pneumonia, 35 to deficiency disease, 14 to colitis, 8 to injuries, 5 to executions, 6 to tuberculosis, and 10 to miscellaneous disease. Total population 1,859 (126) 6.7%.

I yelled for help and got someone's attention. Several guys came and joined in my battle with the ballooned parachute and finally got it cut loose before my legs were amputated. When my heart stopped pounding, I shuddered to think of how close I had come to losing my legs, possibly my life, here at the end of the war!

**Unloading relief supplies** *dropped at Omori PW camp near Toyoko; 083045, history-army-mil.com; Public Domain*

\* \* \* \* \* \* \*

Everyone was restless to be moving on. Liberty gradually became as intoxicating as the *saki*. We started venturing beyond the confining walls to the outside world, going to town or anywhere else we desired.

We boarded the train without money whenever we took the notion. In town, we confiscated whatever we wanted, although there wasn't much to be had anyway.

Some of the guys went to the women barbers in town for a shave and haircut. I didn't let any of them get a razor around my head. I had been over there too long to trust them. I walked on by and didn't go in any of those places.

They had some clippers and razors in a barber shop in camp and I got them to shave my head in August, and we left in September.

* * * * * *

I met Duck Hunter, one of the mine foremen who had beaten me up, on the road as I was headed toward town; he was returning from town. I probably wouldn't have bothered him, I don't guess, but he had tried to make me bow and treat him like he was Mr. High and Mighty. When he met me, he started bowing and scraping, so I straightened him up and laid him out with my fist. Then I told him, "Get up and walk like a man instead of stooping to everyone."

Duck Hunter shook himself off and started down the road again. Soon, he met a group of ex-POWs and walked by them, straight and tall, without bowing. It was his second mistake. They told him to bow and salute. Then they knocked him around for not showing respect. From then on, he stayed out of sight because he couldn't seem to do anything right!

After the war, a few of the Japanese who had been cruel to prisoners vanished, one way or another. Some moved out, went into hiding, or mysteriously disappeared from the face of the earth.

Those who had acted favorably toward us wanted to be even better because they didn't know what to expect. They feared that we might go on a rampage and kill them. And they weren't far from wrong. The mean ones that got caught went missing, if you know what I mean. They not only beat up on them, they hung them to the wall, or met other types of retribution. Flange Face was beaten to death. There were irate prisoners with bottled up frustrations who found their own revenge for being humiliated and mistreated.

The Japanese had practiced mass abuse or punishment. For instance, in the Philippines, when a Filipino was caught or suspected of hiding an American, the Japs might force a man to stand and watch while his whole family was brutally tortured or shot. In the camps, when someone stole something, everyone suffered for it.

Americans didn't retaliate in that manner. If we had something against one of the Japs, we didn't bother his family.

Recalling the many cruelties, we had suffered, a buddy and I agreed it was payback time. We knew where the guards lived, so we went Jap hunting.

**Example of camps marking their roofs for intended airdrops.**
*Aerial view of Wali Coal Mine POW camp. Mansell.com*[105]

---

105        Immediately upon the surrender of Japan, Gen MacArthur instructed the Japanese officials to account for all POWs under its jurisdiction. Each POW camp was to have a PW sign painted on the roof top of each internment facility for the purpose of dropping food, clothing & medicines to the POWs by aircraft." *Mansell.com*

**Liberated POWs confront Japanese guard.**
*Mansell.com*

**Former Japanese guards bow to liberated POWs.** *Mansell.com*

**Newspaper headlines about atomic bomb and victory.**
*US National Archives, WWII Headlines.*

**Liberated soldiers waving their home national flags in victory.**
*Released POWs at Omori, 29 Aug 1945. Multicolored parachutes were gathered from the relief supplies dropped by the B-29s and made into clothing and flags. P.O.W. Experience. Photo courtesy of Linda V. Dahl-Mansell.com*

**Soldiers victoriously display the captured Japanese war flag.**
*www.ww2incolor.com/us-army/life_153.html.*
*Image may be subject to copyright.*

# CHAPTER 36

## LIBERATION

CLARENCE Daubenspeck, a buddy from Nashville, Tennessee, and I set out on foot to do some serious head knocking. Like me, he had threatened to even the score with one of the Japs who had likewise knocked him in the head with a saw. The one that gave us the most trouble was a Jap who was raised in the States and spoke good English. We knew where the guard lived.

We paid a friendly visit to the homes of several Japs on our "Most Wanted" list first, but none of them were to be found. We concluded that word had traveled through their grapevine that we were after them. They left town.

We proceeded to the local train depot, described the Japs to the attendant, and asked if he had seen them.

"*Shiranai!*" (I don't know!), he replied.

One of us grabbed him by the collar so high that his toes dangled off the ground, repeated the question, and demanded an answer.

"*Kono-saki!*" (up ahead), he squawked, pointing up the track. We figured he was trying to tell us the guy was on the train ahead of us.

We boarded a car, which happened to be loaded with armed Japanese soldiers. The train pulled out of the station. Next stop, we climbed off and went around asking about the missing Japs. That depot attendant started the *"shiranai"* business, but we pulled him up on his toes, and he yelped, *"kono-saki!"* too.

We rode most of the day further away from camp in hot pursuit on the trail of our two fugitives. Tired and hungry, we arrived at Fukuoka, a sizable place in which anyone could be swallowed up and disappear, especially in a sea of similar faces, while ours stood out distinctly. We took a vote and decided it was a hopeless quest.

Upon return to the station near our Camp 17, we met nine guys walking toward town. Bob Harp, Wayne Carringer, Brownie, Bill Lee, and George E. Chumley were among them.

"They've turned us loose," one of them informed us. "The Americans have landed at the airfield. They're ready to fly us out. Come on and go with us," they urged.

"We haven't eaten anything all day and we're starved. If you'll wait on us, we'll go with you," we responded.

"No, we're itching to put this place far behind," they said, shaking their heads impatiently. They went directly to the airport and caught a flight out to the Philippines.

We ate and spent the night in camp, planning to go down to the airport the next day. Big mistake! As luck would have it, rain poured down all night. Numerous typhoons hit the area during that time. The Americans didn't fly back into the airport, and it was one month later before we could catch a ship.

The war had officially been declared as over; thus, it wasn't necessary for the Americans to come in and liberate us. Our actual liberation date was September 2, 1945. The U.S. forces calmly arrived at Camp 17 to process us out around September 11th.

We later learned some sobering facts about how timely our deliverance was brought about by the atomic bombs. Japanese high command had a master plan to exterminate all the POW slave laborers, possibly to cover up their horrible treatment.

When the Rangers marched into camp, the commanding lieutenant spoke with a familiar accent.

"Where's your home, Lieutenant?" I asked.

"I'm from Augusta, Georgia," he said, slowly drawling out the syllables.

"You sure are!" I chuckled, his Southern accent welcome to my ears.

The Rangers took two days to process us. On September 13th, we were transported to the train, bound for Nagasaki.[106]

As we approached Nagasaki, nearly one month after the atomic bomb, all the trees seemed to salute toward us, leaning at a curious slant away from the town. Progressively, they became shorter until there were only charred stumps. At the outskirts, there weren't even any stumps. Then there wasn't anything but cement left.

I remember seeing one structure where a big cement smoke stack was all that remained standing; the rest of the building was a pile of melted steel. Railroad tracks, trains, everything resembled melted candle wax. The town, like so many of its inhabitants, was dead.[107]

New railroad tracks had already been laid, but there weren't any buildings, nothing but rubble remained. No signs of life, other than our own men. The people were either dead or had been carried elsewhere. No city, only ashes; no people, just melted steel. Only the cement survived.

---

106     Of the original group of 500 men and officers who came in August. 1943, at least 15 died. On September 2, there were 1,721 prisoners in the camp, including British, Australian, Dutch, and American. *Mansell.com*

107     The atomic bombings led to the death of *90,000 – 166,000 people* in Hiroshima and *60,000 – 80,000* in Nagasaki with nearly half of these casualties occurring on the days of the bombing. "Ten Facts About the Bombings of Hiroshima and Nagasaki" by Anirudh – June 9, 2014. *https://learnodo-newtonic.com/hiroshima-and-nagasaki-facts*

**Nagasaki after atomic bomb, looking toward hospital area.** *Bing.com Source unknown. Image may be subject to copyright.* [108]

**Nagasaki after Atomic Bomb.** *August 9, 1945 picture shows burnt ruins with the only structure, a torii (gate) for a shrine, left standing in Nagasaki. (Archive: public domain.)*

---

108         Damage Report: Leveled Area = 6.7 million square meters; damaged houses = 18,409; Casualties: killed = 73,884; injured = 74,909; total = 148,793 (Large numbers of people died in the following years from the effects of radioactive poisoning). *http://www.nuclearfiles.org/images/gallery/aga/index.html.*

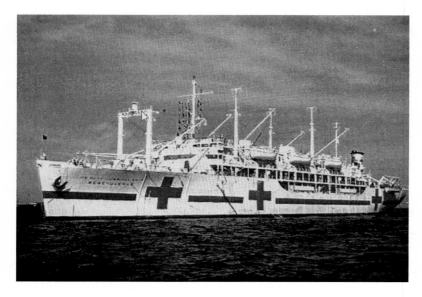

**US Navy Hospital Ship Benevolence.** *Mansell.com**

* * * * * * *

The American ship was docked in the harbor at Nagasaki. When we got off the train, we were directed to a long tent where doctors stood in line, each looking for specific ailments and symptoms. We were ordered to strip to the skin and march down the aisle. A makeshift net or cloth separated us from the doctors.

Thinking I had it licked, I was stepping pretty high by the time I got down to the last two doctors. To my consternation, one of the doctors motioned me aside.

"You come here," he ordered.

I stepped out. My swollen feet, caused by wet beriberi, had not escaped his attention.

He sent me to the hospital ship. I propped my feet on the hammock ropes, higher than my head, knowing the elevated position would cause the fluid to move back up into my body; then I'd just look fat instead of swollen!

Next morning, a medic came in and asked, "Is there anyone that's able to come off this ship? We just found a camp where all the men are in critical condition. We need more hospital space."

I jumped up and said, "I'm ready to go."

"What are you in here for?" he inquired.

"I don't know." I shrugged innocently.

"Who was your doctor?" he asked.

"I don't know," I replied.

"What do you know?" he countered.

"I know I'm ready to go home!" I stated emphatically.

Six other guys said the same thing. When the doctor didn't come to examine us, they put us on a boat and carried us out to the aircraft carrier docked nearby.

As I was walking up the gangplank, I looked up and saw a guy standing on the ship deck.

"Hello, Alabama," he said.

"How did you know I'm from Alabama?" I replied.

"It's written all over you. I could just tell," he grinned.

"Where are you from?" I asked.

"Dothan, Alabama," he stated.

"Anybody else on here from Alabama?" I inquired.

"Yes, a guy named Lindsey from Bexar, Marion County, Alabama, and a Crow from Hamilton," he said.

I had gone to school with the Crow boy. Hamilton was about fifteen miles from home.

\* \* \* \* \* \* \*

**September 2, 1945:** "Some of the men of the 27th were able to watch the Japanese surrender that took place aboard the *USS Missouri*, then off to Manila to the 29th Replacement Depot. We were always looking for a familiar face, wondering who was still alive and who was not. The first familiar face we saw was General William Hipps."[109]

**September 11, 1945:** "On board the ship, while sailing to the Philippines, it was like a reunion among the guys coming in from other camps. We swapped information about who was alive and what happened to the ones who were missing. Out of 1200 men that left Savannah Air Base for 'Operation Plum,' about 350 were still alive. All were very tired, had suffered a great loss of weight, but were very happy to still be alive."[110]

\* \* \* \* \* \* \*

When I got on the aircraft carrier, I met the guy named Lindsey. After we got acquainted, I used his APO address number, so my mail would go through, and wrote Daddy and Mother a letter for the first time in over three years. They didn't have a phone, so I couldn't call them in person.

I was transferred to eight or nine different ships en route to the Philippines. I'd be on one awhile, then they'd put me off ship onto another one, trying to make it back. I transferred to an Australian ship, a Dutch ship, and an English ship, among a few.

I caught up with my group from Camp 17 in the Philippines at a repatriation center east of Manila, at Clark Airfield, where they were taking all the POWs as we returned. Our service history and medical status were verified. They intended to beef us up so that we wouldn't look so scrawny for our hero's homecoming.

Dr. H. J. Blakeney examined me. Later, he set up practice in Amory, Mississippi, and became the Chandler family doctor, and he's still my doctor today.

Before coming home, I was issued new American clothes. I fit into a pair of 29-29 pants. I still have that pair of pants, but I sure can't wear them now. I weighed a strapping 118 pounds. I was fattened up so fast that I looked bloated when I got home.

Before they could get us shipped out, the West Coast and San Francisco shipping went on strike and no ships were permitted to leave port from the

---

109     *27th Bombardment Group—39th Anniversary Program, Nov. 2–4, 1979.*

110     *Ibid.*

States to come pick us up. All the people connected with the ships were on strike.

After enduring all our hardships, that seemed unbearable. We were raring to come home, and the frustration was almost a slap in the face. I haven't been favorable toward unions since then.

The ships were eventually released and one finally arrived. They called us out at 4:00 a.m. to load up in trucks for the ship. They started counting them off, but then they stopped two men ahead of me.

"From here back, return to your tents. That's the quota. We can't carry anybody else."

Muttering and cursing, everyone turned to go back to the camp. I guess I was a little incredulous and a lot stubborn. Another fellow and I kept standing there, frustrated. We didn't move out.

Shortly, the driver of the truck came back and said, "We've got room for two more."

Man, I hopped on that truck like a jackrabbit!

The guy cautioned me, "Buddy, you were one of the last ones on the truck. You better not be one of the last ones on that ship when they pull the line."

When we got down to the ship, I was the first to scramble out of the truck and walk up the gangplank. I didn't want to hear that there was one too many. I had missed my chance back in Japan and wasn't about to *miss the boat* again!

**Navy band greets POWs with familiar songs.** *As the trains arrive, the USS Witchita band strikes up "Hail, Hail, the gang's all here," "Beer Barrel Polka," and other favorites, bringing tears of joy to the faces of prisoners, as well as Navy faces. Mansell.com\**

**Red Cross serves donuts and coffee.** *While lining up for processing, 1,000 POWs per day were served donuts and coffee by the Red Cross. Ibid \**

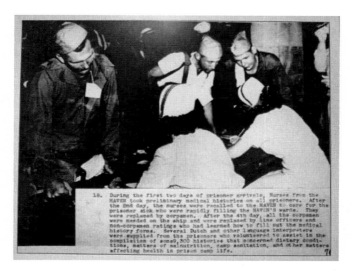

**Red Cross nurses take preliminary records.** *Medical histories are recorded that concerned POWs' dietary condition, matters of malnutrition, camp sanitation and other matters affecting health of prisoners. Ibid\**

**Medical examiner decides** *whether to issue clothing for POW to proceed to release for transport or given pjs and sent aboard hospital ship for medical care.\**

**POWs process through medical exams and then receive new sea bag and clothes.** *Photographer: Kroger, Mansell.com\**

**POWs receive articles for personal needs.**
*Having been issued clothes and dressed, soldier passes second Red Cross line and receives articles for his personal hygiene, comfort, pleasure, and personal needs. Ibid.\**

**POW stretcher cases from Camp #17,
Omuta, shown here arriving at Nagasaki, Japan in stretcher car.** *Ibid.**

**Liberated invalid POWs are carried out of camp.** *Ibid.**

**Liberated camp invalids skip the lines and are lifted to the Red Cross
hospital ship for immediate medical care.** *Ibid.* *

*\*Previous photos in this section are from "Finding Our POWs – The
Recovery and Evacuation of POWs from Japan, 1945" Mansell.com.*

# CHAPTER 37

## HOMECOMING

**OCTOBER 8, 1945:** I finally headed home.

On board the ship, it was like another happy family reunion. It was great to see a guy I didn't know was still alive and had survived, and hear his story.

Grady "Shorty Red" Palmatier from Deland, Florida, and J.P. Lollar from Vernon, Alabama, and Pappy Stein from Shreveport, Louisiana, and I were on the same ship coming back. We sat together reminiscing on the deck of the ship.

Since we had shipped out of San Francisco together, we figured the ship would dock there again. Halfway there, the ship changed course. Everyone began to question what was happening. We were informed that Seattle, Washington, was our destination.

The turn of events was unsettling to many of the married men who had gotten telegrams to their wives; they had planned to meet them in San Francisco.

A good friend of mine, E.N. "Fireball" Adams of the 91st, from Texas, had made contact with his wife, who was planning to meet him in San Francisco. He got word to her that our course had changed; she started up to Seattle and had a wreck on the trip up. It was sad and unnerving that she almost got killed before he could see her after surviving insurmountable odds.

Another band of our guys was returning home by airplane when something happened and it crashed out from Guam. I never could find out how many and exactly who went down. I don't know if I lost friends on that flight.[111]

\* \* \* \* \* \* \*

**October 28, 1945:** When I arrived at Tacoma, Washington, all of the POWs were given 400 dollars regardless of rank. They carried us to the hospital, gave us a pair of pajamas, and took all of our clothes, informing us we were to stay there for the night. But they didn't take our overcoats. We all put on our overcoats and headed downtown. We didn't intend to be kept prisoners ever again.

Shorty Red came by and said, "I'm going to blow my money and have a good time. Here is 100 dollars I want you to hold for me. I'll need that when I get home."

We loaded onto the crowded bus going into town from the base. There was a lot of jostling and pushing, so that I couldn't tell when someone got into my pocket. When I got out at the end of the line, I didn't have a bill-fold or any money. We went ahead and partied, but somebody else paid for it.

After I got home and got the rest of the money, I bought a money order and sent it to Shorty; he went to town and cashed it. So, I lost 500 dollars, plus I paid back the 'mad money'— apt description—which I had borrowed from the other guy.

From Tacoma, Washington, we took the train to Atlanta. They switched some cars and then we were bound for Augusta, Georgia. When we got to Atlanta, there were five or six men missing who had gotten out while they were switching cars. The guards were supposed to keep us on board.

In Augusta, the guys began to call their families as soon as we arrived. I called Aunt Jess, mother's sister, in Birmingham, Alabama. Mom and Dad didn't have a phone so I couldn't tell them I was on the way.

---

111     On Sept.10, 1945, Typhoon Ursula downed a fleet of six U.S. aircraft transporting liberated prisoners of war to the Philippines. The planes were flying from Okinawa to the Philippines, as part of a larger effort to repatriate 32,000 Allied war prisoners... An estimated 120 servicemen, both former POWs and aircrew, plus another 23 servicemen on the ground were also killed by the storm. Hurricane Research Division, NOAA/OAR/Atlantic Oceanographic and Meteorological Laboratory, Sept. 9, 2015.

The government was giving us one dollar per day for ration money for leave time. We were granted a ninety-day leave. If you stayed and picked up your leave, you could draw your ration money, but if you left before picking it up, you couldn't collect it later.

J.P. Lollar's dad came and got him that night. He came looking for me to go back with him. I said, "Shoot, I haven't made 90 dollars in a day since I've been gone. I'll wait until tomorrow so I can get my money."

I had gotten to know a boy from Yazoo City, Mississippi, on the ship coming back. His mother and two sisters came after him the next day. When we met in the hall he asked, "Where do you live, Alabama? We're going through Birmingham. Will that be a help to you?"

"You bet!" I exclaimed.

When I got to Birmingham, they dropped me off at Aunt Jess's house. A big old long-legged boy was out front, but I walked past him. I didn't recognize my brother, Doyle, after four years. He was twelve when I left for service. Now, he was seventeen years old and a handsome young man.

Next day, Doyle and I went to the bus station. As we stepped up to get on the Greyhound bus, the driver attempted to pull the door closed, but I stuck my foot in the door.

"We've got a load," he said. "We can't take you."

I was in uniform. "I've driven a bus and whether you go or not, I can drive this bus. I'm going. Suit yourself."

"I believe you mean that," he said.

"I do mean it," I assured him.

"Move back! Two more are coming on," he announced.

It was pretty cold and nearly dark when we got off the bus at Hamilton and began to look for a way to travel the last stretch home. I went to the AMOCO station. Raymond Jeffers worked there and knew me.

"You looking for a ride home? Mr. Cook's right over yonder. He's going home."

Cook lived about six to eight miles up close to Round Top, not far from home, so I asked him for a lift.

"You'll have to ride in the back of the truck," he offered.

We climbed on and he dropped us out on the road, but not at the house.

"How much do I owe you?" I asked.

He charged me four dollars for riding on the back of the truck about six miles. I never did get over that.

**November 9, 1945:** I got home at dusk. Momma and Daddy were living in my present home, but it was only three rooms at the time: no inside bathroom, no phone. We added the other half years later.

Daddy was in bed with his heart, sick out of his head. He didn't know I was alive or that I had gotten home. Momma and Diane (pronounced Deon), my baby sister, were there. I can't remember where Birdie—my married sister, Roberta, with family—or Yank, my youngest brother, Ray, were at the time. Doyle came home with me. Uncle Troy, Dad's brother, came to see me that night.

My family had gotten my letter about 2:00 p.m. and I got there around 4:00 p.m. That was the first time they knew I was still alive!

Cordy Sagers was already home from the war. His mother heard I was home, and they came by to see me. She was known for bootlegging, but she was one of the first people to come over to welcome me home. Cordy had been in prison for making whiskey, and he had been given a choice of serving out his time in the pen or going into the Army. Cordy wound up in the Pacific, too. He had come up through those jungles, fighting his way back in.

I said, "Cordy, did you make any whiskey while you made your way through the jungles?"

"Naw, but I seen a lot of good places."

Later in the day, somebody brought Jim Dyer to the house. I saw him coming. He got off a truck and started running toward me. We met about halfway and locked up. I didn't know that Jim's family had moved from near my home over to Hamilton. He came all that way to look me up. Jim and I reminisced and he finally told me about how he escaped.

\* \* \* \* \* \* \*

My brother, Doyle, had planted a crop that spring. When I got home, he left for the Navy. He had already tried to run away three times prior to join; he said he wanted to rescue me from the Japanese. The military would not allow him to enlist because he wasn't eighteen years old yet. Finally, the third time, Daddy agreed to sign the paperwork so he could sign up at age seventeen.

I worked out the crop he had planted that summer and brought in the harvest. Three months later I had to report back to the hospital.

When I had been home for three or four years, the government paid us a dollar a day for meals we didn't get while we were prisoners of war. I was a POW for 1,252 days, so I got 1,252 dollars.

I received 1.25 dollars a day backpay for the whole time I was over there. At the time I went in, a private earned 21 dollars a month. I was still a private but I had specialist rating, thus, I drew the same amount as a corporal. I was supposed to get that pay when I was fighting or whatever.

A lot of people who weren't even in the army when I was captured made master sergeant, and when I came out, they raised me to sergeant, which means I moved up one pay grade in four years. I made corporal before I was captured, in about one year. Well, I earned the same pay scale as a corporal in six months, but what time I was staying the same rank, fighting and POW, men that came in after I did were moving up in rank and getting paid more.

1.25 dollars a day was corporal's pay at that time. I was paid 3,300 dollars when I got back. That was all the pay we received, period.

* * * * * * *

They had a case where they were going back and paying 20,000 dollars to the Japanese families who were interned in the United States during the war. I can't agree with that when our own fighting men didn't collect that much for actually fighting to defend our country.

In the meantime, Uncle Sam sent the Japanese families' boys to college and while they got four years college, I was getting four years in POW camp. Still they were awarded 20,000 dollars because they felt they had been mistreated when they were transferred to internment camps. Actually, they were moved off the West Coast inland for their protection. If they had stayed on the West Coast, the Filipinos would have killed them, because there were a lot of Filipinos located in that area. Moving them was doing them a favor, and then we paid them 20,000 dollars to boot![112]

\* \* \* \* \* \* \*

*Lamar Democrat* newspaper reported about some of the local boys during the war. The Sulligent coach owned part of the newspaper, and he liked to boast about his undefeated team in the paper. Everybody knew me because I was on the winning team. When I was captured, they ran a story featuring what little information they could obtain.

When I came home, the government had a program, called "52–20," where a veteran could draw 20 dollars per week unemployment for a year until he found a job. I decided to stay around home awhile and draw my 52–20 while farming. When I went in to their office to sign up, they asked if I'd take a job, if one were offered to me. "Yeah, I'll take a job."

I was directed to the Superintendent of Education's office to take a test. Several college guys were there taking it, too. I just had a high school degree, but I got the job for agriculture teacher at Sulligent, because I made a better grade than the college boys.

I taught agriculture at Sulligent for two years and was teaching school when I got married. My class was written up in the paper, with a commendation for being one of the best, after Mr. Meadows, Superintendent of Education, had visited my class. He visited all agriculture classes to see

---

112     [There was some misunderstanding of the reason the money was paid out.]

Feb. 19, 1942—President Roosevelt authorized evacuation of all persons (Japanese) deemed a threat to national security (some worked in airplane factories and other military facilities, which was a perceived threat of sabotage or espionage). Approximately a hundred and twenty-two thousand men, women, children were...confined in isolated, fenced, and guarded relocation centers known as internment camps, located in ten sites in six Western states. Nearly seventy thousand were American citizens. They lost homes, businesses, farms, etc. Thirty-three thousand Japanese Americans served with distinction during the Second World War in segregated units, with approximately eight hundred killed in action. Many of the veterans took advantage of the G.I. Bill to get college educations. In 1948, Congress provided token payments directly to individuals for property losses. See: "Japanese Relocation During WWII," National Archives @ archives.gov, also *www.ourdocuments. gov*, and "Japanese Americans in Military during WWII," *Densho Encyclopedia*.

whether they were meeting standards. The men in my class were commended for being such good students.

Later, I got a job as rural mail carrier for the U.S. Post Office and continued to serve the government in that capacity for thirty-six years.

I married Evelyn Flynn of Sulligent, Alabama, on May 17, 1948. We have five children: Larry Chandler of Birmingham, Alabama[113]; Wanda Davidson of Tupelo, Mississippi; Jerry Harp (after friend, Bob Harp) Chandler, also of Tupelo, Mississippi[114]; Dale Chandler of Sulligent, Alabama; Tommie Chandler of Detroit, Alabama. We now have seven grandchildren and two great grandchildren. It has been a hard, but good life after all. I've been serving the Lord to the best of my ability for nigh on sixty years.

I've spoken at schools and various events over the years and shared my experiences. Being able to talk about what I went through has made it easier for me to recover, although you can never be the same after experiencing war firsthand. I attended POW reunions often and listened to the stories of other men who could understand my emotions and the impact of those memories.

## To God be the glory!
### I'm just glad that He never, never, never gave up on me!

---

113     DOD: 02/22/14

114     Retired year 2000, thirty-year veteran, USAF E9 Chief Master Sergeant

# EPILOGUE

## Sgt. Drolan Chandler
## Date of service: October 11, 1940 – July 30, 1946
## U. S. Army Air Corp, Savannah Air Base, GA,
## 27th Bomb Group, Headquarters' Squadron

DROLAN Chandler, born June 15, 1919, died at his residence on January 4, 2003, at age 83. He had been awarded the Bronze Star. He was a member of Detroit Church of God and served in various capacities of ministries. Drolan, Bob Harp, and Jim Dyer and others remained life-long friends until their deaths. They maintained contact with fellow comrades by attending annual POW reunions throughout the years.

His spouse, Evelyn Flynn Chandler (DOB: October 7, 1929; DOD: October 29, 2007), with whom he had been married fifty-four years at the time of his death, died at age 78.

**Photo of Drolan** *in The Progressive Shopper, Vol. 1 Number 7, August 1983, article by Ed Woodward, "Drollan Chandler: Another view of WWII". (Note: Drolan is misspelled in article.) Image may be subject to copyright.*

**Photo of Drolan Chandler,** *taken from the informative article, "Prisoner of War Medal Awarded to Droland Chandler," in The Lamar Democrat and The Sulligent News, In 92nd Year, No. 38, Wed., June 15, 1988. Veterans Officer David Barnes presented Drolan with the Prisoner of War Medal in front of the WWI and WWII monument in Vernon, Alabama on June 9, 1988. (Note: Drolan is misspelled.) Image may be subject to copyright.*

**Family photo after Drolan's return from war.** *Front Row (l–r): Drolan, Minos "Daddy Mike" (father), Rayburn "Yank" Chandler, Doyle Chandler, Ordle Rye with Dennis. Back Row (l–r): Juler (Mother) "Momma Juler" Chandler, Mavis (Yank's wife), Diane (Deon) Chandler McDonald, and Roberta Chandler Rye*

**Drolan Chandler, home at last!**

**Drolan with his young family:** *Back Row (l-r): Drolan, Larry, Evelyn Chandler; Middle Row (l-r): Jerry, nicknamed "Butch" – in front of Drolan, and Wanda, in front of Evelyn; Front Row (l-r): Tommie (the baby) and Dale. Photo taken in 1956 (approximately).*

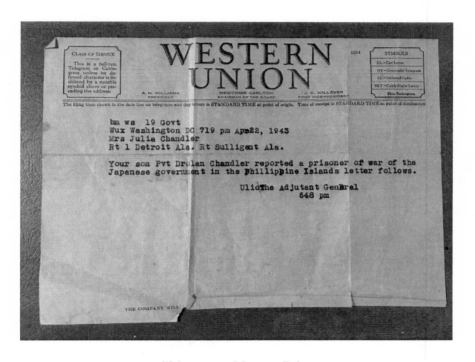

**Telegram to Momma Juler**

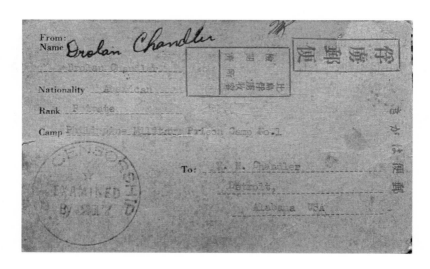

**Postcard 1**: *Line 1–I am interned at Philippine Military Prison Camp #1; Line 5–See that everything is taken care of; Line 6–Family: love to all don't worry; Line 7–Best regard to Roberta (sister).*

**Postcard 1**: *Front of card: Nationality American; Rank Private; Camp Philippine Military Prison Camp No. 1; To: M. N. Chandler, Detroit, Alabama USA*

**Postcard 2**: *Front*

**Postcard 2:** 6 (Re:Family)–Answer via International Red Cross Geneva Switzerland; best regards to all

**Postcard 3**: *front*

**Postcard 3**: *back*

**Drolan's Shadowbox of Medals** *(from right angle)*

**Shadowbox with Medals** *(left side of box)*

These photos were supplied by Jerry Chandler who compiled the contents and had the shadowbox made especially for his Dad. The left side features a carved wood replica of the Philippine Islands. The right side has a carved wood replica of Japan. The background is made from the brown khaki material used to make military uniforms. Jerry went to great lengths to obtain medals from the 1940-1945 era that Drolan deserved and for which he was eligible. He was also helpful to me with clarification of military terms, ranks, facts, etcetera.

**Shadowbox of Medals** *(from center view)*

**Shadowbox of Medals** *(from right view)*

**Drolan viewing shadowbox.** *Photo from Tombigbee Electric publication Community Heroes Series, taken from the Alabama Living magazine November 2002.*

**From Drolan's grave - military foot marker**

**CHANDLER, DROLAN**, age 83, of Detroit, AL died Saturday, January 4, 2003 at his residence.

Born in Detroit, AL, he is the Son of the late Minos and Juler Real Chandler. He had lived in Detroit all of his life, was a member of the Detroit Church Of God, a Veteran of World War II having served in the US Army Air Core, received the Bronze Star, and was a Japanese prisoner for 3 1/2 years. He retired from the post office after 36 years as a rural letter carrier. He had been married for 54 years.

Survived by his wife, Evelyn Flynn Chandler of Detroit, AL, a

daughter, Wanda Davidson of Tupelo, MS, four sons, Larry Chandler of Birmingham, AL, Jerry Chandler of Aventura, FL, Dale Chandler of Sulligent and Tommie Chandler of Detroit, AL, seven grandchildren, and two great grandchildren, two sisters, Roberto Finney of Wetumpka, AL and Diane Shelton of Birmingham, AL; and a brother, Doyle Chandler of Pensacola, FL.

He was preceded in death by a brother, Rayburn Chandler and a granddaughter, Christy Williams.

Services held Tuesday, January 7, 2003 2:00 PM from the Norwood Funeral Home Chapel with burial in the Kingsville Cemetery. Bro. Charles Gilbert officiating.

Norwood Funeral Home of Sulligent, AL directing.

**Clipping of Drolan's newspaper obituary** - *source unknown*

**Photo of Drolan Chandler** *(date unknown)*

**Drolan at 27th Bomb Group Reunion** *(year unknown). Drolan is on 2nd row behind the man on the first row with 27th Bomb Group sign.*

**Drolan at another 27th Bomb Group Reunion,** *(year unknown). Drolan is on the front row, second from left.*

**Drolan at yet another 27th Bomb Group Reunion**
*(year unknown). Drolan is on the 2nd row, far right; it is possible that Bob Harp is on the front right, 4th man (far right).*

# CHAPTER 38

## Robert (Bob) R. Harp

*BOB Harp's daughter, Mandy Harp Vassey, graciously supplied the following information and personal photos, with permission to use them. I (Myra) met Bob when Drolan and I traveled to his home to visit and interview him about his experiences in the Bataan Death March and POW camps.*

### Sgt. Robert R. Harp - April 2, 1920 – September 28, 1991
### U. S. Army Air Corp, Savannah Air Base, GA,
### 27th Bomb Group, Headquarters' Squadron

Robert R. (Bob) Harp was in Manila, Philippine Island when Pearl Harbor was bombed on December 7, 1941. Originally trained to be a tail gunner on an airplane, he had no plane. He and the other brave men had arrived on the island with little or no supplies or equipment. They fought as best and as long as they could until April 9, 1942. At that time, he became part of the infamous Bataan Death March. Bob was able to hang on to his military canteen during the 3 ½ years that followed. He scratched names, places and dates into the metal to record significant events as they occurred. The following list of places are on the canteen; they represent the timeline of his military experience:

- Savannah Air Base, GA
- Manila, Philippine Island
- Bataan
- O'Donnell Prison Camp
- Tayabas Road Detail
- Billibid Prison
- Cabanatuan Prison Camp

- Japan Coal Mines

Crosses are scratched in the metal along with names of his buddies who perished during the ordeal. Bob recounted that when victory was declared no one had to tell them at the prison camp. They woke up that morning unguarded. There were no Japanese in sight. He and some of his buddies, including Wayne Carringer, left the camp and took a train to meet the American troops before they made it to the prison to liberate the men. He noted that the Japanese people felt they were dishonored because they had lost the war and that the Japanese people they encountered were humble and of no threat to them. He had suffered malaria, starvation and dehydration and back injuries as a result of his ordeals. He weighed approximately 92 lbs when he was admitted to the military hospital. Bob and his bride, Athleen Lewis Harp, had been married a mire five months when Bob was shipped over to the Philippines. She met him back on American soil exactly 4 years (to the day) in Tacoma, Washington. They were married 41 years before she preceded him in death in 1982. Family members never heard a lot of the details of his war experiences. They always felt it was too painful for him to discuss. Most of the stories and recounts of experiences were learned from POW reunions that he attended each year. The men were able to talk among themselves of things they couldn't with others because they shared the experiences. Hearing these conversations is how the family learned most of the events that happened. Submitted by: Mandy Harp Vassey (daughter) Jackie Howell Hutchinson (granddaughter)

* * * * * * *

Bob's post-war career was as a contractor / builder. He was superintendent for a hotel built in the Dominican Republic. He was known to be quite an artisan when it came to art deco and was reportedly one of the best builders in Miami for that style of buildings. At one time, he owned a business in Miami, but moved back home to Irvinville, Georgia. He and his wife, Athleen, owned Crystal Lake Resort in Abbeyville, Georgia, formerly owned by her parents, which was where they met and hung out on dates because there was so much to do. There, they could bowl at the Duck Pin Bowling Alley, skate at the roller rink, go to dances, fish, swim, etcetera.

Mandy told me that her parents laughed when they recounted how they first met at Crystal Lake. Bob sent a friend to ask Athleen if she would dance with him. She replied, "I'm not going to dance with that little guy." She was 5'11" and Bob was 5'8". They married May 21, 1941, five months before he shipped out.

**Athleen and Bob Harp**

**Drolan visits with Bob and his wife.** *Drolan is on the right with Bob's wife, Athleen; Drolan's wife, Evelyn, is in the center at far end of table; couple on left unknown. Bob took the photo.*

Bob Harp is fifth man from left (carrying pan) at Camp O'Donnell. This photo clipping was featured in LIFE magazine. One of the family members saw it and notified the others that he was still alive!

*National Archives.gov*

**Sick Area – Tayabas (2010.06.41), by Ben Steele.** *Images courtesy Montana Museum of Art and Culture (All sketches are charcoal on paper.)* [115]

115      The **Tayabas Road detail** arrived at the work site on 29 May 1942 with 300 men. Around 1 July 1942 Dr. Ashton and two medics arrived. On 28 July 1942 the Japanese ended the work detail, only 187 men were still alive. During the work detail, the POWs had no place set up to sleep, so had to sleep on the rocks next to the river. corregidor.proboards.com.

*Note:* Bob said he and a guy built a treehouse-type shelter to sleep in. They put rice in a wheel- barrow and pushed it into the river to wash off, then pushed the wheelbarrow over a fire to cook; they had plenty to eat including corned beef hash. Bob said he was cautious about eating it, the others (including Japanese) chowed down on it and got severe diarrhea. They didn't make much progress on the road because it was such hard digging through jungle roots, muddy muck, hard as cement. "We didn't get much accomplished," Bob concluded.

**Beating – Tayabas Road (2010.06.37), by Ben Steele.** *Images courtesy Montana Museum of Art and Culture (All sketches are charcoal on paper.)*

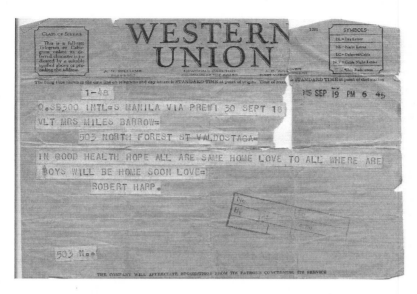

**Telegram 1** – *From: Bob, Manila to Mother,*
*Mrs. Miles Barrow, Sep 29 1945.*

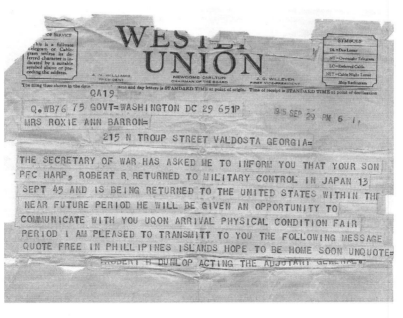

**Telegram 2** – *Official notice from the government to Bob's family.*

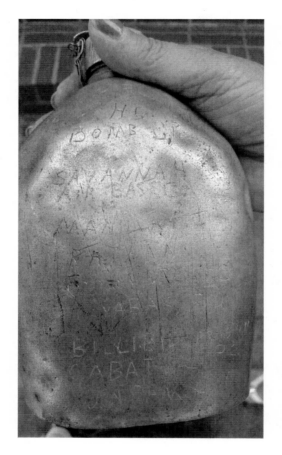

**Places scratched on Bob's Canteen:** *HQ Bomb Grp, Savannah Air Base, Manila, Bilibid, Cabanatuan, Japan are a few of the places listed.*

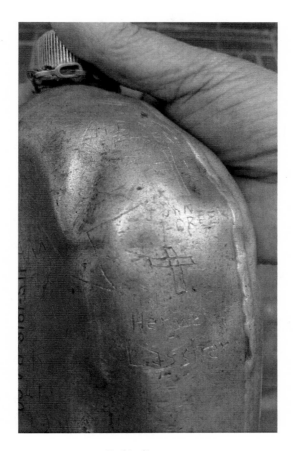

**Bob's Canteen:**
*Names of fallen comrades and cross scratched on sides of canteen*

**Bob's Canteen:** *Bob kept a record of POW camps, fallen comrades, events and dates, scratched on his canteen which he carried throughout the war. Comrade names who had died were scratched on the canteen included the following: Cap Bundy, Henry Rogers, John Greer, Herman Lassiter; star points in center, skull with cross bones with helmet, Bataan War; 12-8-41 (bomb Philippines), 4-9-42 (Bataan Death March); 7-18-45 (end of war).*

# CHAPTER 39

## JAMES (JIM) FRED DYER

## James Fred Dyer

**February 28, 1919 – July 16, 1974**

**First Sergeant US Army, 27th Bomb, Transportation Group**

**Description:** Weight: 143 lb., Eyes: brown, Hair: brown, Height: 5'7"

**DOS:** 05/14/42 to 07/1944; WWII Philippines, Death March, POW at Negros Island, escape – joined Filipino guerillas

**Parents:** Arthur Griffin Dyer (1875-1943); Ila Estell Sullivan Dyer (1884-1987)

**Spouse:** Evah E. Ballard Dyer (1907-1962)

**Siblings:** Estelle Dyer Holloway (1904-2008); Jewel Inez Dyer (1908-2002); Erie Riggan Dyer (1912-1944); Ancil Lee Dyer (1914-2001); Murray Wright Dyer (1923-1994) - Other information was not available.

AFTER being captured in the Philippines, Jim and nine other American prisoners were transported to the Island of Negros to work as mechanics. The Japanese informed the group that they would be shot to death when they were finished with them, because there were too few to bother with carrying elsewhere to camp. The men determined that, at the first feasible opportunity, they would take fate into their own hands to attempt an escape. They felt they had nothing to lose anyway.

The Japs were planning a big festivity on July 4th, which was not a Japanese holiday and could have been a coincidence. The ten POWs hastily planned their escape to take place during the merriment.

During the course of their mechanic work, the prisoners drove trucks out the gate, past the guard, for a test run, then back into camp. That day, they removed the distributor cap from all the trucks, except the one for their getaway.

One lone Jap guard was assigned to them while the others were off celebrating. He made the mistake of leaning back against a building and falling asleep. He never woke up; one of the prisoners took care of that possibility.

Time came for their escape. Nine of the guys piled into the truck with two in the cab and the other seven hidden in the back. One man got cold feet and chickened out of going with them at the last minute. He climbed out and sent them off to their fate.

The driver sped past the guard at the gate. By the time the Japs realized the mechanics were not making a test run, they rushed to the trucks, but none would crank.

The fugitives ditched the truck further down the road, knowing the Japs would call ahead to the next camp for someone to intercept them.

They used their captured rifle to shoot holes in the gas tank and set it on fire.

Luckily, the guy who stayed behind was spared because his captors knew there would be a record of his whereabouts when the others got away. He was transferred to Cabanatuan where he told the other Americans about the nine making an escape.

The escapees came close to being recaptured when Jap soldiers came searching for them. They hid underwater, breathing through a reed, for more than two hours. When they could no longer hear their enemy tramping through the brushes, they dared to come up for air.

Jim and the other eight soldiers fled into the mountains and located a band of Filipino guerrillas known to be in the area. Jap trucks got shot at from time to time; therefore, the Americans knew that finding the Filipinos would give them a place of refuge.

They met up with Marcos and his Filipino guerrilla band, and fought alongside them in their resistance efforts. They performed intelligence gathering roles; one of their activities was to radio American ships regarding Japanese activity in that area.

Eventually, Jim and his eight comrades made contact with American soldiers. His comrades included Captain Mark M. Wohlfeld (Oct. 10, 1912 – May 8, 1978; USAF-Philippine Scout, 26th Cavalry) Rgmt, Silver Star, who had escaped from Mindanao prison. They were provided with transportation, by submarine, back to the United States and home before the end of the war.

James Dyer served as Tax Assessor for Marion County in Hamilton, Alabama during 1967 to 1974. He continued to work and live in the Hamilton area until his death.

**Note:** *Thank you to employees at the Marion County Courthouse, Hamilton, Alabama, for career information, supplied by telephone. Thank you to my cousin (Drolan's son), Dale Chandler, for traveling to the Courthouse to take a photo of the picture of Jim which is displayed in the Courthouse hallway.*

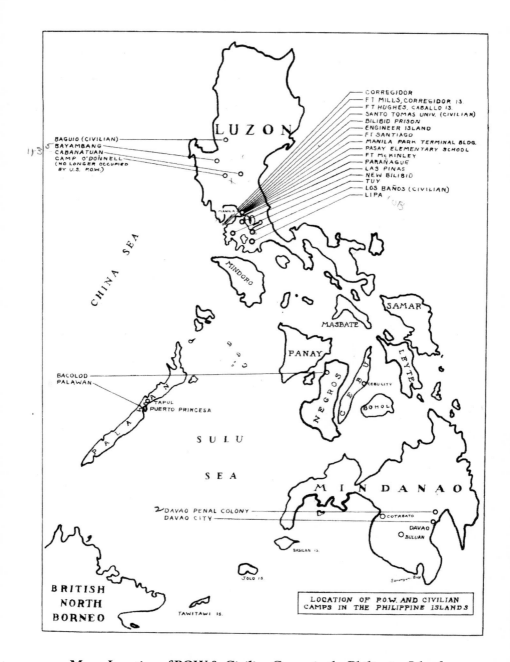

**Map – Location of POW & Civilian Camps in the Philippine Islands.**
*May be See location of Island of Negros where Jim was in Bacolod POW
camp near Bago. Mansell.com*

# CHAPTER 40

## POST WAR – TRIBUNAL VERDICTS FOR WAR CRIMES

**International Military Tribunal for War Crimes, Tokyo, Japan, April 1947.**
*Mansell.com*

THE Tokyo trial featured only one chief prosecutor – American Joseph B. Keenan, a former assistant to the U.S. Attorney General. However, other nations, especially China, contributed to the proceeding, and Australian judge William Flood Webb presided. In addition to the central Tokyo trial, various tribunals, in more than 2,200 trials, sitting outside Japan judged some 5,600 Japanese guilty of war crimes, of whom more than 900 were executed.[116]

**War Crimes Trial defendants, Hideki Tojo, top row in center with mustache, Tokyo Japan January 6, 1948.** *Mansell.com*

**Death by Hanging,** *Mansell.com*

---

116      This Day in History, "Japanese war criminals hanged in Tokyo," December 23, 1948, History.com Editors

**WWII War Criminals trial.** *Camp 17 Commandant Asao Fukuhara (center-back) was executed after the war for war crimes. The Japanese surgeon (seated back row, left) who forced men to work even when critically ill, was also prosecuted for war crimes. Photo courtesy Linda Dahl, Fukuoka Camp 17, Mansell.com*

\* \* \* \* \* \* \*

Among the most appalling war crimes that were committed were those by Americans themselves.

Lt. Cmdr. Edward N. Little, an American who was mess hall officer at Camp 17, Omuta, was brought up on charges of shocking cruelty and betrayal. Also, T/Sgt. J. P. Bennett, who was in charge of camp duty, collaborated with Jap authorities by reporting infraction of rules. Both men caused fellow prisoners to be tortured by various methods, including electric shock. The men were forced to hold iron bars in each hand. The bars were approximately eight inches long and one inch in diameter. They were attached to electric current of approximately 100 volts. Water would then be poured upon their clothing.

Louis Goldbrun, testified before a Navy court of inquiry that the Annapolis graduate (Lt. Little) was a "cruel marionet who made fellow-Americans grovel for food while he basked in Jap favor." Lt. Little was tried by jury of peers and court martialed. He had squealed on Corporal James Pavlakos, U.S. Marine Corps, and Pvt. William Knight of Warsaw, N.Y., whose lives were taken by the Japs. Pavlakos had obtained two bowls of rice from a Jap soldier and sold one to a fellow prisoner. After Lt. Little reported him, he was taken to the guardhouse an hour later, placed in solitary, and died of slow starvation thirty-eight days later by continually reducing the amount of ration and water. His weight was reported to have gone from 170 to 55 pounds. Knight, while being forced to kneel for long periods of time with a bamboo pole behind his knees, was beaten, kicked, abused—all contributing to his death.

Lt. Little was reported, by POWs who testified against him in court, to have stolen Red Cross supplies because he drank American coffee, ate spam, and smoked American cigarettes.

*[For more details regarding war crime trials, see: Mansell.com, Site Map, POW Resources, Atrocity Reports]*

Lt. Cmdr. Edward Little
Faces possible life sentence.
(AP WIREphoto)

**Lt. Cmdr. Edward Little,**
*newspaper clipping (source unknown), AP Wire Photo*

**Lt. Ed Little** - *middle row, far left. Both photos of **Little** supplied by Linda Dahl, Omuta 17, Fukuoka at Mansell.com.*

# Japanese Order
# Posted in POW Camps 1944

EDITOR'S NOTE: Submitted by the AXPOW Dept. of the Commonwealth of Virginia, the copies of the Japanese order that our men saw posted in their camps are from the original now in the U.S. National Archives at Washington, DC. An English translation of the order follows.

**KILL THEM ALL ORDER**
1/8/1944
Document No. 2701
(Certified as Exhibit "O" in
D.c.No. 2687)
From the Journal of the Taiwan
POW Camp H.Q. in Taihoku
Entry 1st August, 1944
(entries about money, promotions
of Formosans at branch camps,
including promotion of Yo Yu-
toku 1st Cl Keibiin - 5 entries).

The following answer about the extreme measures for POWs was sent to the Chief of Staff of the 11th Unit (Formosa POW Security No. 10).

"Under the present situation if there were a mere explosion or fire, a shelter for the time being could be had in nearby buildings such as the school, a warehouse, or the like. However, at such time as the situation became urgent and it be extremely important, the POWs will be concentrated and confined in their present location and under heavy guard the preparation for the final disposition will be made.

The time and method of this disposition are as follows:

(1) The Time
Although the basic aim is to act under superior orders, individual disposition may be made in the following circumstances:

(a) When an uprising of large numbers cannot be suppressed without the use of firearms.

(b) When escapees from the camp may turn into a hostile fighting force.

(2) The Method
(a) Whether they are destroyed individually or in groups, or however it is done, with mass bombing, poisonous smoke, poisons, drowning, decapitation, or what, dispose of them as the situation dictates.

(b) In any case it is the aim not to allow the escape of a single one, to annihilate them all, and not to leave any traces.

(3) To: The Commanding General
The Commanding General of Military Police reported matters conferred on with the 11th Unit, the Keelung Fortified are H.Q., and each prefecture concerning the extreme security in Taiwan POW Camps."

34

EX-POW BULLETIN, AUGUST 1995

Pre-Surrender of Japan, translated version of orders issued to kill all POWs, Exhibit at War Tribunal. *Mansell.com*

N.B. The Japanese had plans to murder all prisoners starting in September of 1945 (link). However, see this ATIS bulletin excerpt ("Put all prisoners to death"), translated from a Japanese document in the Philippines, March 30, 1944:

(3) Extract, dated 30 March 1944, regarding treatment of prisoners of war, from carbon-copy and handwritten file covering period 19 February to 30 March 1944 containing general instructions regarding intelligence, belonging to DOI Force Headquarters.

"Policy of the Division Commander is to put all prisoners to death, but they must first be sent to Regimental Headquarters after which they will be dealt with at Headquarters (TN: Presumably Headquarters of formation effecting capture)."
(ATIS Document No. 12310, ATIS Bulletin No. 1142, page 15)

From: Bodine Diary Exhibits re killing POWs civilians.pdf

**Pre-Surrender of Japan, translated version of orders issued to kill POWs, Exhibit at War Tribunal,** *Mansell.com, Source: Ex-POW Bulletin, August, 1995*

# CHAPTER 41

## COMMEMORATIONS

IN memory of all those who have given their lives for our freedom in all American wars, and in honor of all the brave men and women who have served, and are currently serving, in all branches of service. Freedom is not free! May God bless all these men and women and their families, who have suffered and sacrificed for our great country, the United States of American. God bless America!

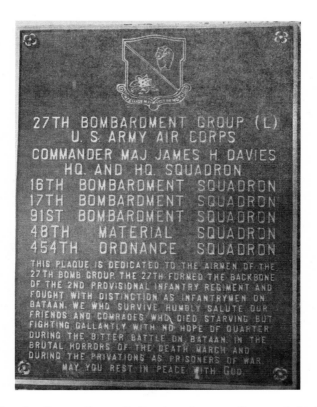

**27th Bombardment Group dedication plaque at Savannah Air Base, Georgia - 35th Anniversary of the Fall of Bataan**

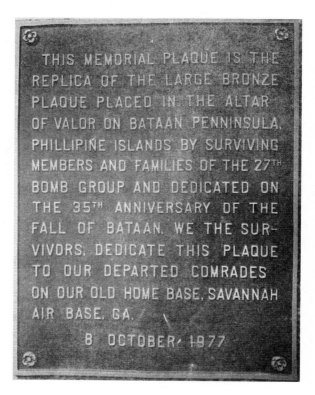

**27th Bombardment Group dedication plaque at Savannah Air Base, Georgia – 35th Anniversary of the Fall of Bataan**

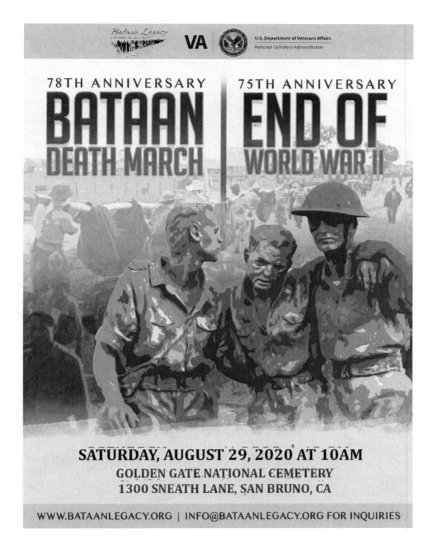

Photograph courtesy of the Bataan Legacy Historical
@ http://www.bataanlegacy.org,
*Designed by Kathrine Colmenar*

# CHAPTER 42

## Honoring Our Family Members

**THE FOLLOWING PAGES ARE PROVIDED TO HONOR OUR OWN FAMILY MEMBERS WHO HAVE SERVED, OR CURRENTLY SERVE, IN THE MILITARY.**

*WE ARE PROUD OF EACH AND EVERY ONE.*
*THANK YOU FOR YOUR SERVICE!*

## GOVAN 'CARLEY' REAL – Drolan's uncle who helped him enlist and took him to basic in Savannah, Georgia

Govan Carley Real, 1920

Govan Carley Real, 1940

**Govan Carley Real, 1950?**

**Govan Carley Real,**
*Military foot stone showing participation in World War I, II, and Korea.*

# DROLAN CHANDLER's – Military Family Members

(*Collage Photo-left photo*) **Ryan Petrae,** *Jerry's son-in-law, Airman First Class E3; injured in basic training, stationed at Aviano Air Base, Italy; 2 ½ years' service; medically retired – 100% disabled.* (**Collage-*Right, upper photo***) **Jerry Chandler** *(Drolan's son) DOB: 1950. CMSGT, USAF, DOS: 1970 to 2000. Stationed in Turkey, Philippines, Hawaii, Japan, plus many more during 30+ years' service.* (***Collage, lower right photo***) **Drolan Chandler.**

**Jerry Chandler, Drolan's son, with wife, Vivian**

# DOYLE CHANDLER (DROLAN'S YOUNGEST BROTHER) – And Military Family Members

**Doyle Chandler**

**Doyle Chandler**

**Doyle Chandler** *(with father, Minos Chandler): DOB: 05/14/28 DOD: 12/01/04; DOS: 04/13/46 thru 12/02/49; Navy – Fireman; Served in Bremerton, WA, and USS Allen M. SUMNER Destroyer Ship.*

**Wade Chandler** *(Doyle's youngest son), DOB: 1952; E4/SGT, USAF, DOS: 1972 to 1976, Radar/Electronics training; West Berlin (1973-1975) – Received WWII Occupation Ribbon.*

**Terry Thorsen**, *DOB: 1961, Sr Airman–Security Police Specialist, USAF; DOS: 1979–1981.*

**Shelby Thorsen** – *Boatswain's Mate 1st Class, U.S. Coast Guard, since 2007. Currently serves at Oak Island, NC.*

**William Knehr**. *DOB: 1975; CTMC(IW/SW) Navy; DOS: Active duty –2004 to 2017, pinned Chief 2013; Reserves, O1E, 2019 to present; Cryptologic Warfare Officer*

**John Knehr**, *DOB 1987; 2nd Class, Navy. DOS 2007–2015; Aviation Machinist Mate.*

**Joshua Strong.** *DOB: 1982; MAJOR (Pilot), USAF; DOS: 2005 to present.*

# (DROLAN'S YOUNGEST SISTER) DIANE CHANDLER MCDONALD MARTIN's –
## Military Family Members

**Damien Moore** - *Medically retired as Petty Officer Second Class – Navy Diver – ND2 (DSW). Served in Operation Enduring Freedom (OEF) and Operation Iraqi Freedom (OIF); Medically retired. DOS: 2006 – 2012. (2nd Row, Left) Diving Salvage Warfare Specialist Qualification – EOD TEU 2-Junior Sailor of the Year award - With Master Diver.*

**Damien Moore** - *(Navy Seals) -*
*Part of EOD TEU 2 – disposing old dynamite*

**Damien Moore - MK-21 Dive Helmet**

**Damien Moore receiving Sailor of the Year Award**

**John Oliver Goode** – *DOB: 09/30/23 DOD: 09/23/03; U.S. Navy,*
*Water Tender First Class WT1c –DOS: Dec 3, 1940 thru Dec 12, 1944*
*– Served aboard Kewaydin, sea tugboat, at Normandy Invasion, WWII.*
*Moved up and down beach, turning ships around so they could fire other side.*

**Jerry Goode,** *DOB: 1946; Staff Sgt, USAF, 1965 to 1971, NCOIC,*
*Airman Personnel Records. RAF Lakenheath, England.*

**Hilton Jones,** *DOB: 09-11-29, DOD: 06-23-01; PFC, Army, Korean Conflict, DOS: 07-20-48 – 07-18-50*

**Hilton Jones** *- pictured on the right, in Korea*

**Albert Woodson Webb, Jr.**, *DOB: 04/23/28 DOD: 11/05/13;
Drafted into U.S. Army; PFC, served in Korean War,
front lines–Mess Sgt. DOS: 1951-1953.*

**Albert Webb – Honor Mess Award**

**James Howard Watts** - *DOB: 03/16/25, DOD: 02/01/05; PFC, DOS: 08/05/43 to 11/11/46, WWII, Italy: He and another soldier shot their way out of a house surrounded by German soldiers; he was wounded while escaping. Medal beneath photo in shadowbox: Sharp Shooter.*

# (DROLAN'S OLDEST SISTER) ROBERTA
# CHANDLER RYE FINNEY's – Military Family Members

**Preston Rye,** *DOB: 1965: A1C, USAF, DOS: 1984-85, injured.*

**Anthony Rye**, *DOB 1983, SGT, Army, DOS: 20007-2014; served in Germany, Afghanistan – injured, Qu wait – injured, DIB/RIB.*

**Julio Rye,**
*DOB 1990, PFC, Army, DOS: 2007–2008, injured in Basic.*

*In Memory of*

**Drolan & Evelyn Chandler, and Larry**

*For: Wanda, Jerry, Dale, Tommie, Molly and their families*


*In Memory of*

**Luther Fred McDonald & Diane Chandler McDonald Shelton**

*For: Linda, Regina, April, Edith & Reba, Martin*

# DEDICATION

*My Love & Deepest Gratitude to each of you for your steadfast love and encouragement:* "my precious" daughter-April Goode Rogers & Michael Rogers-my humorist; Jerry Goode-my encourager; my grandchildren, Blaise & Myka Rogers –" you are my sunshine and inspiration"; and Glenn Jones, my husband– thank you for your immense patience and persistent prodding!

Believe me, if I can accomplish this, with God's help, you can do it and you will see your dreams come true, too, if you'll **Never Give Up!** Ephesians 3:20-21 NKJV *To God be the glory!!!*

\* \* \* \* \* \* \*

**Special Thanks to Deb Kemper, Writing Coach and Mentor** – I couldn't have done this without you! You helped me to cross over the finish line! Words cannot express my appreciation for your invaluable guidance and friendship. Also, the constructive comments from members of the Shelby County Arts Council, Writing Critique Group helped refine the text. Thank you all!

**My appreciation to all my family, friends, and co-workers** who, throughout the years, encouraged me to continue to write and complete this project, and to those who researched, supplied photographs, and information.

# ACKNOWLEDGEMENTS

I am particularly indebted to the excellent, massive website at **Mansell. com**, now called the **Center for Research – Allied POWs Under the Japanese**. It is the primary source of documentation of men and women who served in the Philippines and Japan, which includes names, camps, rosters, maps, etc., by providing links to multitudes of other researchers, such as **Linda Dahl Weeks'** website on Fukuoka #17 Omuta, where the majority of Camp 17 photos for this book were obtained. Linda generously supplied links, photographs, and information pertinent to my enquiries. Photo permissions were provided by **Wes Injerd,** Mansell Website Manager, @ Mansell.com.

**Roger Mansell** (October 8, 1935 to October 25, 2010), Palo Alto, CA, was a dedicated researcher and, along with others, compiled the Research Collection, Concerning World War II Prisoner of War, donated to Hoover Institution Library and Archives. *"We honor them by remembering them."*

I obtained helpful information from the Article, "POW Camps in Japan Proper," POW Research, by Toru Fukubayashi. From that article, I contacted *inquiry@powresearch.jp*. I am grateful to Ms Taeko Sasamoto, the secretary-general of **POW Research Network Japan**, who supplied photos of Miike Coal Mine where the POWs at Fukoka Camp 17 worked, sketches by POWs, museum display photos and data. Ms Sasamoto also diligently fielded my questions regarding mining terms and processes to Mr. Yoshiya Sakai, the director of **Omuta Coal Industry and Science Museum,** and translated his responses. He also supplied photos from the museum.

Jeremy Canwell, PHD, Senior Curator, **Montana Museum of Art and Culture,** granted permission for use of **Ben Steele'**s World War II art and supplied digital images. It is such an honor! Thank you!

I appreciate the privilege of being granted permission to use the cover photograph, provided by **Kelley Hestir,** sculptor of the **"Bataan Death March Memorial"** at Veterans Park, Las Cruces, New Mexico. Her artwork is exhibited internationally. See her beautiful portfolio of creations at the following website: http://www.kelleyhestirsculpture.com/. She also recommended the following websites for more information regarding WWII – Philippines: *http://www.bataandeathmarchmemorial.com/index.html* and *https://www.youtube.com/watch?v=NQc9YF4vCZU*.

Thank you, **Mandy Harp Vassey,** for photographs of your father, Bob Harp, Drolan's friend, from basic throughout the rest of their lives. Thank you to all the POW survivors I interviewed at Fontana, NC, POW Reunion August 27, 1990.

I appreciate permission to use photographs from the following: Lou Gopal, *www.Manilanostalgia.com*, the Bashleben Family for **J.P. Bashleben cartoons**, and James Carter of **South Pacific WWII Museum**. My gratitude to Cecilia Gaerlan, **Bataan Legacy Historical Society** (*http://www.bataanlegacy.org*), and artist Kathrine Colmenar, for the poignant **Anniversary Bataan Death March** poster. Thanks to all others who allowed me to use photographs from their websites.